CHILTON'S
REPAIR & TUNE-UP GUIDE
HONDA
1973 to
1984
All U.S. and Canadian models of Civic, Civic CRX, Accord, Prelude

President LAWRENCE A. FORNASIERI
Vice President and General Manager JOHN P. KUSHNERICK
Executive Editor KERRY A. FREEMAN, S.A.E.
Senior Editor RICHARD J. RIVELE, S.A.E.

CHILTON BOOK COMPANY
Radnor, Pennsylvania
19089

SAFETY NOTICE

Proper service and repair procedures are vital to the safe, reliable operation of all motor vehicles, as well as the personal safety of those performing repairs. This book outlines procedures for servicing and repairing vehicles using safe, effective methods. The procedures contain many NOTES, CAUTIONS and WARNINGS which should be followed along with standard safety procedures to eliminate the possibility of personal injury or improper service which could damage the vehicle or compromise its safety.

It is important to note that repair procedures and techniques, tools and parts for servicing motor vehicles, as well as the skill and experience of the individual performing the work vary widely. It is not possible to anticipate all of the conceivable ways or conditions under which vehicles may be serviced, or to provide cautions as to all of the possible hazards that may result. Standard and accepted safety precautions and equipment should be used when handling toxic or flammable fluids, and safety goggles or other protection should be used during cutting, grinding, chiseling, prying, or any other process that can cause material removal or projectiles.

Some procedures require the use of tools specially designed for a specific purpose. Before substituting another tool or procedure, you must be completely satisfied that neither your personal safety, nor the performance of the vehicle will be endangered.

Although information in this guide is based on industry sources and is as complete as possible at the time of publication, the possibility exists that the manufacturer made later changes which could not be included here. While striving for total accuracy, Chilton Book Company cannot assume responsibility for any errors, changes, or omissions that may occur in the compilation of this data.

PART NUMBERS

Part numbers listed in this reference are not recommendations by Chilton for any product by brand name. They are references that can be used with interchange manuals and aftermarket supplier catalogs to locate each brand supplier's discrete part number.

ACKNOWLEDGMENTS

The Chilton Book Company expresses its appreciation to the Honda Motor Company, Dearborn, Michigan for their generous assistance.

Manufactured in the United States of America
    34567890   32109876

Chilton's Repair & Tune-Up Guide: Honda 1973–84
ISBN 0-8019-7489-5 pbk.
Library of Congress Catalog Card No. 83-45324

CONTENTS

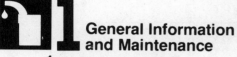
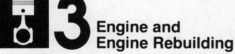

Quick Reference Specifications For Your Vehicle

Fill in this chart with the most commonly used specifications for your vehicle. Specifications can be found in Chapters 1 through 3 or on the tune-up decal under the hood of the vehicle.

 Tune-Up

Firing Order_____

Spark Plugs:

    Type_____

    Gap (in.)_____

Point Gap (in.)_____

Dwell Angle (°)_____

Ignition Timing (°)_____

    Vacuum (Connected/Disconnected)_____

Valve Clearance (in.)

    Intake_____   Exhaust_____

Capacities

Engine Oil (qts)

    With Filter Change_____

    Without Filter Change_____

Cooling System (qts)_____

Manual Transmission (pts)_____

    Type_____

Automatic Transmission (pts)_____

    Type_____

Front Differential (pts)_____

    Type_____

Rear Differential (pts)_____

    Type_____

Transfer Case (pts)_____

    Type_____

FREQUENTLY REPLACED PARTS

Use these spaces to record the part numbers of frequently replaced parts.

PCV VALVE

Manufacturer_____

Part No._____

OIL FILTER

Manufacturer_____

Part No._____

AIR FILTER

Manufacturer_____

Part No._____

General Information and Maintenance

HOW TO USE THIS BOOK

Chilton's Repair & Tune-Up Guide for the Honda is intended to teach you more about the inner workings of your car and save you money on its upkeep. The first two chapters will be used the most, since they contain maintenance and tune-up information and procedures. The following chapters concern themselves with the more complex systems of your Honda. Operating systems from engine through brakes are covered to the extent that we feel the average do-it-yourselfer should get involved. This book will not explain such things as rebuilding the differential for the simple reason that the expertise required and the investment in special tools make this task uneconomical. We will tell you how to change your own brake pads and shoes, replace points and plugs, and many more jobs that will save you money, give you personal satisfaction, and help you avoid problems.

A secondary purpose of this book is as a reference for owners who want to understand their car and/or their mechanics better. In this case, no tools at all are required.

Before removing any parts, read through the entire procedure. This will give you the overall view of what tools and supplies will be required.

The sections begin with a brief discussion of the system and what it involves, followed by adjustments, maintenance, removal and installation procedures, and repair or overhaul procedures. When repair is not considered feasible, we tell you how to remove the part and then how to install the new or rebuilt replacement. In this way, you at least save the labor costs. Backyard repair of such

components as the alternator is just not practical.

Two basic mechanic's rules should be mentioned here. One, whenever the left side of the Honda or engine is referred to, it is meant to specify the driver's side of the Honda. Conversely, the right side of the Honda means the passenger's side. Secondly, most screws and bolts are removed by turning counterclockwise, and tightened by turning clockwise. Safety is always the most important rule. Constantly be aware of the dangers involved in working on an automobile and take the proper precautions. Use jackstands when working under a raised vehicle. Don't smoke or allow an exposed flame to come near the battery or any part of the fuel system. Always use the proper tool and use it correctly; bruised knuckles and skinned fingers aren't a mechanic's standard equipment. Always take your time and have patience; Once you have some experience, working on your Honda will become an enjoyable hobby.

TOOLS AND EQUIPMENT

It would be impossible to catalog each and every tool that you may need to perform all the operations included in this book. It would also not be wise for the amateur to rush out and buy an expensive set of tools on the theory that he may need one of them at some time. The best approach is to proceed slowly, gathering together a good quality set of those tools that are used most frequently. Don't be misled by the low cost of bargain tools. It is far better to spend a little more for quality, name brand tools. Forged wrenches,

10 or 12 point sockets and fine-tooth ratchets are by far preferable to their less expensive counterparts. As any good mechanic can tell you, there are few worse experiences than trying to work on a car or truck with bad tools. Your monetary savings will be far outweighed by frustration and mangled knuckles.

Begin accumulating those tools that are used most frequently; those associated with routine maintenance and tune-up. In addition to the normal assortment of screwdrivers and pliers, you should have the following tools for routine maintenance jobs:

1. SAE wrenches, sockets and combination open end/box end wrenches;
2. Jackstands—for support;
3. Oil filter wrench;
4. Oil filler spout or funnel;
5. Grease gun—for chassis lubrication;
6. Hydrometer—for checking the battery;
7. A low flat pan for draining oil;
8. Lots of rags for wiping up the inevitable mess.

In addition to the above items, there are several others that are not absolutely necessary, but are handy to have around. These include oil drying compound, a transmission funnel, and the usual supply of lubricants, antifreeze and fluids, although these can be purchased as needed. This is a basic list for routine maintenance, but only your personal needs can accurately determine your list of tools.

The second list of tools is for tune-ups. While the tools involved here are slightly more sophisticated, they need not be outrageously expensive. There are several inexpensive tach/dwell meters on the market that are every bit as good for the average mechanic as a $100.00 professional model. Just be sure that it goes to at least 12000–1500 rpm on the tach scale, and that it works on 4, 6, and 8 cylinder engines. A basic list of tune-up equipment could include:

1. Tach/dwell meter;
2. Spark plug wrench;
4. Timing light (preferably a DC light that works from the van's battery);
4. A set of flat feeler gauges;
5. A set of round wire spark plug gauges.

In addition to these basic tools, there are several other tools and gauges you may find useful. These include:

1. A compression gauge. The screw-in type is slower to use, but eliminates the possibility of a faulty reading due to escaping pressure;
2. A manifold vacuum gauge;
3. A test light;
4. An induction meter. This is used for determining whether or not there is current in a wire. These are handy for use if a wire is broken somewhere in a wiring harness. As a final note, you will probably find a torque wrench necessary for all but the most basic work. The beam type models are perfectly adequate, although the newer click type are more precise.

Special Tools

Normally, the use of special factory tools is avoided for repair procedures, since these are not readily available for the do-it-yourself mechanic. When it is possible to perform the job with more commonly available tools, it will be pointed out, but occasionally, a special tool was designed to perform a specific function and should be used. Before substituting another tool, you should be convinced that neither your safety nor the performance of the vehicle will be compromised.

SERVICING YOUR VEHICLE SAFELY

It is virtually impossible to anticipate all of the hazards involved with automotive maintenance and service but care and common sense will prevent most accidents.

The rules of safety for mechanics range from "don't smoke around gasoline," to "use the proper tool for the job." The trick to avoiding injuries is to develop safe work habits and take every possible precaution.

Do's

• Do keep a fire extinguisher and first aid kit within easy reach.
• Do wear safety glasses or goggles when cutting, drilling, grinding or prying. If you wear glasses for the sake of vision, then they should be made of hardened glass that can serve also as safety glasses, or wear safety goggles over your regular glasses.
• Do shield your eyes whenever you work

around the battery. Batteries contain sulphuric acid; in case of contact with the eyes or skin, flush the area with water or a mixture of water and baking soda and get medical attention immediately.

• Do use safety stands for any under-car service. Jacks are for raising vehicles; safety stands are for making sure the vehicle stays raised until you want it to come down. Whenever the vehicle is raised, block the wheels remaining on the ground and set the parking brake.

• Do use adequate ventilation when working with any chemicals. Asbestos dust resulting from brake lining wear can cause cancer.

• Do disconnect the negative battery cable when working on the electrical system. The primary ignition system can contain up to 40,000 volts.

• Do follow manufacturer's directions whenever working with potentially hazardous materials. Both brake fluid and antifreeze are poisonous if taken internally.

• Do properly maintain your tools. Loose hammerheads, mushroomed punches and chisels, frayed or poorly grounded electrical cords, excessively worn screwdrivers, spread wrenches (open end), cracked sockets, slipping ratchets, or faulty droplight sockets can cause accidents.

• Do use the proper size and type of tool for the job being done.

• Do when possible, pull on a wrench handle rather than push on it, and adjust your stance to prevent a fall.

• Do be sure that adjustable wrenches are tightly adjusted on the nut or bolt and pulled so that the face is on the side of the fixed jaw.

• Do select a wrench or socket that fits the nut or bolt. The wrench or socket should sit straight, not cocked.

• Do strike squarely with a hammer to avoid glancing blows.

• Do set the parking brake and block the drive wheels if the work requires that the engine be running.

Don'ts

• Don't run an engine in a garage or anywhere else without proper ventilation— EVER! Carbon monoxide is poisonous; it is absorbed by the body 400 times faster than oxygen; it takes a long time to leave the human body and you can build up a deadly supply of it in your system by simply breathing in a little every day. You may not realize you are slowly poisoning yourself. Always use power vents, windows, fans or open the garage doors.

• Don't work around moving parts while wearing a necktie or other loose clothing. Short sleeves are much safer than long, loose sleeves. Hard-toed shoes with neoprene soles protect your toes and give a better grip on slippery surfaces. Jewelry such as watches, fancy belt buckles, beads or body adornment of any kind is not safe working around a car. Long hair should be hidden under a hat or cap.

• Don't use pockets for toolboxes. A fall or bump can drive a screwdriver deep into your body. Even a wiping cloth hanging from the back pocket can wrap around a spinning shaft or fan.

• Don't smoke when working around gasoline, cleaning solvent or other flammable material.

• Don't smoke when working around the battery. When the battery is being charged, it gives off explosive hydrogen gas.

• Don't use gasoline to wash your hands; there are excellent soaps available. Gasoline may contain lead, and lead can enter the body through a cut, accumulating in the body until you are very ill. Gasoline also removes all the natural oils from the skin so that bone dry hands will suck up oil and grease.

• Don't service the air conditioning system unless you are equipped with the necessary tools and training. The refrigerant, R-12, is extremely cold and when exposed to the air, will instantly freeze any surface it comes in contact with, including your eyes. Although the refrigerant is normally non-toxic, R-12 becomes a deadly poisonous gas in the presence of an open flame. One good whiff of the vapors from burning refrigerant can be fatal.

SERIAL NUMBER IDENTIFICATION

Vehicle Identification (Chassis) Number

Vehicle identification numbers are mounted on the top edge of the instrument panel and are visible from the outside. In addition, there is a Vehicle/Engine Identification plate

The chassis number and engine number are both stamped on the tag under the hood

under the hood on the hood mounting bracket.

Engine Serial Number

The engine serial number is stamped into the clutch casing. The first three digits indicate engine model identification. The remaining numbers refer to production sequence. This same number is also stamped onto the Vehicle/Engine Identification plate mounted on the hood bracket.

Transmission Serial Number

The transmission serial number is stamped on the top of the transmission/clutch case.

Air cleaner element replacement

ROUTINE MAINTENANCE

Air Cleaner

A conventional circular air cleaner element, housed above the carburetor, must be replaced every 12,000 miles (1973–74 models) or 15,000 (1975 and later models). To remove, unscrew the wing nut from the container top, then remove the top and the air cleaner element. Be sure to clean out the container before installing a new element.

NOTE: *Air cleaner elements are not interchangeable, although they appear to be.*

Positive Crankcase Ventilation (PCV)

The Honda is equipped with a "Dual Return" PCV system in which blow-by gas is returned to the combustion chamber through the intake manifold and the air cleaner.

Maintenance on the system is relatively simple and can be conducted by observing the following steps:

1. On 1973–75 models, squeeze the lower end of the drain tube and drain any oil or water which may have collected. On 1976 and later models, remove the tube, invert and drain it.

After all condensation has drained out, install it.

2. Make sure that the intake manifold T-joint is clear. You first have to remove the air cleaner to where the joint is located. To clear the joint, pass the shank end of the appropriate size drill through both ends (both orifices) of the joint.

3. Check for loose, disconnected, or deteriorated tubes and replace if necessary.

For further information on the servicing of Honda emission control components. check the "Emission Controls" section of Chapter 4.

Evaporative Charcoal Canister

The charcoal canister is part of the Evaporative Emission Control System. This system prevents the escape of raw gasoline vapors from the fuel tank and carburetor.

The charcoal canister is designed to absorb fuel vapors under certain conditions (for a more detailed description, see the "Evaporative Emission Control System" section in

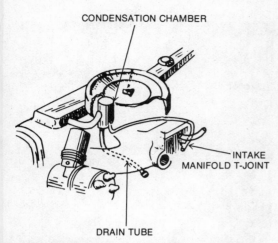

Typical PCV system component location. 1973 model shown

1976 and later drain tube location. Disconnect the tube from the condensation chamber and invert it to drain

Remove this Phillips head screw to disconnect the condensation chamber from the air cleaner

1975 and later CVCC PCV system orifice location

Removing the air cleaner housing bolts from the engine

Chapter 4). Maintenance on the canister consists of testing and inspection at 12,000 mile intervals (1973–74 models), or 15,000 mile intervals (1975 and later models), and replacement at 24,000 miles (1973–74 models), or 30,000 miles (1975 and later models). See Chapter 4 for testing procedures.

The canister is a coffee can-sized object located in the engine compartment. Label the hoses leading to the canister before disconnecting them. Then, simply remove the

Evaporative canister

Check the belt tension midway between the two pulleys

old canister from its mounting bracket and discard it. Install the new canister and connect the hoses as before.

Belts

CHECKING AND ADJUSTING TENSION

The initial inspection and adjustment to the alternator drive belt should be performed after the first 3,000 miles or if the alternator has been moved for any reason. Afterwards, you should inspect the belt tension every 12,000 miles. Before adjusting, inspect the belt to see that it is not cracked or worn. Be sure that its surfaces are free of grease and oil.

1. Push down on the belt halfway between pulleys with moderate force. The belt should deflect approximately ½ inch.

2. If the belt tension requires adjustment, loosen the adjusting link bolt and move the alternator with a pry bar positioned against the front of the alternator housing.

CAUTION: *Do not apply pressure to any other part of the alternator.*

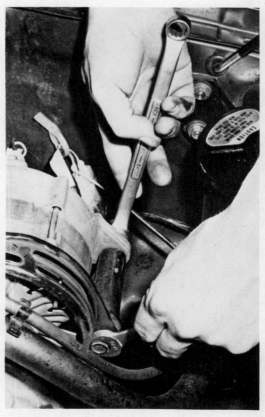

Loosen the pivot bolt before loosening the adjusting bolt

How To Spot Worn V-Belts

V-Belts are vital to efficient engine operation—they drive the fan, water pump and other accessories. They require little maintenance (occasional tightening) but they will not last forever. Slipping or failure of the V-belt will lead to overheating. If your V-belt looks like any of these, it should be replaced.

Cracking or weathering

This belt has deep cracks, which cause it to flex. Too much flexing leads to heat build-up and premature failure. These cracks can be caused by using the belt on a pulley that is too small. Notched belts are available for small diameter pulleys.

Softening (grease and oil)

Oil and grease on a belt can cause the belt's rubber compounds to soften and separate from the reinforcing cords that hold the belt together. The belt will first slip, then finally fail altogether.

Glazing

Glazing is caused by a belt that is slipping. A slipping belt can cause a run-down battery, erratic power steering, overheating or poor accessory performance. The more the belt slips, the more glazing will be built up on the surface of the belt. The more the belt is glazed, the more it will slip. If the glazing is light, tighten the belt.

Worn cover

The cover of this belt is worn off and is peeling away. The reinforcing cords will begin to wear and the belt will shortly break. When the belt cover wears in spots or has a rough jagged appearance, check the pulley grooves for roughness.

Separation

This belt is on the verge of breaking and leaving you stranded. The layers of the belt are separating and the reinforcing cords are exposed. It's just a matter of time before it breaks completely.

Loosen the adjusting bolt and pry the alternator outward

The sight glass is located on top of the receiver-drier

3. After obtaining the proper tension, tighten the adjusting link bolt.

CAUTION: *Do not overtighten the belt; damage to the alternator bearings could result.*

Air Conditioning

This book contains no repair or maintenance procedures for the air conditioning system. It is recommended that any such repairs be left to trained technicians who are well aware of the hazards and who have the proper equipment.

CAUTION: *The compressed refrigerant used in the air conditioning system expands into the atmosphere at a temperature of −21.7°F or lower. This will freeze any surface, including your eyes, that it contacts. In addition, the refrigerant decomposes into a poisonous gas in the presence of flame. Do not open or disconnect any part of the air conditioning system.*

When placing the unit in service at the beginning of the summer season, make the following checks:

1. Operate the engine at approximately 1,500 rpm. Locate the sight glass, located on top of the receiver-drier, a small, black cylinder which is in the engine compartment.

2. Have someone turn the blower to high speed and switch the AIR lever to A/C position while you watch the sight glass. The glass should first become clouded with bubbles, and then clear up. Operate the unit for five minutes while watching the glass. If outside temperature is 68°F or above, the glass should be perfectly clear. If there is a continuous stream of bubbles, it indicates that the system has a slight leak and will require additional refrigerant. If the system starts and runs and no bubbles appear, the entire refrigerant charge has been lost. *Stop the system and do not operate it until it has been repaired.*

3. Inspect all lines for signs of oil accumulation, which would indicate leakage. If leaks are indicated, have the leak repaired by a professional mechanic. Do not attempt to tighten fittings or otherwise repair the system unless you have been trained in refrigeration repair as the system contains high pressure. Do not operate the system if it seems to have leaks as this can aggravate possible damage to the system.

4. Check the tension and condition of the compressor drive belt and adjust its tension or replace as necessary.

5. Test the blower to make sure that it operates at all speeds and have it repaired if it does not.

In winter, operate the air conditioner for 10 minutes with the engine at 1,500 rpm once a month to circulate oil to the compressor seal, thus preventing leakage.

Fluid Level Checks
ENGINE OIL LEVEL

Checking the oil level is one of the simplest and most important checks and it should be done FREQUENTLY.

This is the oil filler plug on the five-speed. The four-speed and the Hondamatic have a dipstick located here instead of a simple filler plug

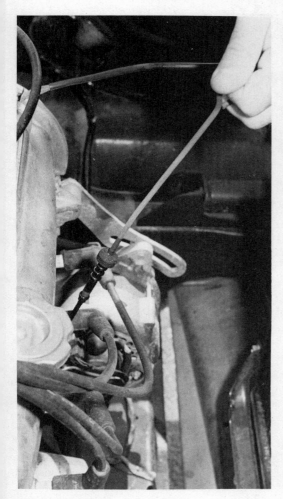

Removing dipstick to check oil

NOTE: *If the engine has been running, let it sit for a few minutes until all the oil accumulates in the sump, before checking the oil level.*

To check the oil level, simply raise the hood, pull the oil dipstick from the engine and wipe it clean. Insert the dipstick into the engine until it is fully seated, then remove it and check the reading. The oil level on all Hondas should register within the crosshatch design on the dipstick. Do not add oil if this is the case. If the level is below the crosshatch, ADD oil but do not overfill. The length covered by the crosshatching on the dipstick is roughly equivalent to one quart of oil.

TRANSMISSION FLUID LEVEL

The transmission fluid should be checked about once a month and replaced after the first 3,000 miles (every 24,000 miles thereaf-

ter). Both the 4-speed manual transmission and the Hondamatic automatic transmission use a threaded dipstick with a crosshatch pattern. The dipstick is located beneath the battery. Approximately ¾ qt. will bring the fluid level from the ADD (lower) to the FULL (upper) line.

On automatic transmission equipped cars, the fluid is checked with the engine running. It is also necessary to warm up the transmission by driving the car a few miles, starting and stopping frequently. Then park the car on level ground and let the engine idle with the transmission in park. Unscrew the dipstick, wipe it clean, and insert it. DO NOT SCREW IT IN, as this would result in an erroneous reading. Top up, as necessary, with DEXRON® type automatic transmission fluid. Add the fluid, if necessary, in small amounts, taking care not to overfill.

On the 5-speed transmission, a dipstick is not used. Instead, there is an oil level checking bolt on the side of the case. To check the oil level, loosen the bolt until transmission oil

Five-speed oil level checking bolt location

begins to run out, then quickly tighten it. If oil runs out, the level is OK, but if oil does not run out, you'll have to add some through the oil cap bolt (directly beneath the battery).

COOLANT LEVEL

To check the coolant level, simply discern whether the coolant is up to the "FULL" line on the expansion tank. Add coolant to the expansion tank if the level is low, being sure to replenish with clean water. Be sure to use a high quality coolant, designed for use in aluminum engines. Never add cold water to a hot engine as damage to both the cooling system and the engine could result.

The radiator cap should be removed only for the purpose of cleaning or draining the system.

CAUTION: *The cooling system is under pressure when hot. Removing the radiator cap when the engine is warm or overheated will cause coolant to spill or shoot out, possibly causing serious burns. The system should be allowed to cool before attempting removal of the radiator cap or hoses. If any coolant spills on painted portions of the body, rinse it off immediately.*

COOLANT CHANGE AND BLEEDING

The radiator coolant should be changed every 24,000 miles (1973–74 models) or 30,000 miles (1975 and later models). When following this procedure, be sure to follow the same precautions as detailed in the above "Coolant Level" section.

1. Remove the radiator cap.

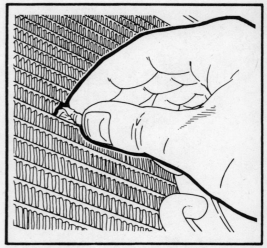

Clean the radiator fins periodically for maximum cooling

2. Slide a drip pan underneath the radiator. Then loosen the drain bolt at the base of the radiator and drain the radiator.

3. Drain the coolant in the reservoir tank.

4. Mix a solution of 50% ethylene glycol (designed for use in aluminum engines) and 50% clean water. Tighten the drain bolt and fill the radiator all the way to the filler mouth. The radiator coolant capacity is about 4.2 qts.

5. Loosen the cooling system bleed bolt to purge air from the system. When coolant flows out of the bleed port, close the bolt and refill the radiator with coolant up to the mouth.

6. To purge any air trapped in other parts of the cooling system, start the engine, set it to fast idle and allow it to warm up. Do not tighten down the radiator cap, and leave the heater control in the "hot" position.

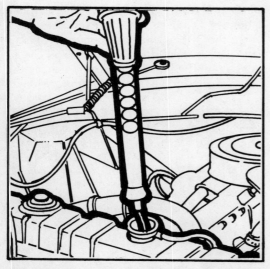

Check the degree of protection with an inexpensive tester

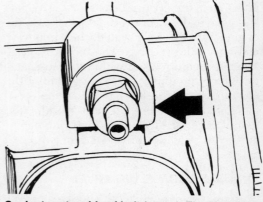

Coolant system bleed bolt (arrow). The bleed bolt is always located in the vicinity of the thermostat housing

How To Spot Bad Hoses

Both the upper and lower radiator hoses are called upon to perform difficult jobs in an inhospitable environment. They are subject to nearly 18 psi at under hood temperatures often over 280°F., and must circulate nearly 7500 gallons of coolant an hour—3 good reasons to have good hoses.

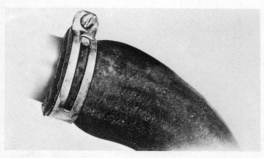

Swollen hose

A good test for any hose is to feel it for soft or spongy spots. Frequently these will appear as swollen areas of the hose. The most likely cause is oil soaking. This hose could burst at any time, when hot or under pressure.

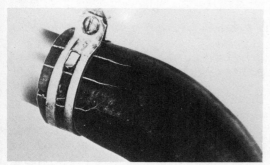

Cracked hose

Cracked hoses can usually be seen but feel the hoses to be sure they have not hardened; the prime cause of cracking. This hose has cracked down to the reinforcing cords and could split at any of the cracks.

Frayed hose end (due to weak clamp)

Weakened clamps frequently are the cause of hose and cooling system failure. The connection between the pipe and hose has deteriorated enough to allow coolant to escape when the engine is hot.

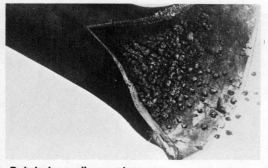

Debris in cooling system

Debris, rust and scale in the cooling system can cause the inside of a hose to weaken. This can usually be felt on the outside of the hose as soft or thinner areas.

Coolant reserve tank located next to windshield washer reservoir

When the engine reaches normal operating temperature, top up the radiator and keep checking until the level stabilizes.

Then fill the coolant reservoir to the "full" mark and make sure that the radiator cap is properly tightened.

BRAKE AND CLUTCH MASTER CYLINDER FLUID LEVEL

Brake and clutch master cylinder fluid level should be checked every few weeks for indication of leaks or low fluid level due to normal wear. Infrequent topping-off will be required in normal use due to brake pad wear.

On all Hondas there is a fill line on the brake fluid reservoir(s) as well as an arrow on the reservoir cap(s) which should face forward when installed. When adding brake fluid, the following precautions should be observed:

1. Use only recommended brake fluid—DOT 3 or DOT 4; SAE J 1703b HD type.

2. Never reuse brake fluid and never use fluid that is dirty, cloudy, or has air bubbles.

3. Store brake fluid in a clean dry place in the original container. Cap tightly and do not puncture a breather hole in the container.

4. Carefully remove any dirt from around the master cylinder reservoir cap before opening.

5. Take special care not to spill the fluid. The painted surface of the vehicle will be damaged by brake fluid.

BATTERY LEVEL

The battery electrolyte level should be checked at least once a month to see if the fluid level is between the "Lower" and "Upper Level" lines on the outside of the

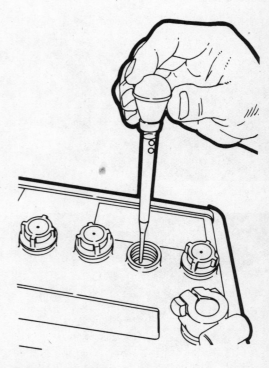

An inexpensive hydrometer will quickly test the state of charge of the battery

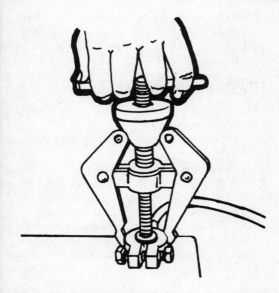

Top terminal battery cables can be removed with a puller available at most parts stores

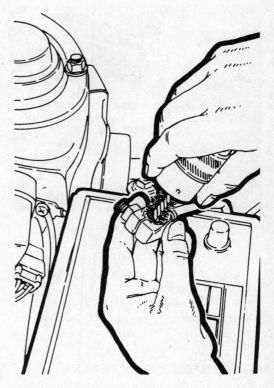

Cleaning the terminal ends of the cable with a wire cleaner

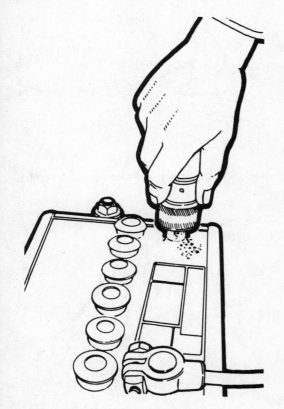

Cleaning the battery post with a wire brush

battery. Should the level be low, you can fill it with ordinary tap water.

NOTE: *If you live in an area having exceptionally hard water, use only distilled water.*

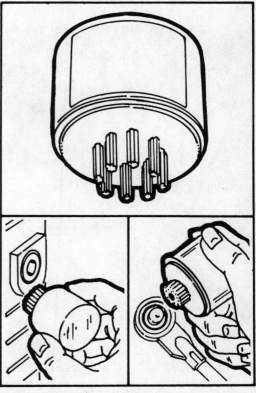

Side terminal batteries require a small, stiff wire brush for cleaning

Checking the battery electrolyte level

Be sure not to overfill the battery, or the elctrolyte may run out giving you a useless battery filled with water.

CAUTION: *The battery gives off highly explosive hydrogen gas. Never hold an open flame, such as a lighted match, near the top of the battery.*

POWER STEERING RESERVOIR

The fluid in the power steering reservoir should be checked every few weeks for indications of leaks or low fluid level.

Power steering fluid reservoir. Use only genuine Honda power steering fluid

NOTE: *Only genuine Honda power steering fluid may be used when adding fluid. The use of any other fluid will cause the seals to swell and create leaks.*

Tires and Wheels

When buying or changing tires, you should remember two things:

1. Do not mix tires of different sizes on the same axle.

2. Never mix radial and bias-ply tires. Not only is it a potentially dangerous practice, but many states prohibit the mixing of the two tire types.

CAUTION: *In no case should you ever mix tires of different construction (bias and radial) on the same axle. Handling will deteriorate dangerously.*

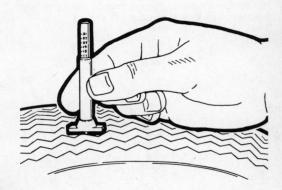

Using a depth gauge to determine tread depth

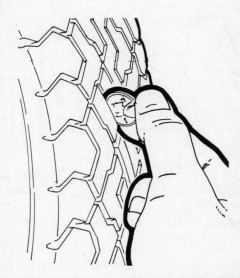

Using a Lincoln penny to determine tread depth. If the top of Lincoln's head is visible, in 2 adjacent grooves, replace the tire

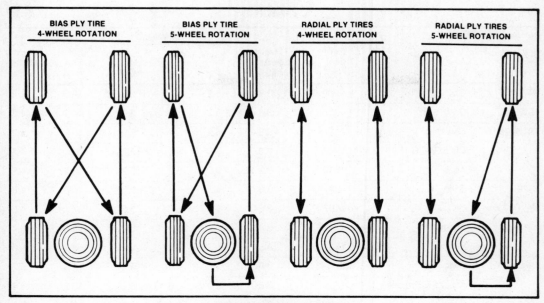

BIAS PLY TIRE 4-WHEEL ROTATION	BIAS PLY TIRE 5-WHEEL ROTATION	RADIAL PLY TIRES 4-WHEEL ROTATION	RADIAL PLY TIRES 5-WHEEL ROTATION

Tire rotation diagrams

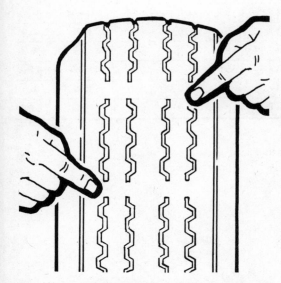

Since 1968 wear indicators have been built into tires. When these bands become visible on the tire's surface, replace the tire

the steering wheel is released, is also a clue to alignment problems. The cause of irregular tire wear should always be investigated and corrected.

And if you want to get the *maximum* life out of your tires, you can rotate them every 5,000 miles (except snow tires, of course) according to the diagram.

Tire life will also be increased if the tires are kept properly inflated. Excessive wear on the outer edges is an indication of underinflation, while too much center wear is usually a sign of overinflation. The air pressure in your tires should be checked at least once a month. Do this when the tires are cold; since tire pressure increases with temperature, an improper reading will result if you measure the pressure when the tires are hot.

NOTE: *When measuring tire pressure, always use a tire pressure gauge. Use the gauge even when adding air, as gas station air pumps are often inaccurate.*

A plate located on the left door will tell you the proper pressure for your tires.

Tires must also be checked regularly for damage and signs of uneven wear. The tire tread should wear evenly across the width of the tire. If an uneven wear pattern is evident (such as cupping or severe wear on only one side of the tire) then front end alignment or wheel balance is out of adjustment. Steering wheel vibration is usually an indication of front-end tire imbalance or misalignment. "Straying" from the direction of travel, when

Fuel Filter Replacement

All cars use a disposable-type fuel filter which cannot be disassembled for cleaning. On 1973–74 models, the recommended replacement interval is 24,000 miles. On 1975 and later models, the filter is replaced after

Capacities

Year	Model	Engine Displ. (cc)	Engine Crankcase (qts) [2]	Transmission (pts) Manual 4-sp	Transmission (pts) Manual 5-sp	Auto. [3]	Gasoline Tank (gals)	Cooling System (qts)
1973	Civic	1170	3.8	5.2	—	5.2	10.0	4.2
1974	Civic	1237	3.8	5.2	—	5.2	10.0	4.2
1975–78	Civic	1237	3.8	5.2	—	5.2	10.6	4.2
	Civic CVCC	1487	3.8	5.2	5.2	5.2	10.6 [1]	4.2
	Accord	1600	3.8	5.2	5.2	5.2	13.2	4.2
1979	Civic	1237	3.8	5.2	—	5.2	10.6	4.8
	Civic	1487	3.8	5.2	5.6	5.2	10.6 [1]	4.8
	Accord	1751	3.8	5.2	5.2	5.2	13.2	6.4
	Prelude	1751	3.8	5.2	5.2	5.2	13.2	6.0
1980–81	Civic	1335, 1487	3.8	4.8	5.2	5.2	10.8	5.2
	Accord & Prelude	1751	3.8	5.0	5.0	5.2	13.2	6.4
1982	Civic	1335, 1487	3.7	5.6	5.6	5.2	10.8	5.2
	Accord	1751	3.7	5.0	5.0	5.2	15.8	6.0
	Prelude	1751	3.7	5.0	5.0	5.2	13.2	6.0
'83	Civic	1335, 1487	3.7	5.2	5.2	5.2	10.4 [4]	4.8 [5]
	Accord	1751	3.7	5.0	5.0	6.0	15.8	6.0
	Prelude	1829	3.7	—	5.0	5.8	15.9	6.3
'84–'85	Civic	1342, 1488	3.7	5.0	5.0	6.0	11.9 [6]	4.8 [7]
	Accord	1829	3.7	—	5.0	6.0	15.8	6.4
	Prelude	1829	3.7	—	5.0	5.8	15.9	6.3 [8]

[1] Sta. Wgn.: 11.0
[2] Includes filter
[3] Does not include torque converter. Total capacity from dry is 8.8 pts.
[4] 4-dr sedan: 12.1
[5] 1335cc: 4.0
[6] CRX: 10.8
[7] 1342cc: 3.6
[8] Auto. Tran.: 7.1 qts

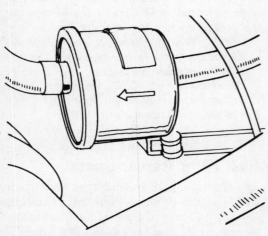

Fuel filter—non-CVCC Civic (arrow)

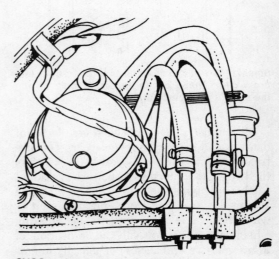

CVCC sedan fuel pump and filter location

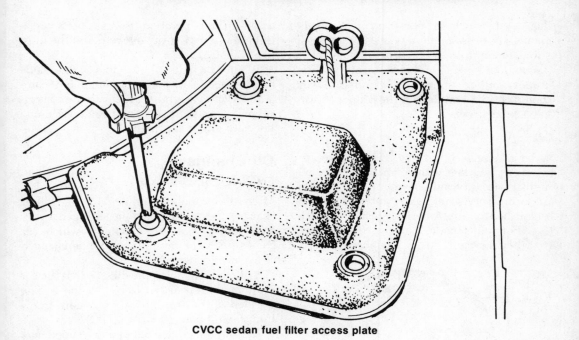

CVCC sedan fuel filter access plate

the first 15,000 miles, and every 30,000 miles thereafter.

CAUTION: *Before disconnecting any fuel lines, be sure to open the gas tank filler cap to relieve any pressure in the system. If this is not done, you may run the risk of being squirted with gasoline.*

On all 1973–74 Civics, as well as 1975 and later Civics with the air-injection 1237 cc (AIR) engine, the filter is located in the engine compartment, inline between the fuel pump and carburetor. Replacement is a simple matter of pinching the lines closed, loosening the hose clamps and discarding the old filter.

On all CVCC Sedan models, the filter is located beneath a special access cover under the rear seat on the driver's side. The rear seat can be removed after removing the bolt at the rear center of the cushion and then pivoting the seat forward from the rear.

Then, remove the four screws retaining the access cover to the floor and remove the cover. The filter, together with the electric fuel pump, are located in the recess. Pinch the lines shut, loosen the hose clamps and remove the filter.

On all 1975 and later wagon Accord and Prelude models, the filter is located under the car, in front of the spare tire, together with the electrical fuel pump. To replace the fuel filter, you must raise the rear of the car, support it with jackstands, and clamp off the fuel lines leading to and from the filter. Then, loosen the hose clamps and, taking note of which hose is the inlet and which is the outlet, remove the filter. Some replacement filters have an arrow embossed or printed on the filter body, in which case you want to install the new filter with the arrow pointing in the direction of fuel flow. After installing the new filter, remember to unclamp the fuel lines. Check for leaks.

LUBRICATION

Oil and Fuel Recommendations
FUEL

All Hondas are designed to run on regular gasoline; high-octane (premium) gasoline is not required. The octane number is used as a measure of the anti-knock properties of a gasoline and the use of a higher octane gasoline

Accord and Prelude fuel filter location (arrow) —wagon similar

than that which is necessary to prevent engine knock is simply a waste of money. If your Honda does knock (usually heard as a pinging noise), it is probably a matter of improper ignition timing, in which case you should check Chapter 2 for the proper adjustment procedure.

OIL

As far as engine oil is concerned, there are two types of ratings with which you should be familiar: viscosity and service (quality). There are several service ratings, resulting from tests established by the American resulting Institute. For your Honda, use only SE rated oil. No other service rating is acceptable.

Typical oil rating location on can

You can buy oil in two different types of viscosity ratings, single and multi-viscosity. Single viscosity oil, designated by only one number (SAE 30), maintains the same viscosity, or thickness, over a wide range of temperatures. A multi-viscosity oil rating is given in two numbers (SAE 10W-40) and changes viscosity, within the range of the rating, according to various engine temperature conditions, such as cold starts and eventual engine

warm-up and operation. Because of its versatility, a multi-viscosity oil would be the most likely choice.

When you add oil, try to use the same brand since all oils are not completely compatible with each other. Refer to the "Lubrication" chart in this chapter for service and viscosity rating information.

Oil Changes
ENGINE OIL CHANGE

After the initial 600 miles oil and filter change, the oil should mile changed every 3,000 miles or every 3 months, whichever comes first. The oil filter should be changed at every oil change.

1. Before changing the oil, see that the car is situated on a flat surface with the engine warmed up. Warm oil will flow more freely from the oil pan.

2. Shut the engine off, open the hood, and remove the oil filler cap from the top of the engine valve cover.

   CAUTION: *Hot oil can burn you. Keep an inward pressure on the plug until the last thread is cleared. Then quickly remove it.*

3. Place a container underneath the oil pan large enough to catch the oil. A large, flat drain pan is the most desirable.

4. Using a proper-size wrench, remove the oil drain plug and allow the oil to drain completely. When the oil has finished draining, install the drain plug tight enough to prevent oil leakage. Remove the drain pan from under the engine.

5. Add the correct amount of recommended oil into the oil filler hole on top of

Oil pan drain plug location

Lubricant Specifications

Engine Oil	6000 mile motor oil (MS or SE sequence tested)

Single Viscosity Oils	
When outside temperature is consistently	Use SAE Viscosity Number
−4°F to +32°F	10W
+32°F to +59°F	20W-20
+59°F to +86°F	30
Above 86°F	40

Multiviscosity Oils	
Above 5°F	10W/40
+5°F to +86°F	10W/30
Above 32°F	20W/40
	20W/50
Manual Transmission and Differential Gear Oil	Use engine oil according to the above specifications
Automatic Transmission	Automatic Transmission Fluid—Dexron® type

the valve cover. Be sure that the oil level registers near the full line on the oil dipstick.

6. Replace the filler cap, start the engine, and allow it to idle. The oil pressure light on the instrument panel should go out after a few seconds of running.

7. Shut the engine off after a few minutes of running and recheck the oil level. Add oil if necessary. Be sure to check for oil leaks, as this is a common problem on early production models using the Japanese filter.

OIL AND FILTER CHANGE

A conventional spin-on oil filter is used.
NOTE: *Only oil filters which have an integral by-pass should be used.*

1. Before removing the filter it is advisable to have an oil filter wrench which is inexpensive and makes the job much easier. Follow Steps 1–4 of the above oil change procedure before removing the filter.

2. Place the oil drain pan underneath the filter. The filter retains some oil which will drain when removed.

3. Loosen the oil filter with the oil filter wrench. Unscrew it by hand.

4. Clean the filter mounting surface of the cylinder block with a clean cloth. Apply a thin coat of oil to the new filter gasket and install the filter.
NOTE: *Hand-tighten the filter only. Do not use a wrench for tightening.*

5. Fill the engine with oil and replace the filler cap.

6. Run the engine for a few minutes and check for leakage. Be sure to recheck the oil level.

TRANSMISSION FLUID CHANGE

Both the manual and automatic transmission models have drain plugs located on the bottom of the transmission for draining. To change the fluid, remove the drain plug and drain the fluid into a drain pan. Refit the plug and fill the transmission with the specified fluid (MT—API service SE or SD; AT—DEXRON®) through the transmission fluid dipstick hole.
NOTE: *Although the specified quantity of fluid in both the manual and automatic transmissions is 2.5 liters, or 2.6 quarts, be sure that the required quantity of fluid is always slightly less than the specified quantity, due to the remaining fluid left in the transmission housing recesses. While changing fluid, always check the level with the dipstick as you are pouring the fluid to see that you do not overfill the transmission.*

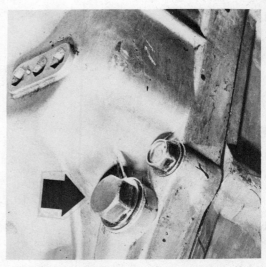

Manual transmission drain plug location—automatic similar

WHEEL BEARINGS

Refer to the appropriate section in Chapter 9 for procedures on wheel bearing assembly and repacking. The front wheel bearings should be inspected and repacked (or replaced) every 30,000 miles. To check the wheel bearings for any play, jack up each wheel to clear the ground. Hold the wheel and shake it to check the bearings for any play. If any play is felt, tighten the castellated spindle nut to the specified torque (87–130 ft lbs) and reinspect. If play is still present, replace the bearing.

Checking wheel bearings for excessive play

NOTE: *Overtightening the spindle nuts will cause excessive bearing friction and will result in rough wheel rotation and eventual bearing failure.*

BODY LUBRICATION

Lubricate all locks and hinges with multi-purpose grease every 6000 miles or 6 months.

PUSHING AND TOWING

Pushing

Hondas equipped with a standard transmission can be push-started. Make sure that the bumpers match as a damaged bumper and/or fender could result from push-starting. To push-start your Honda, turn the ignition switch ON, push the clutch in, and select Second or Third gear. As the car picks up speed (10–15 mph), slowly release the clutch pedal until the engine fires up.

If your Honda is equipped with an automatic transmission, it cannot be push-started.

Towing

If your Honda's rear axle is operable, then you can tow your car with the rear wheels on the ground. Due to its front wheel drive, the Honda is a relatively easy vehicle to tow with the front wheels up. Before doing so, you should release the parking brake.

If the rear axle is defective, the car must then be towed with the rear wheels off the ground. Before attempting this, a dolly should be placed under the front wheels. If a dolly is not available, and you still have to tow it with the rear wheels up, then you should first shift the transmission into Neutral and then lock the steering wheel so that the front wheels are pointing straight ahead. In such a position, the car must not be towed at speeds above 20 mph or for more than short distances (5–10 miles).

JACKING AND HOISTING

Your Honda came equipped with a scissors jack. This jack is fine for changing a flat tire or other operations where you do not have to go beneath the car. There are four lifting points where this jack may be used; one behind each front wheel well and one in front of each rear wheel well in reinforced sheet metal brackets beneath the rocker panels (see illustration).

A more convenient way of jacking is the use of a garage or floor jack. You may use the floor jack beneath any of the four scissors jacking points, or you can raise either the entire front or entire rear of the car using the special jacking brackets beneath the front center or rear center of the car. On station wagon models, the rear of the car may be jacked beneath the center of the rear axle beam.

CAUTION: *The following safety points cannot be overemphasized;*
• *always block the opposite wheel or wheels to keep the car from rolling off the jack.*
• *when raising the front of the car, firmly apply the parking brake.*
• *when raising the rear of the car, place the transmission in low or reverse gear.*
• *always use jack stands to support the car when you are working underneath.*

JUMP STARTING A DEAD BATTERY

The chemical reaction in a battery produces explosive hydrogen gas. This is the safe way to jump start a dead battery, reducing the chances of an accidental spark that could cause an explosion.

Jump Starting Precautions

1. Be sure both batteries are of the same voltage.
2. Be sure both batteries are of the same polarity (have the same grounded terminal).
3. Be sure the vehicles are not touching.
4. Be sure the vent cap holes are not obstructed.
5. Do not smoke or allow sparks around the battery.
6. In cold weather, check for frozen electrolyte in the battery.
7. Do not allow electrolyte on your skin or clothing.
8. Be sure the electrolyte is not frozen.

Jump Starting Procedure

1. Determine voltages of the two batteries; they must be the same.
2. Bring the starting vehicle close (they must not touch) so that the batteries can be reached easily.
3. Turn off all accessories and both engines. Put both cars in Neutral or Park and set the handbrake.
4. Cover the cell caps with a rag—do not cover terminals.
5. If the terminals on the run-down battery are heavily corroded, clean them.
6. Identify the positive and negative posts on both batteries and connect the cables in the order shown.
7. Start the engine of the starting vehicle and run it at fast idle. Try to start the car with the dead battery. Crank it for no more than 10 seconds at a time and let it cool off for 20 seconds in between tries.
8. If it doesn't start in 3 tries, there is something else wrong.
9. Disconnect the cables in the reverse order.
10. Replace the cell covers and dispose of the rags.

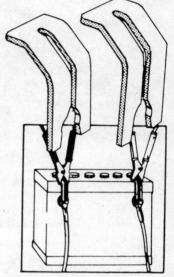

Side terminal batteries occasionally pose a problem when connecting jumper cables. There frequently isn't enough room to clamp the cables without touching sheet metal. Side terminal adaptors are available to alleviate this problem and should be removed after use.

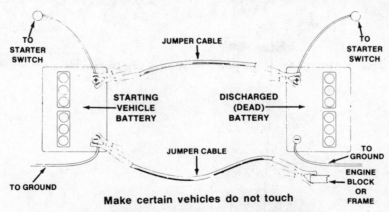

TO STARTER SWITCH   JUMPER CABLE   TO STARTER SWITCH

STARTING VEHICLE BATTERY   DISCHARGED (DEAD) BATTERY

JUMPER CABLE

TO GROUND

TO GROUND   ENGINE BLOCK OR FRAME

Make certain vehicles do not touch

This hook-up for negative ground cars only

Reinforced lifting point on the side of the Honda (arrow)

Place the stands beneath the scissors jacking brackets. Before climbing underneath, rock the car a bit to make sure it is firmly supported.

If you are going to have your Honda serviced on a garage hoist, make sure the four hoist platform pads are placed beneath the scissors jacking brackets. These brackets are reinforced and will support the weight of the entire vehicle.

The correct method of raising the Honda with a garage hoist

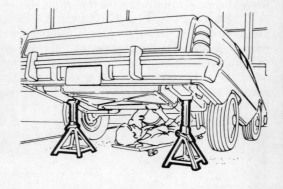

Always use jackstands when working under the car

Tune-Up and Performance Maintenance

2

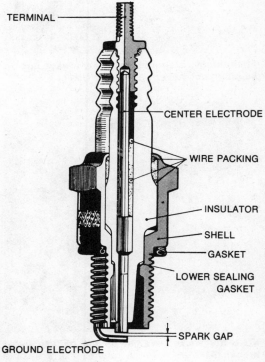

TUNE-UP PROCEDURES

The procedures in this section are specifically intended for your Honda and intended to be as basic and complete as possible.

Spark Plugs

Most people know that the spark plug ignites the air/fuel mixture in the cylinder, which in turn forces the piston downward, turning the crankshaft. This action turns the drivetrain (clutch, transmission, drive axles) and moves the car. What many people do not know, however, is that spark plugs should be chosen according to the type of driving done. The plug with a long insulator nose retains heat long enough to burn off oil and combustion deposits under light engine load conditions. A short-nosed plug dissipates heat rapidly and prevents pre-ignition and detonation under heavy loaded conditions. Under normal driving conditions, a standard plug is just fine.

Spark plug life is largely governed by operating conditions and varies accordingly. To ensure peak performance, inspect the plugs at least every 6,000 miles. Faulty or excessively worn plugs should be replaced immediately. It is also helpful to check plugs for types of deposit and degree of electrode wear, as an indication of engine operating condition. Excessive or oily deposits could be an indication of real engine trouble, and it would be wise to investigate the problem thoroughly until the cause is found and corrected.

Underhood emissions control sticker containing tune-up information

Spark plug cross-section

REMOVAL

1. Place a piece of masking tape around each spark plug wire and number it according to its corresponding cylinder.

2. Pull the wires from the spark plugs, grasping the wire by the end of the rubber boot and twisting off.

NOTE: *Avoid spark plug removal while the engine is hot. Since the cylinder head spark plug threads are aluminum, the spark plug becomes tight due to the different coefficients of heat expansion. If a plug is too tight to be removed even while the engine is cold, apply a solvent around the plug followed with an application of oil once the solvent has penetrated the threads. Do this only when the engine is cold.*

3. Loosen each spark plug with a $^{13}/_{16}$ in. spark plug socket. When the plug has been loosened a few turns, stop to clean any material from around the spark plug holes. Compressed air is preferred; however, if air is not available, simply use a rag to clean the area.

NOTE: *In no case should foreign matter be allowed to enter the cylinders. Severe damage could result.*

4. Finish unscrewing the plugs and remove them from the engine.

INSPECTION AND CLEANING

Before attempting to clean and re-gap plugs, be sure that the electrode ends aren't worn or damaged and that the insulators (the white porcelain covering) are not cracked. Replace the plug if this condition exists.

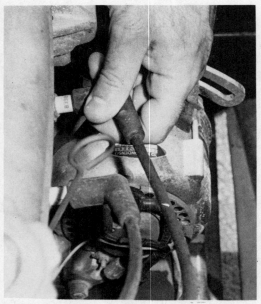

When removing spark plug wires, always pull on the plug boot, never on the wire itself

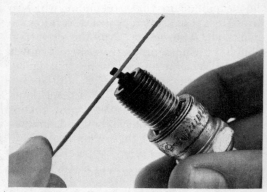

Use a small file to clean and square up the electrode if the plug is still usable

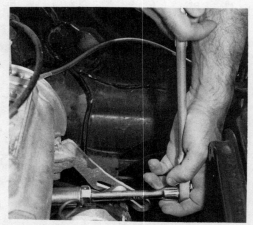

Keep the socket straight on the plug to avoid breaking the insulator. A ratchet with a flexible head is helpful

When gapping plugs, new or used, make sure the wire gauge passes through the gap with just a slight drag. Don't use a flat feeler gauge

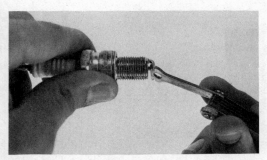

Bend the side electrode carefully using a spark plug gapping tool

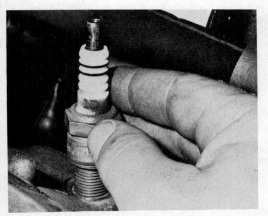

Always start the plugs by hand to avoid crossthreading them

Clean reusable plugs with a small file or a wire brush. The plug gap should be checked and readjusted, if necessary, by bending the ground electrode with a spark plug gapping tool.

NOTE: *Do not use a flat gauge to check plug gap; an incorrect reading will result. Use a wire gauge only.*

INSTALLATION

1. Lightly oil the spark plug threads and hand tighten them into the engine.

2. Tighten the plugs securely with a spark plug wrench (about 10 ft lbs of torque).

CAUTION: *Do not overtighten because of the aluminum threads.*

3. Connect the wires to the plugs, making sure that each is securely fitted.

Breaker Points and Condenser

The points and condenser function as a circuit breaker for the primary circuit of the ignition system. The ignition coil must boost the 12 volts (V) of electrical pressure supplied to it by the battery to about 20,000 V in order to fire the spark plugs. To do this, the coil depends on the points and condenser for assistance.

The coil has a primary and a secondary circuit. When the ignition key is turned to the "on" position, the battery supplies voltage to the primary side of the coil which passes the voltage on to the points. The points are connected to ground to complete the primary circuit. As the cam in the distributor turns, the points open and the primary circuit collapses. The magnetic force in the primary circuit of the coil cuts through the secondary circuit and increases the voltage in the secondary circuit to a level that is sufficient to fire the spark plugs. When the points open, the electrical charge contained in the primary circuit jumps the gap that is created between the two open contacts of the points. If this electrical charge was not transferred elsewhere, the material on the contacts of the points would melt and that all-important gap between the contacts would start to change. If this gap is not maintained, the points will not break the primary circuit. If the primary circuit is not broken, the secondary circuit will not have enough voltage to fire the spark plugs. Enter the condenser.

The function of the condenser is to absorb the excessive voltage from the points when they open and thus prevent the points from becoming pitted or burned.

There are two ways to check breaker point gap: with a feeler gauge or with a dwell meter. Either way you set the points, you are adjusting the amount of time (in degrees of distributor rotation) that the points will remain open. If you adjust the points with a feeler gauge, you are setting the maximum amount the points will open when the rubbing block on the points is on a high point of the distributor cam. When you adjust the points with a dwell meter, you are measuring the number of degrees (of distributor cam rotation) that the points will remain closed before they start to open as a high point of the distributor cam approaches the rubbing block of the points.

If you still do not understand how the points function, take a friend, go outside, and remove the distributor cap from your engine. Have your friend operate the starter (make sure the transmission is not in gear) as you look at the exposed parts of the distributor.

Tune-Up Specifications

Year	Model	Engine Displ. (cc)	Spark Plug Type	Gap	Point Dwell (deg)	Point Gap (in)	Ignition Timing (deg) MT	Ignition Timing (deg) AT	Intake Valve Opens (Deg)	Fuel Pump Pressure (psi)	Idle Speed MT	Idle Speed AT
1973	Civic	1170	B-6ES	.030	49–55	.020	TDC	TDC	32B	2.5	750–850[1]	700–800[1]
1974	Civic	1237	B-6ES	.030	49–55	.020	5B	5B	31B	2.5	750–850[1]	700–800[1]
1975	Civic CVCC	1487	B-6ES	.030	49–55	.020	TDC	3A	—	2.5	800–900[1]	700–800[1]
1975–78	Civic AIR	1237	B-6ES	.030	49–55	.020	7B	7B	31B	2.5	750–850[1]	700–800[1]
1976–78	Civic CVCC	1487	B-6ES	.030	49–55	.020	2B[3]	2B[2]	—	2.5	800–900[1]	700–800[1]
1975–78	Accord	1600	B-6ES	.030	49–55	.020	6B	2B	—	2.5	800–900[1]	700–800[1]
1979	Civic CVCC	1487	B-6EB	.030	49–55	.020	2B	6B	10A	2.5	650–750	600–700
	Civic AIR	1237	B-6ES	.030	49–55	.020	2B	2B	—	2.5	650–750	650–750
	Accord	1751	B-7EB	.030	Electronic		6B[4]	4B[5]	—	2.5	650–750	650–750
	Prelude	1751	B-7EB	.030	Electronic		6B[4]	4B[5]	—	2.5	650–750	650–750
1980	Civic CVCC	1487	B-7EB11	.042	Electronic		15B[6]	TDC[7]	—	2.5	700–800	700–800
	Civic AIR	1335	W20ES-L11	.042	Electronic		2B	TDC	10A	2.5	700–800	700–800
	Accord	1751	B-7EB	.030	Electronic		4B	TDC	—	2.5	750–850	750–850
	Prelude	1751	B-7EB	.030	Electronic		TDC	TDC	—	2.5	750–850	750–850
1981	Civic	1487	B6EB-11	.042	Electronic		10B[8]	2A	10A	2.5	700–800	700–800
	Civic	1335	W20ES-L11	.042	Electronic		2B	2B	10A	2.5	700–800	750–850
	Accord	1751	B6ER-L11	.042	Electronic		TDC	TDC	10A	2.5	750–850	750–850
	Prelude	1751	B6EB-L11	.042	Electronic		TDC	TDC	10A	2.5	750–850	750–850

Year	Model	Displacement	Spark Plug	Gap	Ignition	Timing	Timing			Idle Speed	Idle Speed
1982	Civic	1487	B6REB-L11	.042	Electronic	18B	18B	10A	2.5	650–750	650–750
	Civic	1335	W20ESR-L11	.042	Electronic	20B	—	10A	2.5	650–750	—
	Accord	1751	BR6EB-L11	.042	Electronic	16B (9)	16B	10A	2.5	750–850	750–850
	Prelude	1751	BR6EB-L11	.042	Electronic	12B (10)	16B	10A	2.5	700–800	700–800
'83	Civic	1487	BR6EB-11	0.042	Electronic	18B (11)	18B (11)	10A	2.5	650–750 (1)	650–750 (12)
	Civic	1335	BR6EB-11	0.042	Electronic	18B (11)(13)	—	10A	2.5	600–750 (1)	—
	Accord	1751	BR6EB-L11	0.042	Electronic	16B (9)	16B (11)	10A	2.5	700–800 (1)	650–750 (12)
	Prelude	1829	BUR6EB-11	0.042	Electronic	10B (11)(9)	12B (11)	N.A.	2.5	750–850 (1)	700–800 (12)
'84–'85	Civic	1488	BUR6EB-11	0.042	Electronic	(11)	(11)	N.A.	3.0	650–750	650–750
	Civic	1342	BUR6EB-11	0.042	Electronic	(11)	(11)	N.A.	3.0	650–750	—
	Accord	1829	BUR6EB-11	0.042	Electronic	22B (14)	18B	N.A.	2.5	700–800	650–750
	Prelude	1829	BPR6EY-11	0.042	Electronic	20B	12B	N.A.	2.5	750–850	750–850

(1) With headlights on
(2) Sta. Wgn.: TDC
(3) 5-speed sedan from engine #2500001 and up: 6B
(4) Calif. and high altitude: TDC
(5) Calif. and high altitude: 2B
(6) 49 states station wagon: 10B
(7) Calif. and high altitude: TDC
(8) Wagon/Sedan-4B, Calif.-2A
(9) Calif. 12B
(10) Calif., High altitude: 16B
(11) Use red mark (yellow mark on '78–'79 Accord w/M.T.) on flywheel or torque converter drive plate; distributor vacuum hose connected; @ idle
(12) In Drive; headlights on
(13) 4-sp: 20B
(14) Calif. 18B

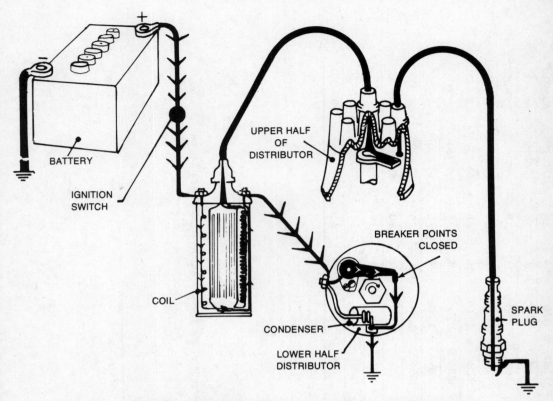

Primary side of ignition circuit is energized when breaker points are closed

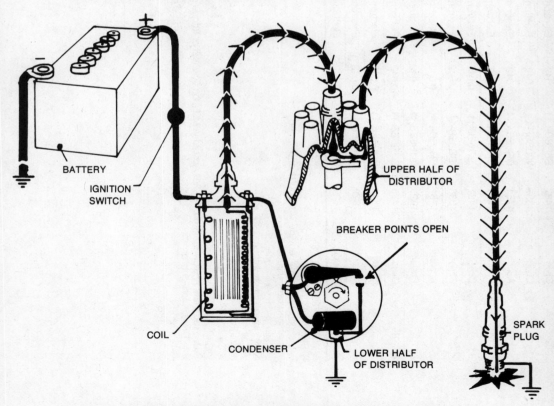

Secondary side of ignition circuit is energized when breaker points are open

NOTE: *There are two rules that should always be followed when adjusting or replacing points. The points and condenser are a matched set; never replace one without replacing the other. If you change the point gap or dwell of the engine, you also change the ignition timing. Therefore, if you adjust the points, you must also adjust the timing.*

INSPECTION

1. Disconnect the high-tension wire from the coil.

2. Unfasten the two retaining clips to remove the distributor cap.

3. Remove the rotor from the distributor shaft by pulling it straight up. Examine the condition of the rotor; if it is cracked or the metallic tip is excessively burned, replace it.

4. Pry the breaker points open with a screwdriver and examine the condition of the contact points. If the points are excessively worn, burned, or pitted they should be replaced.

NOTE: *Contact points which have been used for several thousand miles will have a gray, rough surface, but this is not necessarily an indication that they are malfunctioning. The roughness between the points matches so that a large contact area is maintained.*

5. If the points are in good condition, polish them with a point file.

NOTE: *Do not use emery cloth or sandpaper as they may leave particles on the points which could cause them to arc.*

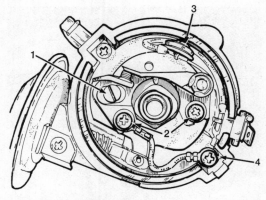

1. Point gap adjusting screw
2. Breaker point retaining screws
3. Primary lead wire connection
4. Ground wire connection

Distributor breaker plate details—all except CVCC Hondamatic. Notice that the rubbing block is on the high spot of the cam lobe

Primary wire removal

After polishing the points, refer to the section following the breaker point replacement procedures for proper adjustment. If the points need replacing, refer to the following procedure.

REMOVAL AND INSTALLATION

1. Remove the small nut from the terminal screw located in the side of the distributor housing and remove the nut, screw, condenser wire, and primary wire from the terminal. Remove the terminal from the slot in the distributor housing.

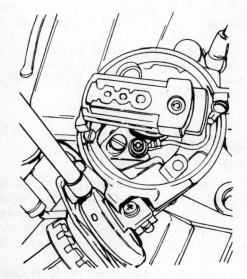

Pull the rotor straight up to remove it

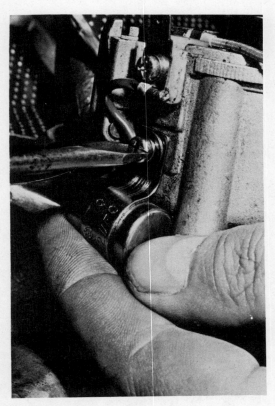

Condenser removal

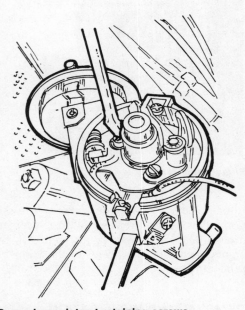

Removing point set retaining screws

2. Remove the screw(s) which attaches the condenser to the outside of the distributor housing (most models), or to the breaker plate inside the distributor (CVCC Hondamatic models), and remove the condenser.

Crankshaft pulley bolt access window—CVCC models

3. Unscrew the Phillips head screw which holds the ground wire to the breaker point assembly and lift the end of the ground wire out of the way.

4. Remove the two Phillips head screws which attach the point assembly to the breaker plate and remove the point assembly.

NOTE: *You should use a magnetic or locking screwdriver. Trying to locate one of these tiny screws after you've dropped it can be an excruciating affair.*

5. Wipe all dirt and grease from the distributor plate and cam with a lint-free cloth. Apply a small amount of heat-resistant lubricant to the distributor cam. Although the lube is supplied with most breaker point kits, you can buy it at any auto parts store if necessary.

6. Properly position the new points on the breaker plate of the distributor and secure with the two point screws. Attach the ground wire, with its screw, to the breaker plate assembly. Screw the condenser to its proper position on the distributor housing, or breaker plate.

7. Fit the terminal back into its notch in the distributor housing and attach the condenser and primary wires to the terminal screw and fasten with the nut.

ADJUSTMENT

With a Feeler Gauge

1. Rotate the crankshaft pulley until the point gap is at its greatest (where the rubbing block is on the high point of the cam lobe). This can be accomplished by using either a remote starter switch or by rotating the crankshaft pulley by hand.

2. At this position, insert the proper sized feeler gauge between the points. A slight

Adjusting point gap with feeler gauge

5. Recheck the point gap to be sure that it did not change when the breaker point attaching screws were tightened.

6. Align the rotor with the distributor shaft and push the rotor onto the shaft until it is fully seated.

7. Reinstall the distributor cap and the coil high-tension wire.

Rotating crankshaft pulley by hand

Dwell Angle

Dwell or cam angle refers to the amount of time the points remain closed, and is measured in degrees of distributor rotation. Dwell will vary according to the point gap, since dwell is a function of point gap. If the point gap is too wide, they open gradually, and dwell angle (the time they remain closed) is small. This wide gap causes excessive arcing at the points, leading to point burning. The insufficient dwell doesn't give the coil sufficient time to build up maximum energy, so coil output decreases. If the point gap is too small, dwell is increased and the idle becomes rough and starting is difficult. When setting points, remember: the wider the point opening, the smaller the dwell, and the smaller the point opening, the larger the dwell. When connecting a dwell meter, connect one lead (usually the black or negative lead) to a good ground on the engine, and the red or positive lead to the negative or distributor side of the coil. This terminal is easy to find; simply look for the terminal which has the small wire that leads to the distributor.

Closeup of the points showing the rubbing block exactly on one of a high spot of the cam

drag should be felt. Point gap should be 0.018–0.022 in.

3. If no drag is felt, or if the feeler gauge cannot be inserted, loosen, but do not remove the two breaker point set screws.

4. Adjust the points as follows:

Insert a screwdriver through the hole in the breaker point assembly and into the notch provided on the breaker plate. Twist the screwdriver to open or close the points. When the correct gap has been obtained, re-tighten the point set screws.

SETTING THE DWELL ANGLE

1. Connect a dwell-tach according to the manufacturer's instructions. See the preced-

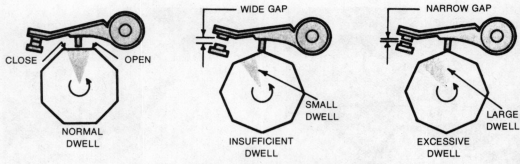

Dwell angle as a function of point gap

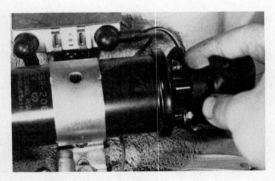

Ignition coil primary terminals

Taking a dwell reading. Notice the ground wire location

ing section for instructions on connecting the dwell meter.

2. With the engine warmed up and running at the specified idle speed, take a dwell reading.

3. If the point dwell is not within specifications, shut the engine off and adjust the point gap, as outlined earlier. Remember, increasing the point gap decreases the dwell angle and vice versa.

4. Check the dwell reading again and adjust it as required.

Electronic Ignition

All 1979 and later Hondas are equipped with a magnetic pulse type electronic ignition system. This system eliminates the points and condenser, and requires no periodic maintenance.

Ignition Timing

Ignition timing is the measurement, in degrees of crankshaft rotation, of the instant the spark plugs in the cylinders fire, in relation to the location of the piston, while the piston is on its compression stroke.

Ideally, the air/fuel mixture in the cylinder will be ignited (by the spark plug) and just beginning its rapid expansion as the piston passes top dead center (TDC) of the compression stroke. If this happens, the piston will be beginning the power stroke just as the compressed (by the movement of the piston) and ignited (by the spark plug) air/fuel mixture starts to expand. The expansion of the air/fuel mixture will then force the piston down on the power stroke and turn the crankshaft.

It takes a fraction of a second for the spark

from the plug to completely ignite the mixture in the cylinder. Because of this, the spark plug must fire before the piston reaches TDC, if the mixture is to be completely ignited as the piston passes TDC. This measurement is given in degrees (of crankshaft rotation) *before* the piston reaches *top dead center* (BTDC). If the ignition timing setting for your engine is six degrees (6°) BTDC, this means that the spark plug must fire at a time when the piston for that cylinder is 6° before top dead center of its compression stroke. However, this only holds true while your engine is at idle speed.

As you accelerate from idle, the speed of your engine (rpm) increases. The increase in rpm means that the pistons are now traveling up and down much faster. Because of this, the spark plugs will have to fire even sooner if the mixture is to be completely ignited as the piston passes TDC. To accomplish this, the distributor incorporates means to advance the timing of the spark as engine speed increases.

The distributor has two means of advancing the ignition timing. One is called centrifugal advance and is actuated by weights in the distributor. The other is called vacuum advance and is controlled in that large circular housing on the side of the distributor.

In addition, some Honda distributors have a vacuum-retard mechanism which is contained in the same housing on the side of the distributor as the vacuum advance. Models having two hoses going to the distributor vacuum housing have both vacuum advance *and* retard. The function of this mechanism is to regulate the timing of the ignition spark under certain engine conditions. This causes more complete burning of the air/fuel mixture in the cylinder and consequently lowers exhaust emissions.

If ignition timing is set too far advanced (BTDC), the ignition and expansion of the air/fuel mixture in the cylinder will try to force the piston down the cylinder while it is still traveling upward. This causes engine "ping." If the ignition timing is too far retarded (after, or ATDC), the piston will have already started down on the power stroke when the air/fuel mixture ignites and expands. This will cause the piston to be forced down only a portion of its travel. This will result in poor engine performance and lack of power.

IGNITION TIMING CHECKING AND ADJUSTING

Honda recommends that the ignition timing be checked at 12,000 mile intervals (1973–74), or 15,000 mile intervals (1975–78 later models), on 1979–82 models, check the timing only when problems are suspected. Also, the timing should always be adjusted after installing new points or adjusting the dwell angle. On all non-CVCC engines, the timing marks are located on the crankshaft pulley, with a pointer on the timing belt cover; all visible from the driver's side of the engine compartment. On all CVCC engines, the timing marks are located on the flywheel (manual transmission) or torque converter drive plate (automatic transmission), with a pointer on the rear of the cylinder block; all visible from the front right-side of the engine compartment after removing a special rubber access plug in the timing mark window. In all cases, the timing is checked with the engine warmed to operating temperature (176°F), idling in Neutral (manual trans.) or 2nd gear (Hondamatic), and with all vacuum hoses *connected.*

1. Stop the engine, and hook up a tachometer. The positive lead connects to the distributor side terminal of the ignition coil, and the negative lead to a good ground, such as an engine bolt.

NOTE: *On some models you will have to pull back the rubber ignition coil cover to reveal the terminals.*

2. Hook up a DC stroboscopic timing light to the engine. The positive and negative leads connect to their corresponding battery terminals and the spark plug lead to No. 1 spark plug. The No. 1 spark plug is the one at the driver's side of the engine compartment.

3. Make sure that all wires are clear of the cooling fan and hot exhaust manifolds. Start the engine. Check that the idle speed is set

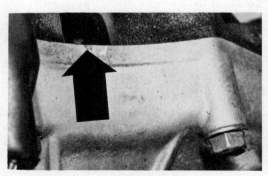

CVCC timing mark window location

Timing marks on the non-CVCC engines. The white mark is TDC

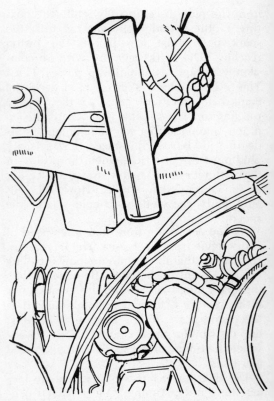

Checking the timing on a CVCC engine

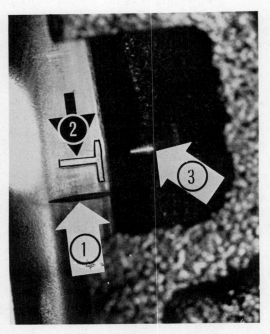

Details of CVCC engine timing marks. Arrow 1 is the red notch, which is the ignition timing mark. Arrow 2 is the TDC mark. The T has been outlined for clarity in this picture. Arrow 3 is the ignition timing pointer

CAUTION: *Make sure that the parking brake is firmly applied and the front wheels blocked to prevent the car from rolling forward when the automatic transmission is engaged.*

4. Point the timing light at the timing marks. On Non-CVCC cars, align the pointer with the "F" or red notch on the crankshaft pulley. On CVCC cars, align the pointer with the red notch on the flywheel or torque converter drive plate (except on cars where the timng specification is TDC in which case the "T" or white notch is used).

NOTE: *The timing light flashes every time the spark plug for the No. 1 cylinder fires. Since the timing light flash makes the crankshaft pulley or flywheel seem stationary, you will be able to read the exact position of No. 1 piston on the timing scale.*

5. If necessary, adjust the timing by loosening the larger distributor hold-down (clamp) bolt and slowly rotate the distributor in the required direction while observing the timing marks.

CAUTION: *Do not grasp the top of the distributor cap while the engine is running as you might get a nasty shock. Instead, grab the distributor housing to rotate.*

to specifications with the transmission in Neutral (manual transmission) or 2nd gear (Hondamatic). If not, adjust as outlined in this chapter. At any engine speed other than the specified idle speed, the distributor advance or retard mechanisms will actuate, leading to an erroneous timing adjustment.

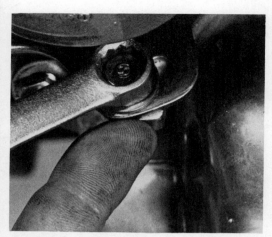

Loosen this distributor hold-down (clamp) bolt to rotate the distributor for ignition timing adjustments

If the timing cannot be adjusted within the range of the upper (larger) clamp bolt, this smaller one can be loosened to provide extra adjustment

After making the necessary adjustment, tighten the hold-down bolt, taking care not to disturb the adjustment.

NOTE: *There are actually two bolts which may be loosened to adjust ignition timing. There is a smaller bolt on the underside of the distributor swivel mounting plate. This smaller bolt should not be loosened unless you cannot obtain a satisfactory adjustment using the upper bolt. Its purpose is to provide an extra range of adjustment, such as in cases where the distributor was removed and then installed one tooth off.*

Valve Adjustment

Valve adjustment is one factor which determines how far the intake and exhaust valves will open into the cylinder.

If the valve clearance is too large, part of the lift of the camshaft will be used up in removing the excessive clearance, thus the

Valve Clearance Specifications

Year	Engine	Intake	Exhaust	Auxiliary
1973	1170	0.005–0.007	0.005–0.007	—
1974–79	1237	0.004–0.006	0.004–0.006	—
1975–78	1487	0.005–0.007	0.005–0.007	0.005–0.007
	1600	0.005–0.007	0.005–0.007	0.005–0.007
1979–80	1487	0.005–0.007	0.007–0.009	0.005–0.007
	1751	0.005–0.007	0.010–0.012	0.005–0.007
1980	1237	0.005–0.007	0.007–0.009	—
1981	1487	0.005–0.007	0.007–0.009	0.005–0.007
	1335	0.005–0.007	0.007–0.009	0.005–0.007
	1751	0.005–0.007	0.010–0.012	0.005–0.007
1982	1487	0.005–0.007	0.007–0.009	0.005–0.007
	1335	0.005–0.007	0.007–0.009	0.005–0.007
	1751	0.005–0.007	0.010–0.012	0.005–0.007
1983	1487	0.005–0.007	0.005–0.007	0.007–0.009
	1335	0.005–0.007	0.005–0.007	0.007–0.009
	1751	0.005–0.007	0.005–0.007	0.010–0.012
	1829	0.005–0.007	0.005–0.007	0.010–0.012
1984–85	1488	0.007–0.009	0.007–0.009	0.009–0.011
	1342	0.007–0.009	0.007–0.009	0.009–0.011
	1829	0.005–0.007	0.005–0.007	0.010–0.012

valves will not be opened far enough. This condition has two effects, the valve train components will emit a tapping noise as they take up the excessive clearance, and the engine will perform poorly, since the less the intake valves open, the smaller the amount of air/fuel mixture that will be admitted to the cylinders. The less the exhaust valves open, the greater the backpressure in the cylinder which prevents the proper air/fuel mixture from entering the cylinder.

If the valve clearance is too small, the intake and exhaust valves will not fully seat on the cylinder head when they close. When a valve seats on the cylinder head it does two things, it seals the combustion chamber so none of the gases in the cylinder can escape and it cools itself by transferring some of the heat it absorbed from the combustion process through the cylinder head and into the engine cooling system. Therefore, if the valve clearance is too small, the engine will run poorly (due to gases escaping from the combustion chamber), and the valves will overheat and warp (since they cannot transfer heat unless they are touching the seat in the cylinder head).

Distributor rotor at no. 1 piston Top Dead Center (TDC) position

Honda recommends that the valve clearance be checked at 12,000 mile intervals (1973–74 models), or 15,000 mile intervals (1975 and later models).

NOTE: *While all valve adjustments must be as accurate as possible, it is better to have the valve adjustment slightly loose than slightly tight, as burned valves may result from overly tight adjustments.*

All Non-CVCC Models

1. Adjust valves when the engine is cold (100°F or less).
2. Remove the valve cover and align the TDC (Top Dead Center) mark on the crankshaft pulley with the index mark on the timing belt cover. The TDC notch is the one immediately following the red 5° BTDC notch used for setting ignition timing.
3. When No. 1 cylinder is at TDC on the compression stroke, check and adjust the following valves (numbered from the crankshaft pulley end of the engine):
   • Intake—Nos. 1 and 2 cylinders
   • Exhaust—Nos. 1 and 3 cylinders
   Adjust the valves as follows
   a. Check valve clearance with a feeler gauge between the tip of the rocker arm and the top of the valve. There should be a slight drag on the feeler gauge;

Valve adjustment—CVCC and non-CVCC models

b. If there is no drag or if the gauge cannot be inserted, loosen the valve adjusting screw locknut;

c. Turn the adjusting screw with a screwdriver to obtain the proper clearance;

d. Hold the adjusting screw and tighten the locknut;

e. Recheck the clearance before reinstalling the valve cover.

4. Then rotate the crankshaft 360° and adjust:

- Intake—Nos. 3 and 4 cylinders
- Exhaust—Nos. 2 and 4 cylinders

CVCC Models

1. Make sure that the engine is cold (cylinder head temperature below 100°F).

2. Remove the valve cover. From the front of the engine, take a look at the forward face of the camshaft timing belt gear. When No. 1 cylinder as at Top Dead Center (TDC), the keyway for the woodruff key retaining the

Adjusting auxiliary valve clearance—CVCC models

timing gear to the camshaft will be facing up. On 1976 and later models, the word "UP" will be at the top of the gear. You can double-check this by distributor rotor position. Take some chalk or crayon and make where the No. 1 spark plug wire goes into the distributor cap on the distributor body. Then, remove the cap and check that the rotor points toward that mark.

3. With the No. 1 cylinder at TDC, you can adjust the following valves (numbered from the crankshaft pulley end of the engine):

- Intake—Nos. 1 and 2 cylinders
- Auxiliary Intake—Nos. 1 and 2 cylinders
- Exhaust—Nos. 1 and 3 cylinders

Adjust the valves as follows:

a. Check valve clearance with a feeler gauge between the tip of the rocker arm and the top of the valve. There should be a slight drag on the feeler gauge;

b. If there is no drag or if the gauge cannot be inserted, loosen the valve adjusting screw locknut;

c. Turn the adjusting screw with a screwdriver to obtain the proper clearance;

d. Hold the adjusting screw and tighten the locknut;

e. Recheck the clearance before reinstalling the valve cover.

4. To adjust the remaining valves, rotate the crankshaft to the No. 4 cylinder TDC position. To get the No. 4 cylinder to the TDC position, rotate the crankshaft 360 degrees. This will correspond to an 180 degree movement of the distributor rotor and camshaft timing gear. The rotor will now be pointing opposite the mark you made for the No. 1 cylinder. The camshaft timing gear keyway or "UP" mark will now be at the bottom (6 o'clock position). At this position, you may adjust the remaining valves:

- Intake—Nos. 3 and 4 cylinders
- Auxiliary Intake—Nos. 3 and 4 cylinders
- Exhaust—Nos. 2 and 4 cylinders

Carburetor Adjustments

This section contains only carburetor adjustments which apply to engine tune-up—namely, idle speed and mixture adjustments. Descriptions of the carburetors used and complete adjustment procedures can be found in the "Emission Controls" and "Fuel Systems" sections of Chapter 4.

Carburetor idle speed and mixture adjustment is the last step in any tune-up. Prior to making the final carburetor adjustments, make sure that the spark plugs, points and condenser, dwell angle, ignition timing, and valve clearance have all been checked, serviced, and, if necessary, adjusted. If any of these tune-up items have been overlooked, it may be difficult to obtain a proper carburetor adjustment.

NOTE: *All carburetor adjustments must be made with the engine fully warmed up to operating temperature (176°F).*

IDLE SPEED AND MIXTURE ADJUSTMENT

1973 Civic 1170 CC with Hitachi 2-bbl

1. Adjust the idle speed with the headlights on and the cooling fan off. The cooling fan can be disconnected by removing the leads from either the fan motor or the thermoswitch screwed into the base of the radiator, on the engine side.

Manual transmission models should be set in Neutral. Cars equipped with Hondamatic transmissions should be set in gear "1". Set the parking brake and block the front wheels.

2. Remove the limiter cap and turn the idle mixture screw counterclockwise, until engine speed drops. Now turn the idle speed screw in the reverse direction (clockwise) until the engine reaches its highest rpm. (If the idle speed reaches now above specification, repeat Steps 1 & 2.)

3. Continue to turn the idle mixture screw clockwise to obtain the specified rpm drop:
   - 4-speed—40 rpm
   - Hondamatic—20 rpm

4. Replace the limiter cap and reconnect the cooling fan lines.

1974 and later non-CVCC Civic with Hitachi 2-bbl

1. The idle speed is adjusted with the headlights on and the radiator cooling fan off. To make sure that the cooling fan stays off while you are making your adjustments, disconnect the fan leads.

NOTE: *Do not leave the cooling fan leads disconnected for any longer than necessary, as the engine may overheat.*

Manual transmission cars are adjusted with the transmission in Neutral. On Hondamatic cars, the idle adjustments are made with the car in gear "1." As a safety precaution, firmly apply the parking brake and block the front wheels.

2. Remove the plastic limiter cap from the idle mixture screw. Hook up a tachometer to the engine with the positive lead connected to the distributor side (terminal) of the coil and the negative lead to a good ground. On 1976 models, disconnect the breather hose from the valve cover.

3. Start the engine and adjust first the mixture screw (turn counterclockwise to richen), and then the idle speed screw for the best quality idle at 870 rpm (manual transmission), or 770 rpm (Hondamatic in gear).

4. Then, lean out the idle mixture (turn mixture screw clockwise), until the idle speed drops to 800 rpm (manual transmission), or 750 rpm (Hondamatic in gear).

5. Replace the limiter cap, connect the cooling fan, and disconnect the tachometer.

CVCC Models with Keihin 3-bbl through 1979

1. The idle speed is adjusted with the headlights on and the radiator cooling fan on. With the engine warmed to operating temperature and idling, the cooling fan should come on. But, if it doesn't, you can load the engine's electrical system (for purposes of adjusting the idle speed), by turning the high-speed heater blower on instead. Do not have both the cooling fan and heater blower operating simultaneously, as this will load the engine too much and lower the idle speed abnormally. Manual transmission cars are adjusted with the transmission in Neutral. On Hondamatic cars, the idle adjustments are made with the car in gear "2" (that's right, Hi gear). As a safety precaution, apply the parking brake and block the front wheels.

Idle speed and mixture screw locations on the Keihin 3-bbl carburetor used on the CVCC engines. Arrow 1 is the idle speed screw, and arrow 2 is the mixture screw. The 2-bbl carburetor used on the non-CVCC engines is similar

2. Remove the plastic cap from the idle mixture screw. Hook up a tachometer to the engine with the positive lead connected to the distributor side (terminal) of the coil and the negative lead to a good ground.

3. Start the engine and rotate the idle mixture screw counterclockwise (rich), until the highest rpm is achieved. Then, adjust the idle speed screw to 910 rpm (manual transmission), or 801 rpm (Hondamatic in Second gear).

4. Finally, lean out the idle mixture (turn mixture screw in clockwise), until the idle speed drops to 850 rpm (manual transmission), or 750 rpm Hondamatic in Second gear).

5. Replace the limiter cap and disconnect the tachometer.

1980 and Later

Changes in the carburetors have made the adjustment of the idle mixture impossible without a propane enrichment system not available to the general public. The idle speed may be adjusted as follows:

1. With the engine at normal operating temperature; remove the vacuum hose from the intake air control diaphragm and clamp the hose end.

2. Connect a tachometer to the engine.

3. With the headlights, heater blower, rear window defroster, cooling fan and air conditioner off, adjust the idle speed by turning the throttle stop screw to the rpm listed in the "Tune-Up Specifications" or underhood sticker.

Engine and Engine Rebuilding

3

ENGINE ELECTRICAL

Distributor

The distributor is bevel gear-driven by the camshaft. On non-CVCC engines, it is located at the crankshaft pulley end of the engine. On CVCC engines, the distributor is located in a special extension housing at the flywheel end of the engine.

All distributors utilize centrifugal advance mechanisms to increase ignition timing as engine speed increases. Centrifugal advance is controlled by a pair of weights located under the breaker point mounting plate. As the distributor shaft spins faster, the weights

Honda distributor. Note the helical teeth on the drive gear (arrow)

are affected by centrifugal force and move away from the shaft, advancing the timing.

In addition, all distributors use some kind of vacuum ignition control, although this varies from model to model.

Vacuum advance works as follows: When the engine is operating under low-load conditions (light acceleration), the vacuum diaphragm moves the breaker point mounting plate in the opposite direction of distributor rotation, thereby advancing the timing.

Vacuum retard, on the other hand, is actuated when the engine is operating under high-vacuum conditions (deceleration or idle), and moves the breaker point mounting plate in the same direction of rotation as the distributor, thereby retarding the spark. On models, equipped with both vacuum advance and retard, both these ignition characteristics are true. You can always tell a dual diaphragm distributor by its *two* hoses.

REMOVAL AND INSTALLATION
Breaker Point Type

1. Disconnect the high tension and primary lead wires that run from the distributor to the coil.

2. Unsnap the two distributor cap retaining clamps and remove the distributor cap. Position it out of the way.

3. Using chalk or paint, carefully mark the position of the distributor rotor in relation to the distributor housing, and mark the relation of the distributor housing to the engine block. When this is done, you should have a line on the distributor housing directly in line with the tip of the rotor, and another line on the engine block directly in line with the mark on the distributor housing.

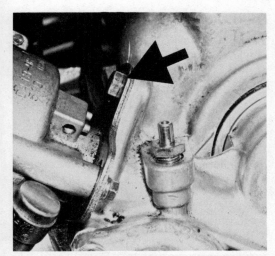

CVCC distributor hold-down bolt; non-CVCC similar

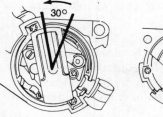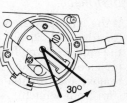

Upon installation the rotor will turn 30 degrees. Allow for this when installing the distributor. The figure on the left shows a typical installation for cars with manual transaxle; the one on the right shows installation for cars with automatic transaxle

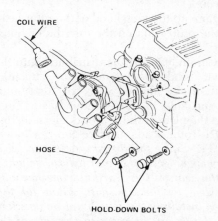

1983 and later Prelude distributor

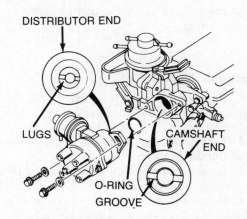

1342, 1488 and 1829cc distributor lug positioning

NOTE: *This aligning procedure is very important because the distributor must be reinstalled in the exact location from which it was removed, if correct ignition timing is to be maintained.*

4. Note the position of the vacuum line(s) on the vacuum diaphragm with masking tape and then disconnect the lines from the vacuum unit.

5. Remove the bolt which attaches the distributor to the engine block or distributor extension housing (CVCC), and remove the distributor from the engine.

CAUTION: *Do not disturb the engine while the distributor is removed. If you attempt to start the engine with the distributor removed, you will have to retime the engine.*

6. To install, place the rotor on the distributor shaft and align the tip of the rotor with the line that you made on the distributor housing.

7. With the rotor and housing aligned, insert the distributor into the engine while aligning the mark on the housing with the mark on the block, or extension housing (CVCC).

NOTE: *Since the distributor pinion gear has helical teeth, the rotor will turn slightly as the gear on the distributor meshes with the gear on the camshaft. Allow for this when installing the distributor by aligning the mark on the distributor with the mark on the block, but poisitioning the tip of the rotor slightly to the side of the mark on the distributor.*

8. When the distributor is fully seated in the engine, install and tighten the distributor retaining bolt.

9. Align and install the distributor cap and snap the retaining clamps into place.

10. Install the high-tension and primary wires onto the coil.

11. Check the ignition timing as outlined in Chapter 2.

INSTALLATION WHEN ENGINE HAS BEEN DISTURBED

If the engine was cranked with the distributor removed, it will be necessary to retime the engine. If you have installed the distributor incorrectly and the engine will not start, remove the distributor from the engine and start from scratch.

1. Install the distributor with No. 1 cylinder at the top dead center position on the compression stroke (the "TDC" mark on the crankshaft pulley (or flywheel) aligned with the index mark on the timing belt cover or crankcase).

2. Line up the metal end of the rotor head with the protrusion on the distributor housing.

3. Carefully insert the distributor into the cylinder head opening with the attaching plate bolt slot aligned with the distributor mounting hole in the cylinder head. Then secure the plate at the center of the adjusting slot. The rotor head must face No. 1 cylinder.

NOTE: *Since the distributor pinion gear has helical teeth, the rotor will turn slightly as the gear on the distributor meshes with the gear on the camshaft. Allow for this when installing the distributor by positioning the tip of the rotor to the side of the protrusion.*

4. Inspect and adjust the point gap and ignition timing.

Electronic Ignition Type

1. Remove the spark plug wires from the cap, numbering them for installation as they are removed.

2. Disconnect the hoses and other wires from the distributor.

3. Remove the holddown bolt and pull the distributor from the head.

4. Crank the engine until #1 piston is at TDC.

5. Install a new O-ring on the distributor housing.

6. Align the raised mark on the lower part of the distributor housing with the punch mark on the distributor gear shaft.

7. Insert the distributor into the head and the rotor will turn to #1 firing position. Loosely install the holddown bolt. Tighten the bolt temporarily and replace the cap.

8. Connect all wires and hoses.

9. Start the engine and adjust the ignition timing.

FIRING ORDER

To avoid confusion, replace spark plug wires one at a time.

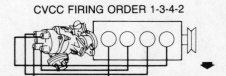

Firing order—1829cc Accord (1984 and later)

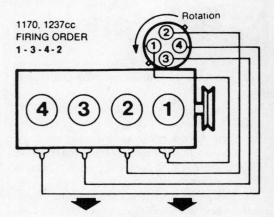

Front of car
Non–CVCC firing order

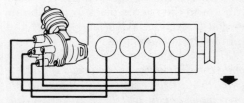

Firing order—1342 & 1488cc Civic (1984 and later)

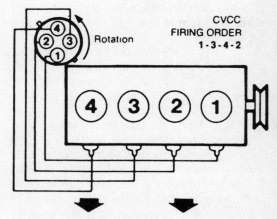

Front of car
Firing order—1978–83 CVCC (exc. 1829cc Prelude)

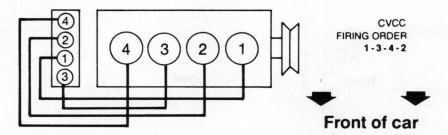

CVCC
FIRING ORDER
1 - 3 - 4 - 2

Front of car

Firing order—1983 and later 1829cc Prelude

Alternator

The alternator converts the mechanical energy which is supplied by the drive belt into electrical energy by electromagnetic induction. When the ignition switch is turned on, current flows from the battery, through the charging system light or ammeter, to the voltage regulator, and finally to the alternator. When the engine is started, the drive belt turns the rotating field (rotor) in the stationary windings (stator), inducing alternating current. This alternating current is converted into usable direct current by the diode rectifier. Most of this current is used to charge the battery and power the electrical components of the vehicle. A small part is returned to the field windings of the alternator enabling it to increase its output. When the current in the field windings reaches a predetermined control voltage, the voltage regulator grounds the circuit, preventing any further increase. The cycle is continued so that the voltage remains constant.

On non-CVCC models, the alternator is located beneath the distributor toward the rear of the engine compartment. On CVCC models, the alternator is located near the No. 1 spark plug at the front of the engine compartment. On CVCC models equipped with air conditioning, the alternator is mounted on a special vibration-absorbing bracket at the driver's side of the engine compartment.

PRECAUTIONS

1. Observe the proper polarity of the battery connections by making sure that the positive (+) and negative (−) terminal connections are not reversed. Misconnection will allow current to flow in the reverse direction, resulting in damaged diodes and an overheated wire harness.

CVCC alternator mounting

Alternator mounting—CVCC models with air conditioning

Alternator wiring connections—CVCC shown

2. Never ground or short out any alternator or alternator regulator terminals.

3. Never operate the alternator with any of its or the battery's leads disconnected.

4. Always remove the battery or disconnect its output lead while charging it.

5. Always disconnect the ground cable when replacing any electrical components.

6. Never subject the alternator to excessive heat or dampness.

7. Never use arc-welding equipment with the alternator connected.

REMOVAL AND INSTALLATION

All Models

1. Disconnect the negative (−) battery terminal.

2. Unplug the wires from the plugs on the rear of the alternator.

3. Loosen and remove the two alternator mounting bolts and remove the V-belt and alternator assembly.

4. To install, reverse the removal procedure. Adjust the alternator belt tension according to the "Belt Tension Adjustment" section below.

BELT TENSION ADJUSTMENT

The initial inspection and adjustment to the alternator drive belt should be performed after the first 3,000 miles or if the alternator has been moved for any reason. Afterwards, you should inspect the belt tension every 12,000 miles. Before adjusting, inspect the belt to see that it is not cracked or worn. Be sure that its surfaces are free of grease and oil.

1. Push down on the belt halfway between pulleys with a force of about 24 lbs. The belt should deflect 0.47–0.67 in. (12–117 mm).

2. If the belt tension requires adjustment, loosen the adjusting link bolt and move the alternator with a pry bar positioned against the front of the alternator housing.
CAUTION: *Do not apply pressure to any other part of the alternator.*

3. After obtaining the proper tension, tighten the adjusting link bolt.
CAUTION: *Do not overtighten the belt; damage to the alternator bearings could result.*

Regulator

The regulator is a device which controls the output of the alternator. If the regulator did not limit the voltage output of the alternator, the excessive output could burn out components of the electrical system, as well as the alternator itself.

REMOVAL AND INSTALLATION

All except 1982–83 Accord

The regulator is inside the engine compartment, attached to the right fenderwall just above the battery.

1. Disconnect the negative (−) terminal from the battery.

2. Remove the regulator terminal lead wires.
NOTE: *You should label these wires to avoid confusion during installation.*

3. Unscrew the two regulator retaining bolts and remove the regulator from the car.

4. To install, reverse the removal procedure.

1982–83 Accord

1. Disconnect the negative (−) terminal from the battery.

2. Remove the four main fuse plate retain-

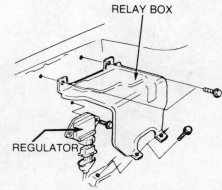

1982–83 Accord voltage regulator mounting

Alternator and Regulator Specifications

Year	Engine Displacement (cc)	Alternator Part No. or Manufacturer	Field Current @ 12 V (amps)	Output (amps) @ 5,000 rpm	Regulator Part No. or Manufacturer	Field Relay Yoke Gap (in.)	Field Relay Point Gap (in.)	Field Relay Volts to Close	Regulator Yoke Gap (in.)	Regulator Point Gap (in.)	Regulator Volts (@ 5,000 rpm)
1973–80	1170, 1237	Hitachi	2.5	40 ① 35 ②	Hitachi	0.008–0.018	0.0016–0.0472	4.5–5.8	0.008–0.024	0.010–0.018	13.5–14.5
1975–83	1487, 1600 CVCC	Nippon Denso	2.5	35 ③ 45 ④	Nippon Denso	—	—	—	—	0.016–0.020	13.5–14.5
1979–83	1751	Nippon Denso	2.5	55	Nippon Denso	0.008–0.024	0.016–0.047	—	0.018–0.022	0.018–0.022	13.5–14.5
'80–'83	1335 CVCC	Nippon Denso	2.5	45	Nippon Denso	0.008–0.018	0.020–0.050	N.A.	0.020	0.016–0.047	13.5–14.5
'84–'85	1342 CVCC	Nippon Denso Mitsubishi	2.5	55	Nippon Denso Mitsubishi ⑥	N.A.	N.A.	N.A.	N.A.	N.A.	13.5–14.5
'84–'85	1488 CVCC	Nippon Denso Mitsubishi	2.5	55	Nippon Denso Mitsubishi ⑥	N.A.	N.A.	N.A.	N.A.	N.A.	13.5–14.5
'83–'85	1829 CVCC	Nippon Denso	2.5	60	Nippon Denso ⑤	N.A.	N.A.	N.A.	N.A.	N.A.	13.5–14.5

① From No. 1011759
② Up to No. 1011158
③ Without A/C
④ With A/C
⑤ Wagon: 7.87
⑥ Wagon: 7.91

ing bolts and remove the main fuse plate to gain access to the solid state regulator.

3. Remove the regulator terminal plug from the regulator.

4. Unscrew the regulator retaining bolts and remove the regulator from the car.

5. To install, reverse the removal procedure.

Starter

The starter is located on the firewall side of the engine block, adjacent to the flywheel or torque converter housing. 1170 cc and 1237 cc models use a direct drive-type starter, while the CVCC uses a gear reduction starter. Otherwise, the two units are similar in operation and service. Both starters are four-pole, series-wound, DC units to which an outboard solenoid is mounted. When the ignition is turned to the "start" position, the solenoid armature is drawn in, engaging the starter pinion with the flywheel. When the starter pinion and flywheel are fully engaged, the solenoid armature closes the main contacts for the starter, causing the starter to crank the engine. When the engine starts, the increased speed of the flywheel causes the gear to overrun the starter clutch and rotor. The gear continues in full mesh until the ignition is switched from the "start" to the "on" position, interrupting the starter current. The shift lever spring then returns the gear to its neutral position.

REMOVAL AND INSTALLATION

1. Disconnect the ground cable at the battery negative (−) terminal, and the starter motor cable at the positive terminal.

2. Disconnect the starter motor cable at the motor.

3. Remove the starter motor by loosening

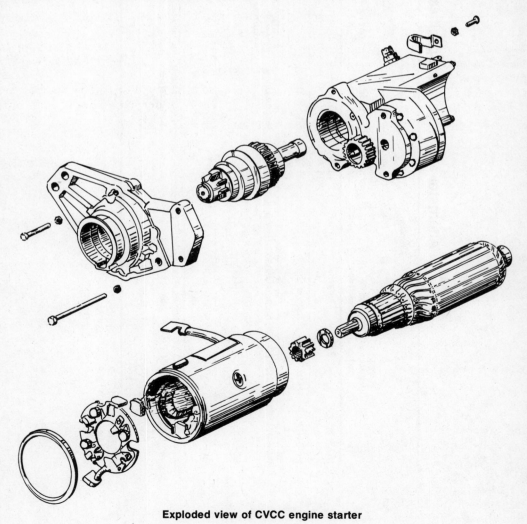

Exploded view of CVCC engine starter

Battery and Starter Specifications

Year	Engine Displacement (cc)	Battery			Starter							Brush Spring Tension (oz)	Min Brush Length (in.)
		Ampere Hour Capacity	Volts	Terminal Grounded	Lock Test			No-Load Test					
					Amps	Volts	Torque (ft. lbs.)	Amps	Volts	RPM			
1973–85	1170, 1237, 1335	45	12	Negative	380 or less	4.9	5.42	Less than 70	12	7000+		56.448	
1975–85	1487, 1600, 1751, 1829 CVCC	45	12	Negative	160 @ 68°F	9.6	—	Less than 80	11.5	—		—	0.39

CVCC starter showing rear bolt (arrow)

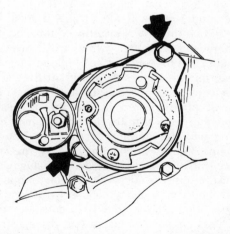

Non-CVCC engine starter showing mounting bolts (arrows)

the two attaching bolts. On CVCC models, the bolts attach from opposing ends of the starter.

4. Reverse the removal procedure to install the motor. Be sure to tighten the attaching bolts to 29–36 ft lbs and make sure that all wires are securely connected.

STARTER DRIVE REPLACEMENT

All Non-CVCC Civics, and California and High Altitude CVCC Civics

1. Remove the solenoid by loosening and removing the attaching bolts.

2. Remove the two brush holder plate retaining screws from the rear cover. Also pry off the rear dust cover along with the clip and thrust washer(s).

3. Remove the two thru–bolts from the rear cover and lightly tap the rear cover with a mallet to remove it.

4. Remove the four carbon brushes from the brush holder and remove the brush holder.

5. Separate the yoke from the case. The yoke is provided with a hole for positioning, into which the gear case lock pin is inserted.

6. Pull the yoke assembly from the gear case, being sure to carefully detach the shift lever from the pinion.

7. Remove the armature unit from the yoke casing and the field coil.

8. To remove the pinion gear from the armature, first set the armature on end with the pinion end facing upward and pull the clutch stop collar downward toward the pinion. Then remove the pinion stop clip and pull the pinion stop and gears from the armature shaft as a unit.

9. To assemble and install the starter motor, reverse the disassembly and removal procedures. Be sure to install new clips, and

Removing pinion gear from armature

be careful of the installation direction of the shift lever.

Reduction Gear Type

A reduction gear starter is used on the Prelude, Accord and the 49 States CVCC Civics.

1. Remove the solenoid end cover. Pull out the solenoid. There is a spring on the shaft and a steel ball at the end of the shaft.

2. Remove the through bolts retaining the end frame to the motor and solenoid housing.

3. Remove the end frame. The over-running clutch assembly complete with drive gear can be removed. The idler and motor pinion gears can be removed separately. The idler gear retains five steel roller bearings.

4. The clutch assembly is held together by a circlip. Push down on the gear against the spring inside the clutch assembly and remove the circlip with a circlip expander. Slide the stopper ring, gear, spring, and washer out of the clutch assembly.

5. Assembly is the reverse. The stopper ring is installed with the smaller end with the lip towards the clutch. Be sure that the steel ball is in place at the end of the solenoid shaft. Grease all sliding surfaces of the solenoid before reassembly.

ENGINE MECHANICAL

Design

The engines used in the Honda Civic, Accord and Prelude are water-cooled, overhead cam, transversely mounted, inline four cylinder powerplants. They can be divided into two different engine families; CVCC and non-CVCC.

The non-CVCC engines have been offered in two different displacements; 1170 cc (1973 only), and 1237 cc (1974 and later). These engines are somewhat unusual in that both the engine and the cylinder head are aluminum. The cylinder head is a crossflow design. The block uses sleeved cylinder liners and a main bearing girdle to add rigidity to the block. The engine uses five main bearings.

The CVCC (Compound Vortex Controlled Combustion) engine is unique in that its cylinder head is equipped with three valves per cylinder, instead of the usual two. Besides the intake and exhaust valve, each cylinder has an auxiliary intake valve which is much smaller than the regular intake valve. This auxiliary intake valve has its own separate precombustion chamber (adjacent to the

Frontal view of CVCC engine

main chamber with a crossover passage), its own intake manifold passages, and its own carburetor circuit.

Briefly, what happens is this; at the beginning of the intake stroke, a small but very rich mixture is introduced into the precombustion chamber, while next door in the main combustion chamber, a large but very lean mixture makes its debut. At the end of the compression stroke, ignition occurs. The spark plug, located in the precombustion chamber, easily ignites the rich auxiliary mixture and this ignition spreads out into the main combustion chamber, where the large lean mixture is ignited. This two-stage combustion process allows the engine to operate efficiently with a much leaner overall air/fuel ratio. So, whereas the 1975 and later non-CVCC engines require a belt-driven air injection system to control pollutants, the CVCC accomplishes this internally and gets better gas mileage.

Engine Removal and Installation

CAUTION: *If any repair operation requires the removal of a component of the air conditioning system (on vehicles so equipped), do not disconnect the refrigerant lines. If it is impossible to move the*

*component out of the way with the lines at-
tached, have the air conditioning system
evaluated by a trained serviceman. The air
conditioning system contains freon under
pressure. This gas can be very dangerous.
Therefore, under no circumstances should
an untrained person attempt to disconnect
the air-conditioner refrigerant lines.*

1170, 1237 cc Models

1. Raise the front of the car and support
it with safety stands.

2. Remove the front wheels.

3. Drain the engine, transmission, and
radiator.

4. Remove the front turn signal lights
and grille.

5. Remove the hood support bolts and
the hood. Remove the fan shroud, if so
equipped.

6. Remove the air cleaner case, and air
intake pipe at the air cleaner.

7. Disconnect the battery and engine
ground cables at the battery and the valve
cover.

8. Disconnect the hose from the fuel
vapor storage canister at the carburetor.

9. Disconnect the fuel line at the fuel
pump.

NOTE: *Plug the line so that gas does not
siphon from the tank.*

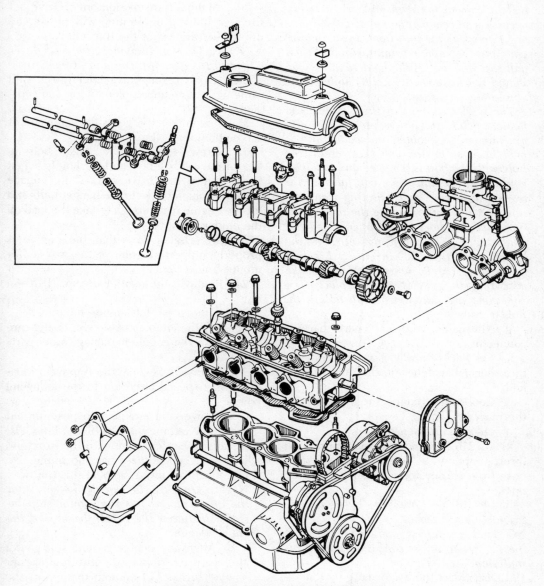

Exploded view of 1170 1237, 1335 cc engine

10. Disconnect the lower coolant hose at the water pump connecting tube and the upper hose at the thermostat cover.

11. Disconnect the following control cables and wires from the engine:

a. Throttle and choke cables at the carburetor;

b. Clutch cable at the release arm;

c. Ignition coil wires at the distributor;

d. Starter motor positive battery cable connection and solenoid wire;

e. Back-up light switch and T.C.S. (Transmission Controlled Spark) switch wires from the transmission casing;

f. Speedometer and tachometer cables;

CAUTION: *When removing the speedometer cable from the transmission, it is not necessary to remove the entire cable holder. Remove the end boot (gear holder seal) and the cable retaining clip and then pull the cable out of the holder. In no way should you disturb the holder unless it is absolutely necessary.*

The holder consists of three pieces: the holder, collar, and a dowel pin. The dowel pin indexes the holder and collar and is held in place by the bolt that retains the holder. If the bolt is removed and the holder rotated, the dowel pin can fall into the transmission case, necessitating transmission disassembly to remove the pin. To insure that this does not happen when the holder must be removed, do not rotate the holder more than 30° in either direction when removing it. Once removed, make sure that the pin is still in place. Use the same precaution when installing the holder.

g. Alternator wire and wire harness connector;

h. The wires from both water temperature thermal switches on the intake manifold;

i. Cooling fan connector and radiator thermoswitch wires;

j. Oil pressure sensor;

k. On 1975–76 models, vacuum hose to throttle opener at opener, and vacuum hose from carburetor insulator to throttle opener;

l. On 1976–77 models, by-pass valve assemble and bracket.

NOTE: *It would be a good idea to tag all of these wires to avoid confusion during installation.*

12. Disconnect the heater hose by removing the "H" connector from the two hoses in the firewall.

13. Remove the engine torque rod from the engine and firewall.

14. Remove the starter motor.

15. Remove the radiator from the engine compartment.

16. Remove the exhaust pipe-to-manifold clamp.

17. Remove the exhaust pipe flange nuts and lower the exhaust pipe.

18. Disconnect the left and right lower control arm ball joints at the knuckle, using a ball joint remover (or special tool 07941-6340000).

19. Hold the brake disc and pull the right and left drive shafts out of the differential case.

20a. Manual transmission only: Drive out the gearshift rod pin (8 mm) with a drift and disconnect the rod at the transmission case.

NOTE: *Do not disconnect the shift lever end of the gearshift rod and extension.*

20b. Hondamatic only: Disconnect shift cable at console and cooler line at transmission.

21. Disconnect the gearshift extension at the engine (man. trans. only).

22. Screw in two engine hanger bolts in the torque rod bolt hole and the bolt hole just to the left of the distributor. Then, engage the lifting chain hooks to the hanger bolts and lift the engine just enough to take the load off the engine mounts.

23. After being sure that the engine is properly supported, remove the two center mount bracket nuts.

24. Remove the center beam (1973–74 only).

25. Remove the left engine mount.

26. Lift the engine out slowly, taking care not to allow the engine to damage other parts of the car.

27. To install, reverse the removal procedure. Pay special attention to the following points:

a. Lower the engine into position and install the left mount. On 1973–74 models, install the center beam with the front end between the stabilizer bar and frame. Do not attach mounting bolts at this time.

NOTE: *On 1973–74 models, be sure that the lower mount has the mount stop installed between the center beam and the rubber mount.*

b. Align the center mount studs with the beam and tighten the nuts and washer several turns (just enough to support the beam). On 1973–74 models, attach the rear end of the center beam to the subframe.

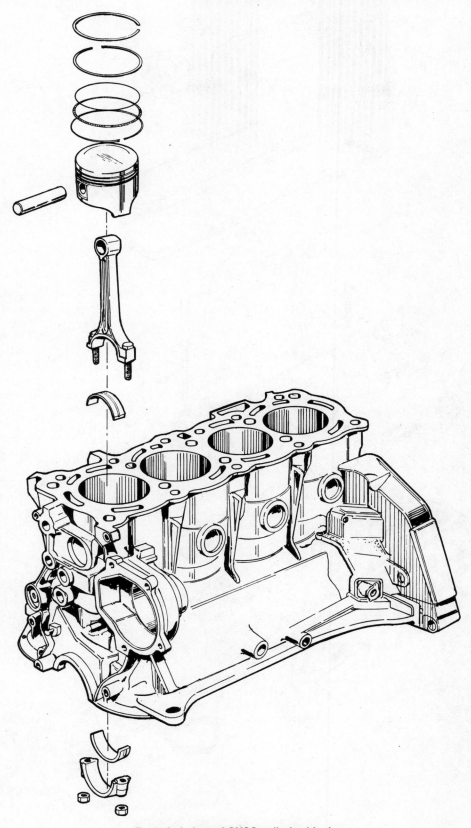

Exploded view of CVCC cylinder block

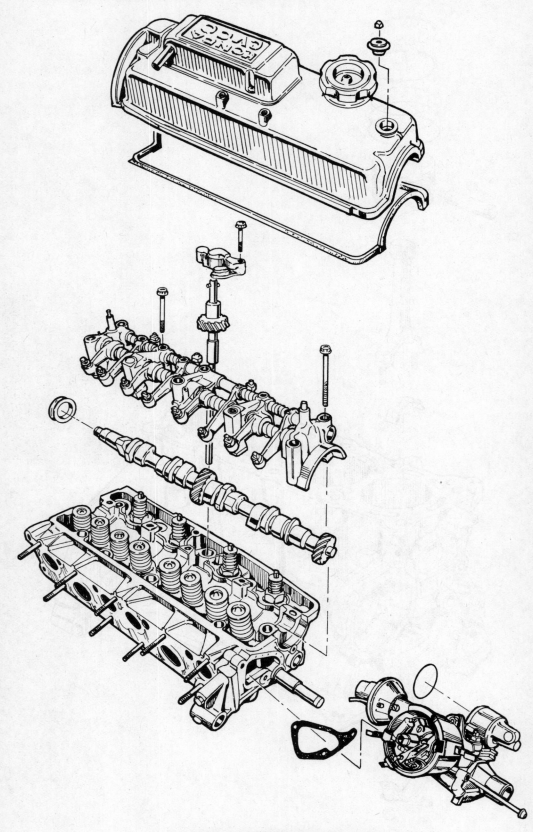

Exploded view of CVCC cylinder head

c. On 1973–74 models, attach the front end of the center beam. Torque the center beam bolts but do not tighten the lower mount nuts. Lower the engine so it rests on the lower mount. Torque the lower mount nuts.

d. Use a new shift rod pin;

e. After installing the driveshafts, attempt to move the inner joint housing in and out of the differential housing. If it moves easily, the driveshaft end clips should be replaced;

f. Make sure that the control cables and wires are connected properly;

g. When connecting the heater hoses, the upper hose goes to the water pump connecting pipe and the lower hose to the intake manifold;

h. Refill the engine, transmission, and radiator with their respective fluids to the proper levels;

i. On Hondamatic cars, check shift cable adjustment.

1335 and 1487 cc CVCC Models

1. Raise the front of the car and support it with jackstands. On models through 1979, remove both front wheels.

2. Remove the headlight rim attaching screws and the rims. On 1980–82 models, remove the battery, tray, and mount.

3. Open the hood. Disconnect both parking light connectors. Remove the parking

Center mount nut locations (arrows)

Thermosensors and coolant temperature sending unit locations. Arrow 1 is the temperature sending unit, arrow 2 is thermosensor "A", and arrow 3 is the thermosensor "B"

Emission control black box—1976 type shown

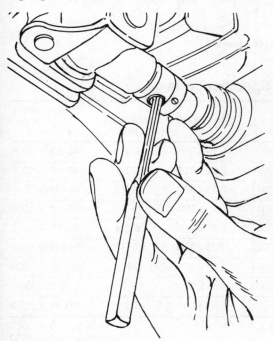

Driving gearshift rod pin out using pin driver

light retaining bolts and backing plate and remove the parking lights.

4. Remove the lower grille molding and remove the six grille retaining bolts and the grille.

5. Disconnect the windshield washer

hose and remove it from the underside of the hood.

6. Disconnect the negative battery cable and the tranmission bracket-to-body ground cable.

7. Remove the upper torque (engine locating) arm.

8. Disconnect the vacuum hose at the power brake booster, thermosensors "A" and "B" at their wiring connectors, and the coolant temperature gauge sending unit wire.

9. Drain the radiator. After all coolant has drained, install the drain bolt finger-tight.

10. Disconnect all four coolant hoses. Disconnect cooling fan motor connector and the temperature sensor. Remove the radiator hose to the overflow tank.

11. On Hondamatic cars only, remove both ATF cooler line bolts.

NOTE: *Save the washers from the cooler line banjo connectors and replace if damaged.*

12. Remove the radiator.

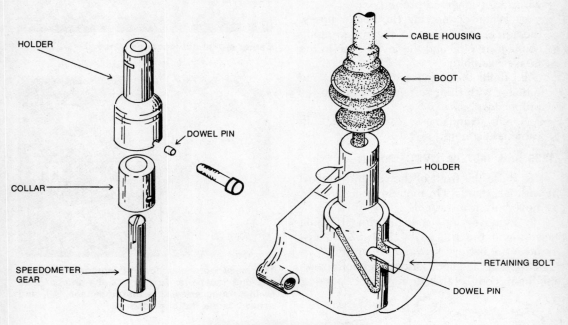

Speedometer cable removal

General Engine Specifications

Year	Engine Displacement (cc)	Horsepower @ rpm	Torque @ rpm (ft. lb.)	Bore x Stroke (in.)	Compression Ratio	Oil Pressure @ rpm (psi)
1973	1170	50 @ 5000	59 @ 3000	2.76 x 2.99	8.3:1	48–59 @ 5000
1974–79	1237	63 @ 5000	77 @ 3000	2.83 x 3.23	7.9:1	48–59 @ 5000
1980–83	1335	68 @ 5000	77 @ 3000	2.83 x 3.23	7.9:1 ③	48–59 @ 5000
1975–82	1488	53 @ 5000	68 @ 3000	2.91 x 3.41	7.9:1 ⑦	48–59 @ 5000
1976–78	1600	68 @ 5000	85 @ 3000	2.91 x 3.66	8.2:1	48–59 @ 5000
1979–82	1751	72 @ 4500	94 @ 3000	3.03 x 3.70	8.0:1 ②	54–59 @ 5000
1983	1751	75 @ 4500	99 @ 3000	3.03 x 3.70	8.8:1	54–59 @ 5000
1983–85	1829	86 @ 5800 ④	99 @ 3500 ⑤	3.15 x 3.58	9.0:1 ⑥	60 @ 5000
1984–85	1488	76 @ 6000	84 @ 3500	2.91 x 341	9.0:1	48–59 @ 5000

① 1975: 8.0:1
   1980: 8.9:1 49 states
      9.0:1 Calif.

② 1980 Prelude: 8.9: 1 Calif.
③ '81: 8.8:1
   '82: 9.3:1

④ Prelude: 100 @ 5500
⑤ Prelude: 104 @ 4000
⑥ Prelude: 9.4:1

Valve Specifications

Year	Engine Displacement (cc)	Seat Angle (deg)	Face Angle (deg)	Spring Installed Height (in.)	Stem to Guide Clearance (in.)			Stem Diameter (in.)		
					Intake	Exhaust	Auxiliary	Intake	Exhaust	Auxiliary
1973 1974–79	1170, 1237	45	45	Inner: 1.6535 Outer: 1.5728	0.005– 0.007	0.005– 0.007	—	0.2591– 0.2594	0.2579– 0.2583	—
1975–78	1487, 1600	45	45	Inner: 1.358 Outer: 1.437 Auxiliary: 0.906	0.0004– 0.0016	0.0020– 0.0031	0.0008– 0.0020	0.2592– 0.2596	0.2580– 0.2584	0.2162– 0.2166
1979	1487	45	45	Intake inner: 1.401 Intake outer: 1.488 Exhaust inner: 1.358 Exhaust outer: 1.437 Auxiliary: 0.906	0.0004– 0.0016	0.0020– 0.0031	0.0008– 0.0020	0.2592– 0.2596	0.2580– 0.2584	0.2162– 0.2166
1979–80	1751	45	45	Intake inner: 1.000 Intake outer: 1.094 Exhaust inner: 1.031 Exhaust outer: 1.109 Auxiliary: 0.875	0.0008– 0.0020	0.0024– 0.0035	0.0009– 0.0023	0.2748– 0.2753	0.2732– 0.2736	0.2587– 0.2593
1981–83	1335, 1487	45	45	Intake inner: 1.402 Intake outer: 1.488 Exhaust outer: 1.402 Exhaust outer: 1.488 Auxiliary: 0.984 ①	0.0008– 0.0020	0.0024– 0.0035	0.0009– 0.0023	0.2591– 0.2594	0.2574– 0.2578	0.2587– 0.2593
1981–83	1751	45	45	Intake inner: 1.402 Intake outer: 1.488 Exhaust inner: 1.402 Exhaust outer: 1.488 Auxiliary: 0.984	0.001– 0.002	0.002– 0.004	0.0009– 0.0023	0.2748– 0.2751	0.2732– 0.2736	0.2587– 0.2593
'83–'85	1829	45	45	Intake: 1.660 Exhaust inner: 1.460 Exhaust outer: 1.670 Auxiliary: 0.984	0.001– 0.002	0.002– 0.004	0.001– 0.002	0.2591– 0.2594	0.2732– 0.2736	0.2587– 0.2593

Valve Specifications (cont.)

Year	Engine Displacement (cc)	Seat Angle (deg)	Face Angle (deg)	Spring Installed Height (in.)	Stem to Guide Clearance (in.)			Stem Diameter (in.)		
					Intake	Exhaust	Auxiliary	Intake	Exhaust	Auxiliary
'84–'85	1342, 1488	45	45	Intake: 1.690 Exhaust: 1.690 Auxiliary: 0.980	0.001– 0.002	0.002– 0.003	0.001– 0.002	0.2591– 0.2594	0.2579– 0.2583	0.2587– 0.2593

① 1980 1335: 0.906

Crankshaft and Connecting Rod Specifications

All measurements given in in.

Year	Engine Displacement (cu in.)	Crankshaft				Connecting Rod		
		Main Brg Journal Dia	Main Brg Oil Clearance	Shaft End Play	Thrust on No.	Journal Dia	Clearance Oil	Side Clearance
1973–78	1170, 1237	1.9685– 1.9673	0.0009– 0.0017	0.0039– 0.0138	3	1.5736– 1.548	0.0008– 0.0015	0.0079– 0.0177 ①
1975–78	1600, 1487 CVCC	1.9687– 1.9697	0.0010– 0.0021	0.0039– 0.0138	3	1.6525– 1.6535	0.0008– 0.0015	0.0059– 0.0118
1979–79	1237	1.9687– 1.9697	0.0009– 0.0017	0.0040– 0.0140	3	1.5739– 1.5748	0.0008– 0.0015	0.006– 0.012
1979–80	1487	1.9687– 1.9697	0.0010– 0.0022	0.0040– 0.0140	3	1.6526– 1.6535	0.0008– 0.0015	0.006– 0.012
1979–83	1751	1.9687– 1.9697	0.0010– 0.0017	0.0040– 0.0140	3	1.6526– 1.6535	0.0008– 0.0015	0.006– 0.012
1980	1335	1.9687– 1.9697	0.0010– 0.0022	0.0040– 0.0140	3	1.6526– 1.6535	0.0008– 0.0015	0.006– 0.012
1981–83	1335	1.9676– 1.9685	0.0010– 0.0022	0.0040– 0.0140	3	1.6526– 1.6535	0.0008– 0.0015	0.006– 0.012
1981	1487	1.9676– 1.9685	0.0010– 0.0021	0.0040– 0.0140	3	1.6525– 1.6535	0.0008– 0.0015	0.0059– 0.0118
1982–83	1487	1.9687– 1.9803	0.0010– 0.0021	0.0039– 0.0138	3	1.6525– 1.6535	0.0008– 0.0015	0.0059– 0.0118
'84–'85	1488	1.9676– 1.9685	0.0009– 0.0017	0.004– 0.014	3	1.7707– 1.7717	0.0008– 0.0015	0.006– 0.012
'83–'85	1829	1.9685– 1.9694	0.0010– 0.0022	0.004– 0.014	3	1.7707– 1.7717	0.0008– 0.0015	0.006– 0.012
'84–'85	1342	1.7707– 1.7717	0.0009– 0.0017	0.004– 0.014	3	1.4951– 1.4961	0.008– 0.0015	0.006– 0.012

① 1974–76 1237 cc engines—0.0059–0.0018 in.

Torque Specifications
All readings are given in ft. lbs.

Year	Engine Displacement (cc)	Cylinder Head Bolts	Main Bearing Bolts	Rod Bearing Bolts	Crankshaft Pulley Bolts	Flywheel to Crankshaft Bolts	Manifold In	Manifold Ex	Spark Plugs	Oil Pan Drain Bolt
1973–79	1170, 1237	30–35 ① 37–42 ②	27–31	18–21	34–38	34–38	13–17	13–17 ③	11–18	29–36
1975–79	1600, 1487 CVCC	40–47	30–35	18–21	34–38	34–38	15–17	15–17	11–18	29–36
1979–83	1335, 1487	33	29	21	61 ④	51	18	18	15 ⑤	33
1979–83	1751	43	48	23 ⑥	61 ⑦	51	18	18	15 ⑤	33
'83–'85	1829	49 ⑧	48	23	83	76 ⑨	16	20	13	33
'84–'85	1342, 1488	43 ⑧	36	20	83	86 ⑨	16	23	13	33

① To engine number EB 1-1019949
② From engine number EB 1-1019950
③ 1975–76 models w/AIR—22–33 ft. lbs.
④ 1980–83: 80 ft. lb.
⑤ 1980–83: 13 ft. lb.
⑥ 1982–83: 21 ft. lb.
⑦ 1981: 83 ft. lb.
  1982–83: 195 ft. lb.
⑧ In two equal steps
⑨ Auto. trans.: 54 ft. lb.

Piston and Ring Specifications
All measurements are given in inches

Year	Engine Displacement (cc)	Piston Clearance	Ring Gap Top Compression	Ring Gap Bottom Compression	Ring Gap Oil Control	Ring Side Clearance Top Compression	Ring Side Clearance Bottom Compression	Ring Side Clearance Oil Control
1973	1170	0.0012–0.0039	0.008–0.016	0.008–0.016	0.008–0.035	0.0008–0.0018	0.0008–0.0018	0.0008–0.0018
1974–79	1237	0.0012–0.0039	0.0098–0.0157	0.0098–0.0577	0.0118–0.0394	0.0008–0.0018	0.0008–0.0018	Snug
1975–78	1600, 1487 CVCC	0.0012–0.0039	0.0079–0.0157	0.0079–0.0157	0.0079–0.0354	0.0008–0.0018	0.0008–0.0018	Snug
1979	1487	0.0012–0.0060	0.0079–0.0157	0.0079–0.0157	0.0079–0.0354	0.0008–0.0018	0.0008–0.0018	Snug
1979–83	1751	0.0008–① 0.0028	0.0059–0.0138	0.0059–0.0138	0.0118–0.0354	0.0008–0.0018	0.0008–0.0018	Snug
1980–81	1335, 1487	0.0004–0.0024	0.006–0.014	0.006–0.014	0.012–0.035	0.0008–0.0018	0.0008–0.0018	Snug
1982–83	1335, 1487	0.0004–0.0025	0.006–0.014	0.006–0.014	0.012–0.035	0.0012–0.0024	0.0012–0.0020	Snug
'83–'85	1829 CVCC	0.0008–0.0016	0.008–0.014	0.008–0.014	0.008–0.035	0.0008–0.0018	0.0008–0.0018	Snug
'84–'85	1342, 1488	0.0004–0.0016	0.006–0.014	0.006–0.014	0.008–0.024	0.0012–0.0024	0.0012–0.0022	Snug

① 1982–83: 0.0004–0.0024

13. Label and disconnect the starter motor wires. Remove the two starter mounting bolts (one from each end of the starter), and remove the starter.

14. Label and disconnect the spark plug wires at the plugs. Remove the distributor cap and scribe the position of the rotor on the side of the distributor housing. Remove the top distributor swivel bolt and remove the distributor (the rotor will rotate 30° as the drive gear is beveled).

15. On manual transmission cars, remove the C-clip retaining the clutch cable at the firewall. Then, remove the end of the clutch cable from the clutch release arm and bracket. First, pull up on the cable, and then push it out to release it from the bracket. Remove the end form the release arm.

16. Disconnect the back-up light switch wires. Disconnect the control valve vacuum hose, the air intake hose, and the preheat air intake hose. Disconnect the air bleed valve hose from the air cleaner. Label and disconnect all remaining vacuum hoses from the underside of the air cleaner. Remove the air cleaner.

17. Label and disconnect all remaining emission control vacuum hoses from the engine. Disconnect the emission box wiring connector and remove the black emission box from the firewall.

18. Remove the engine mount heat shield.

19. Disconnect the engine-to-body ground strap at the valve cover.

20. Disconnect the alternator wiring connector and oil pressure sensor leads.

21. Disconnect the vacuum hose from the start control and electrical leads to both cut-off solenoid valves.

22. Disconnect the vacuum hose from the charcoal canister and both fuel lines to the carburetor. Mark the adjustment and disconnect the choke and throttle cables at the carburetor.

23. On Hondamatic cars only, remove the center console and disconnect the gear selector control cable at the console. This may be accomplished after removing the retaining clip and pin.

24. Drain the transmission oil.

25. Remove the fender well shield under the right fender, exposing the speedometer drive cable. Remove the set screw securing the speedometer drive holder. Then, slowly pull the cable assembly out of the transmission, taking care not to drop the pin or drive

gear. Finally, remove the pin, collar, and drive gear from the cable assembly.

26. Disconnect the front suspension stabilizer bar from its mounts on both sides. Also, remove the bolt retaining the lower control arm to the sub-frame on both sides.

27. Remove the forward mounting nut on the radius rod on both sides. Then, pry the constant velocity joint out about ½ in. and pull the stub axle out of the transmission case. Repeat for other side.

28. Remove the six retaining bolts and remove the center beam.

29. On manual transmission cars only, drive out the pin retaining the shift linkage.

30. Disconnect the lower torque arm from the transmission.

31. On Hondamatic cars only, remove the bolt retaining the control cable stay at the transmission. Loosen the two U-bolt nuts and pull the cable out of its housing.

32. Disconnect the exhaust pipe at the manifold. Disconnect the retaining clamp also.

33. Remove the rear engine mount nut.

34. Attach a chain pulley hoist to the engine. Honda recommends using the threaded bolt holes at the extreme right and left ends of the cylinder head (with special hardened bolts) as lifting points, as opposed to wrapping a chain around the entire block and risk damaging some components such as the carburetor, etc.

35. Raise the engine enough to place a slight tension on the chain, remove the nut retaining the front engine mount. Then, remove the three bolts retaining the front mount. While lifting the engine, remove the mount.

36. Remove the three retaining bolts and push the left engine support into its shock mount bracket to the limit of its travel.

37. Slowly raise the engine out of the vehicle.

38. Installation is the reverse of removal.

1342 and 1488cc Civic CVCC

1. Apply the parking brake and place blocks behind the rear wheels. Raise the front of the car and support it on jackstands.

2. Disconnect both battery cables from the battery. Remove the battery, and then remove the battery tray from the engine compartment.

3. Scribe a line where the hood brackets

meet the inside of the hood. This will help realign the hood during the installation. Unbolt and remove the hood.

4. Remove the engine and wheelwell splash shields.

5. Drain the oil from the engine, the coolant from the radiator, and the transmission oil/fluid from the transmission.

NOTE: *Removal of the filler plug or cap will speed the draining process.*

6. Remove the air cleaner using the following procedure:

a. Disconnect and label all hoses leading to the air cleaner.

b. Remove the air cleaner cover and filter.

c. Remove the three bolts holding down the air cleaner. Lift up the air cleaner and disconnect the temperature sensor wire and the remaining two hoses. Remove the air cleaner.

7. Disconnect the following hoses and wires:

a. The engine compartment sub-harness connector

b. The engine secondary cable

c. The brake booster vacuum hose

d. On engines with A/C, remove the idle control solenoid hoses from the valve and remove the valve.

8. Disconnect the control box connector(s). Remove the control box(es) from the bracket(s), and let it hang next to the engine.

9. Disconnect the purge control solenoid valve vacuum hose at the charcoal canister.

10. Remove the air jet controller (if so equipped).

11. Loosen the throttle cable locknut and adjusting nut, then slip the cable end out of the throttle bracket, removing the cable.

12. Disconnect the fuel line hose from the fuel pump. Remove the fuel pump cover and the pump.

13. Remove the spark plug wires and the distributor from the engine.

14. Remove the radiator and heater hoses from the engine.

NOTE: *Label the heater hoses so they will be reinstalled in their original locations.*

15. On manual transmission cars:

a. Disconnect the transmission ground cable.

b. Loosen the clutch cable adjusting nut and remove the cable from the release arm.

c. Disconnect the shift lever torque rod from the clutch housing.

d. Slide the shift rod pin retainer out of the way, then with a pin punch, drive the pin out and remove the shift rod.

16. On automatic transmission cars:

a. Remove the oil cooler hoses at the transmission, let the fluid drain from the hoses then prop the hoses up out of the way near the radiator.

b. Remove the center console from the inside of the car.

c. Put the shift lever in reverse and remove the lock pin from the end of the shift cable.

d. Unbolt and remove the shift cable holder.

e. Disconnect the throttle control cable end from the throttle lever. Loosen the lower locknut on the throttle cable bracket and remove the cable from the bracket.

NOTE: *Do not move the upper locknut as it will change the transmission shift points.*

17. Remove the speedometer cable clip, then pull the cable out of the holder.

NOTE: *Do not remove the holder from the transmission as it may cause the speedometer gear to fall into the transmission.*

18. Squirt penetrating oil on the 7 nuts (5 front and 2 rear) holding the exhaust header pipe in place. Loosen and remove the nuts and pipe.

19. Remove the driveshafts as follows:

a. Remove the jackstands and lower the car. Loosen the 32mm spindle nuts with a socket. Raise the car and resupport on jackstands.

b. Remove the front wheel, and the spindle nut.

c. Place a floor jack under the lower control arm, then remove the ball joint cotter pin and nut.

NOTE: *Be certain the lower control arm is positioned securely on top of the floor jack so that it doesn't suddenly jump or spring off when the ball joint remover is used.*

d. Using a ball joint puller, separate the ball joint from the front hub.

e. Slowly, lower the floor jack to lower the control arm. Pull the hub outward and off the driveshaft.

f. Using a small pry bar, pry out the inboard CV-joint approximately ½ in. in order to release the spring clip from the groove in the differential.

g. Pull the driveshaft out of the transmission case.

20. Attach a lifting sling to the engine block and raise the hoist to remove the slack from the chain.

21. Remove the rear transmission mount, and remove the bolts from the front transmission mount and the engine side mount.

22. On A/C equipped cars:

   a. Loosen the belt adjusting bolts and remove the belt.

   b. Remove the mounting bolts to the A/C compressor, then wire it up out of the way on the front beam.

NOTE: *DO NOT disconnect the A/C freon lines; the compressor can be moved without discharging the system.*

   c. Remove the lower compressor mounting bracket.

23. Disconnect the alternator wiring harness connectors. Remove the alternator belt. Remove the alternator mounting bolts and remove the alternator.

24. Check that the engine and transaxle are free from any hoses or electrical connectors.

25. Slowly raise the engine up and out of the car.

26. To install, reverse the removal procedures. Pay special attention to the following:

   a. Torque the engine mounting bolts in the proper sequence.

   b. Be sure that the spring clip on the end of each driveshaft "clicks" into the differential.

NOTE: *Always use new spring clips on installation.*

   c. Bleed the air from the cooling system.

   d. Adjust the belt(s) tension, and the throttle cable tension.

   e. Check the clutch pedal free play.

Accord 1600 and Accord and Prelude 1751

1. Disconnect the negative battery terminal.

2. Drain the radiator of coolant, and drain the engine and transmission oil.

3. Jack up the front of the car and remove the front wheels. Be sure to support the car with safety stands.

4. Remove the air cleaner.

5. Remove the following wires and hoses:

   a. The coil wire and the ignition primary wire from the distributor.

   b. The engine subharness and the starter wires. (Mark the wires before removal to ease installation.)

   c. The vacuum tube from the brake booster.

   d. On Hondamatic models, remove the ATF cooler hose from the transmission.

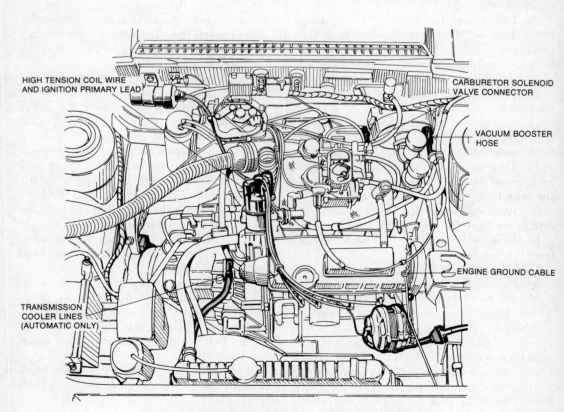

Accord and Prelude component removal points

e. The engine ground cable.

f. Alternator wiring harness.

g. Carburetor solenoid valve connector

h. Carburetor fuel line.

i. On 1981–82 models with California and high altitude equipment, disconnect the hoses at the air controller.

6. Remove the choke and throttle cables.

7. Remove the radiator and heater hoses.

8. Remove the emission control "black box".

9. Remove the clutch slave cylinder with the hydraulic line attached.

10. Remove the speedometer cable. Pull the wire clip from the housing, and remove the cable from the housing. Do not, under any circumstances, remove the housing from the transmission.

11. Attach an engine hoist to the engine block, and raise the engine just enough to remove the slack from the chain.

12. Disconnect the right and left lower ball joints, and the tie rod ends. You will need a ball joint remover tool for this operation. An alternative method is to leave the ball joints connected, and remove the lower control arm inner bolts, and the radius rods from the lower control arms.

13. Remove the driveshafts from the transmission by prying the snap ring off the groove in the end of the shaft. The pull the shaft out by holding the knuckle.

14. Remove the center engine mount.

15. Remove the shift rod positioner from the transmission case.

16. Drive out the pin from the shift rod using a small pin driver.

17. On Hondamatics, remove the control cable.

18. Disconnect the exhaust pipe.

19. Remove the three engine support bolts and push the left engine support into the shock mount bracket.

20. Remove the front and rear engine mounts.

21. Raise the engine carefully and remove it from the car.

22. Install the engine in the reverse order of removal, making the following checks:

a. Make sure that the clip at the end of the driveshaft seats in the groove in the differential. *Failure to do so may lead to the wheels falling off.*

b. Bleed the air from the cooling system.

c. Adjust the throttle and choke cable tension.

d. Check the clutch for the correct free play.

e. Make sure that the transmission shifts properly.

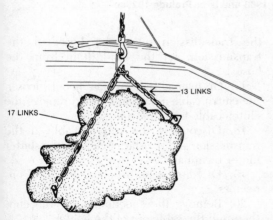

Accord and Prelude engine removal. Note the chain positioning

Accord/Prelude 1829cc

1. Disconnect the negative and then the positive battery terminal.

2. Remove the knob caps covering the headlight manual retracting knobs, then turn the knobs to bring the headlights to the on position (Prelude only).

3. Remove the five screws retaining the grille and remove the grille (Prelude only).

4. Remove the splash guard from under the engine. Unbolt and remove the hood.

5. Remove the oil filler cap and drain the engine oil.

NOTE: *When replacing the drain plug be sure to use a new washer.*

6. Remove the radiator cap, then open the radiator drain petcock and drain the coolant from the radiator.

7. Remove the transmission filler plug, then remove the drain plug and drain the transmission.

8. Label and then remove the wires at the coil and the engine secondary ground cable located on the valve cover.

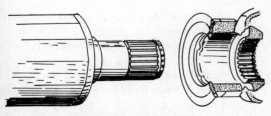

Accord and Prelude driveshaft removal

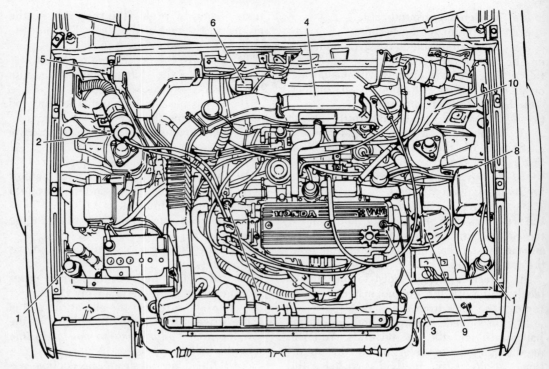

① Headlight retracting knobs
② Ignition coil wires
③ Secondary ground cable
④ Air cleaner assembly
⑤ No. 1 control box connector
⑥ Charcoal canister
⑦ Air bleed bolt for cooling system
⑧ No. 2 control box connector
⑨ Air chamber location (if so equipped)
⑩ Air jet controller location (if so equipped)

Component removal points on 1983 and later Prelude 1829cc

9. Remove the air cleaner cover and filter.

10. Remove the air intake ducts. Remove the two nuts and two bolts from the air cleaner, remove the air control valve, then remove the air cleaner (Accord only).

11. Loosen the locknut on the throttle cable and loosen the cable adjusting nut, then slip the cable end out of the carburetor linkage.

NOTE: *Be careful not to bend or kink the throttle cable. Always replace a damaged cable.*

12. Disconnect the No. 1 control box connector. Remove the control box from its bracket, and let it hang next to the engine.

13. Disconnect the fuel line at the fuel filter and remove the solenoid vacuum hose at the charcoal canister.

14. On California and high altitude models, remove the air jet controller.

15. Disconnect the radiator and heater hoses at the engine. Label the heater hoses so they can be installed correctly.

16. On automatic models, disconnect the transmission oil cooler hoses at the transmission, let the fluid drain from the hoses.

17. On manual transmission models, loosen the clutch cable adjusting nut and remove the clutch cable from the release arm.

18. Disconnect the battery cable at the transmission and the starter cable at the starter motor terminal.

19. Disconnect both engine harness connectors.

20. Remove the speedometer cable clip, then pull the cable out of the holder.

NOTE: *DO NOT remove the holder as the speedometer gear may drop into the transmission.*

21. On models equipped with power steering:

   a. Remove the speed sensor complete with the hoses.

   b. Remove the adjusting bolt and the V-belt.

   c. Without disconnecting the hoses, pull the pump away from its mounting bracket and position it out of the way.

d. Remove the power steering hose bracket from the cylinder head.

22. Remove the center beam beneath the engine. Loosen the radius rod nuts to aid in the later removal of the driveshafts (Accord only).

23. On models equipped with air conditioning:

a. Remove the compressor clutch lead wire.

b. Loosen the belt adjusting bolt.

NOTE: *DO NOT remove the air conditioner hoses. The air conditioner compressor can be moved without discharging the air conditioner system.*

c. Remove the compressor mounting bolts, then lift the compressor out of the bracket with the hoses attached, and hang it to the front bulkhead with a piece of wire.

24. On models with manual transmission, remove the shift rod yoke attaching bolt and disconnect the shift lever torque rod from the clutch housing.

25. On models with automatic transmission:

a. Remove the center console.

b. Place the shift lever in reverse, then remove the lock pin from the end of the shift cable.

c. Unscrew the cable mounting bolts and remove the shift cable holder.

d. Remove the throttle cable from the throttle lever. Loosen the lower locknut, then remove the cable from the bracket.

NOTE: *DO NOT loosen the upper locknut as it will change the transmission shift points.*

26. Disconnect the right and left lower ball joints and the tie-rod ends.

27. Remove the driveshafts as follows:

a. Remove the jackstands and lower the car. Loosen the 32mm spindle nuts with a socket. Raise the car and resupport on jackstands.

b. Remove the front wheel, and the spindle nut.

c. Remove the damper fork and damper pinch bolts. Remove the damper fork (Prelude only).

d. Remove the ball joint bolt and separate the ball joint from the front hub (Accord) or lower control arm (Prelude).

e. Disconnect the tie rods from the steering knuckles.

f. Remove the sway bar bolts (Accord only).

g. Pull the front hub outward and off the driveshafts.

h. Using a small pry bar, pry out the inboard CV-joint approximately ½ in. in order to release the spring clip from the differential, then pull the driveshaft out of the transmission case.

NOTE: *When installing the driveshaft, insert the shaft until the spring clip clicks into the groove. Always use a new spring clip when installing driveshafts.*

28. Remove the exhaust header pipe.

29. Attach a chain hoist to the engine and raise it just enough to remove the slack.

30. Disconnect the No. 2 control box connector, lift the control box off of its bracket, and let it hang next to the engine (if so equipped).

31. On models with air conditioning, remove the idle control solenoid valve.

32. Remove the air chamber (if so equipped).

33. Remove the three engine mount bolts located under the air chamber, then push the engine mount into the engine mount tower.

34. Remove the front engine mount nut, then remove the rear engine mount nut.

35. Loosen and remove the alternator belt. Disconnect the alternator wire harness and remove the alternator.

36. Remove the bolt from the rear torque rod at the engine, then loosen the bolt in the frame mount and swing the rod up and out of the way.

37. Raise the engine carefully from the car checking that all wires and hoses have been removed from the engine/transaxle. Raise the engine all the way up and remove it from the car.

38. Install the engine in the reverse order of removal, making the following checks:

a. Torque the engine mounting bolts in the proper sequence.

b. Bleed the air from the cooling system.

c. Adjust the clutch pedal free play.

d. Adjust the throttle cable tension.

e. Make sure the transmission shifts properly.

Cylinder Head

You will need a 12 point socket to remove and install the head bolts on the CVCC engine.

ENGINE OVERHAUL

Most engine overhaul procedures are fairly standard. In addition to specific parts replacement procedures and complete specifications for your individual engine, this chapter also is a guide to accepted rebuilding procedures. Examples of standard rebuilding practice are shown and should be used along with specific details concerning your particular engine.

Competent and accurate machine shop services will ensure maximum performance, reliability and engine life. Procedures marked with the symbol shown above should be performed by a competent machine shop, and are provided so that you will be familiar with the procedures necessary to a successful overhaul.

In most instances it is more profitable for the do-it-yourself mechanic to remove, clean and inspect the component, buy the necessary parts and deliver these to a shop for actual machine work.

On the other hand, much of the rebuilding work (crankshaft, block, bearings, pistons, rods, and other components) is well within the scope of the do-it-yourself mechanic.

Tools

The tools required for an engine overhaul or parts replacement will depend on the depth of your involvement. With a few exceptions, they will be the tools found in a mechanic's tool kit (see Chapter 1). More in-depth work will require any or all of the following:
• a dial indicator (reading in thousandths) mounted on a universal base
  • micrometers and telescope gauges
  • jaw and screw-type pullers
  • scraper
  • valve spring compressor
  • ring groove cleaner
  • piston ring expander and compressor
  • ridge reamer
  • cylinder hone or glaze breaker

• Plastigage®
• engine stand

Use of most of these tools is illustrated in this chapter. Many can be rented for a one-time use from a local parts jobber or tool supply house specializing in automotive work.

Occasionally, the use of special tools is called for. See the information on Special Tools and the Safety Notice in the front of this book before substituting another tool.

Inspection Techniques

Procedures and specifications are given in this chapter for inspecting, cleaning and assessing the wear limits of most major components. Other procedures such as Magnaflux and Zyglo can be used to locate material flaws and stress cracks. Magnaflux is a magnetic process applicable only to ferrous materials. The Zyglo process coats the material with a flourescent dye penetrant and can be used on any material. Check for suspected surface cracks can be more readily made using spot check dye. The dye is sprayed onto the suspected area, wiped off and the area sprayed with a developer. Cracks will show up brightly.

Overhaul Tips

Aluminum has become extremely popular for use in engines, due to its low weight. Observe the following precautions when handling aluminum parts:
• Never hot tank aluminum parts (the caustic hot-tank solution will eat the aluminum)
• Remove all aluminum parts (identification tag, etc.) from engine parts prior to hot-tanking.
• Always coat threads lightly with engine oil or anti-seize compounds before installation, to prevent seizure.
• Never over-torque bolts or spark plugs, especially in aluminum threads.

Stripped threads in any component can be repaired using any of several commercial repair kits (Heli-Coil, Microdot, Keenserts, etc.)

When assembling the engine, any parts that will be in frictional contact must be pre-lubed to provide lubrication at initial start-up. Any product specifically formulated for this purpose can be used, but engine oil is not recommended as a pre-lube.

When semi-permanent (locked, but removable) installation of bolts or nuts is desired, threads should be cleaned and coated with Loctite® or other similar, commercial non-hardening sealant.

Repairing Damaged Threads

Several methods of repairing damaged threads are available. Heli-Coil® (shown here), Keenserts® and Microdot® are among the most widely used. All involve basically the same principle—drilling out stripped threads, tapping the hole and installing a prewound insert—making welding, plugging and oversize fasteners unnecessary.

Two types of thread repair inserts are usually supplied—a standard type for most Inch Coarse, Inch Fine, Metric Coarse and Metric Fine thread sizes and a spark plug type to fit most spark plug port sizes. Consult the individual manufacturer's catalog to determine exact applications. Typical thread repair kits will contain a selection of prewound threaded inserts, a tap (corresponding to the outside diameter threads of the insert) and an installation tool. Spark plug inserts usually differ because they require a tap equipped with pilot threads and a combined reamer/tap section. Most manufacturers also supply blister-packed thread repair inserts separately in addition to a master kit containing a variety of taps and inserts plus installation tools.

Before effecting a repair to a threaded hole, remove any snapped, broken or damaged bolts or studs. Penetrating oil can be used to free frozen threads; the offending item can be removed with locking pliers or with a screw or stud extractor. After the hole is clear, the thread can be repaired, as follows:

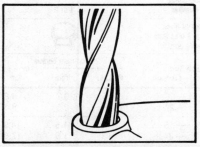

Drill out the damaged threads with specified drill. Drill completely through the hole or to the bottom of a blind hole

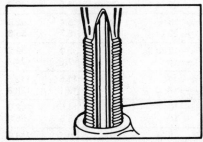

With the tap supplied, tap the hole to receive the thread insert. Keep the tap well oiled and back it out frequently to avoid clogging the threads

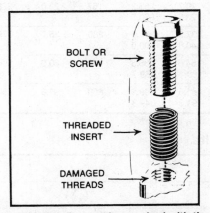

BOLT OR SCREW

THREADED INSERT

DAMAGED THREADS

Damaged bolt holes can be repaired with thread repair inserts

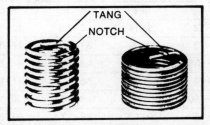

TANG

NOTCH

Standard thread repair insert (left) and spark plug thread insert (right)

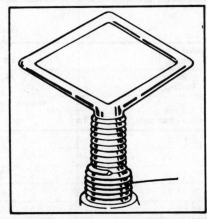

Screw the threaded insert onto the installation tool until the tang engages the slot. Screw the insert into the tapped hole until it is ¼–½ turn below the top surface. After installation break off the tang with a hammer and punch

Standard Torque Specifications and Fastener Markings

In the absence of specific torques, the following chart can be used as a guide to the maximum safe torque of a particular size/grade of fastener.

- There is no torque difference for fine or coarse threads.
- Torque values are based on clean, dry threads. Reduce the value by 10% if threads are oiled prior to assembly.
- The torque required for aluminum components or fasteners is considerably less.

U.S. Bolts

SAE Grade Number	1 or 2			5			6 or 7		
Number of lines always 2 less than the grade number.									
Bolt Size (inches)—(Thread)	Maximum Torque			Maximum Torque			Maximum Torque		
	Ft./Lbs.	Kgm	Nm	Ft./Lbs.	Kgm	Nm	Ft./Lbs.	Kgm	Nm
¼ — 20	5	0.7	6.8	8	1.1	10.8	10	1.4	13.5
— 28	6	0.8	8.1	10	1.4	13.6			
5/16 — 18	11	1.5	14.9	17	2.3	23.0	19	2.6	25.8
— 24	13	1.8	17.6	19	2.6	25.7			
3/8 — 16	18	2.5	24.4	31	4.3	42.0	34	4.7	46.0
— 24	20	2.75	27.1	35	4.8	47.5			
7/16 — 14	28	3.8	37.0	49	6.8	66.4	55	7.6	74.5
— 20	30	4.2	40.7	55	7.6	74.5			
½ — 13	39	5.4	52.8	75	10.4	101.7	85	11.75	115.2
— 20	41	5.7	55.6	85	11.7	115.2			
9/16 — 12	51	7.0	69.2	110	15.2	149.1	120	16.6	162.7
— 18	55	7.6	74.5	120	16.6	162.7			
5/8 — 11	83	11.5	112.5	150	20.7	203.3	167	23.0	226.5
— 18	95	13.1	128.8	170	23.5	230.5			
¾ — 10	105	14.5	142.3	270	37.3	366.0	280	38.7	379.6
— 16	115	15.9	155.9	295	40.8	400.0			
7/8 — 9	160	22.1	216.9	395	54.6	535.5	440	60.9	596.5
— 14	175	24.2	237.2	435	60.1	589.7			
1 — 8	236	32.5	318.6	590	81.6	799.9	660	91.3	894.8
— 14	250	34.6	338.9	660	91.3	849.8			

Metric Bolts

Relative Strength Marking	4.6, 4.8			8.8		
Bolt Markings						
Bolt Size Thread Size x Pitch (mm)	Maximum Torque			Maximum Torque		
	Ft./Lbs.	Kgm	Nm	Ft./Lbs.	Kgm	Nm
6 x 1.0	2–3	.2–.4	3–4	3–6	.4–.8	5–8
8 x 1.25	6–8	.8–1	8–12	9–14	1.2–1.9	13–19
10 x 1.25	12–17	1.5–2.3	16–23	20–29	2.7–4.0	27–39
12 x 1.25	21–32	2.9–4.4	29–43	35–53	4.8–7.3	47–72
14 x 1.5	35–52	4.8–7.1	48–70	57–85	7.8–11.7	77–110
16 x 1.5	51–77	7.0–10.6	67–100	90–120	12.4–16.5	130–160
18 x 1.5	74–110	10.2–15.1	100–150	130–170	17.9–23.4	180–230
20 x 1.5	110–140	15.1–19.3	150–190	190–240	26.2–46.9	160–320
22 x 1.5	150–190	22.0–26.2	200–260	250–320	34.5–44.1	340–430
24 x 1.5	190–240	26.2–46.9	260–320	310–410	42.7–56.5	420–550

CHECKING ENGINE COMPRESSION

A noticeable lack of engine power, excessive oil consumption and/or poor fuel mileage measured over an extended period are all indicators of internal engine wear. Worn piston rings, scored or worn cylinder bores, blown head gaskets, sticking or burnt valves and worn valve seats are all possible culprits here. A check of each cylinder's compression will help you locate the problems.

As mentioned in the "Tools and Equipment" section of Chapter 1, a screw-in type compression gauge is more accurate than the type you simply hold against the spark plug hole, although it takes slightly longer to use. It's worth it to obtain a more accurate reading. Follow the procedures below for gasoline and diesel-engined cars.

Gasoline Engines

1. Warm up the engine to normal operating temperature.
2. Remove all spark plugs.

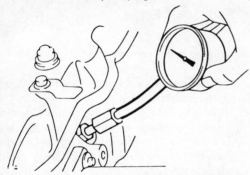

The screw-in type compression gauge is more accurate

3. Disconnect the high-tension lead from the ignition coil.
4. On carbureted cars, fully open the throttle either by operating the carburetor throttle linkage by hand or by having an assistant "floor" the accelerator pedal. On fuel-injected cars, disconnect the cold start valve and all injector connections.
5. Screw the compression gauge into the No. 1 spark plug hole until the fitting is snug.
   NOTE: *Be careful not to crossthread the plug hole. On aluminum cylinder heads use extra care, as the threads in these heads are easily ruined.*
6. Ask an assistant to depress the accelerator pedal fully on both carbureted and fuel-injected cars. Then, while you read the compression gauge, ask the assistant to crank the engine two or three times in short bursts using the ignition switch.

7. Read the compression gauge at the end of each series of cranks, and record the highest of these readings. Repeat this procedure for each of the engine's cylinders. Compare the highest reading of each cylinder to the compression pressure specifications in the "Tune-Up Specifications" chart in Chapter 2. The specs in this chart are maximum values.

A cylinder's compression pressure is usually acceptable if it is not less than 80% of maximum. The difference between each cylinder should be no more than 12–14 pounds.

8. If a cylinder is unusually low, pour a tablespoon of clean engine oil into the cylinder through the spark plug hole and repeat the compression test. If the compression comes up after adding the oil, it appears that that cylinder's piston rings or bore are damaged or worn. If the pressure remains low, the valves may not be seating properly (a valve job is needed), or the head gasket may be blown near that cylinder. If compression in any two adjacent cylinders is low, and if the addition of oil doesn't help the compression, there is leakage past the head gasket. Oil and coolant water in the combustion chamber can result from this problem. There may be evidence of water droplets on the engine dipstick when a head gasket has blown.

Diesel Engines

Checking cylinder compression on diesel engines is basically the same procedure as on gasoline engines except for the following:

1. A special compression gauge adaptor suitable for diesel engines (because these engines have much greater compression pressures) must be used.
2. Remove the injector tubes and remove the injectors from each cylinder.
   NOTE: *Don't forget to remove the washer underneath each injector; otherwise, it may get lost when the engine is cranked.*

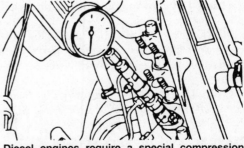

Diesel engines require a special compression gauge adaptor

3. When fitting the compression gauge adaptor to the cylinder head, make sure the bleeder of the gauge (if equipped) is closed.
4. When reinstalling the injector assemblies, install new washers underneath each injector.

Disassembled CVCC cylinder head showing major components

REMOVAL PRECAUTIONS

a. To prevent warping, the cylinder head should be removed when the engine is cold.

b. Remove oil, scale or carbon deposits accumulated from each part. When decarbonizing take care not to score or scratch the mating surfaces.

c. After washing the oil holes or orifices in each part, make sure they are not restricted by blowing out with compressed air.

d. If parts will not be reinstalled immediately after washing, spray parts with a rust preventive to protect from corrosion.

NOTE: *If the engine has already been removed from the car, begin with Step 12 in the following procedure.*

REMOVAL AND INSTALLATION

All except 1342, 1488, 1751 & 1829cc Engines

1. Remove the turn signals, grille, and hood (civic through 1977 only). Disconnect the negative battery cable.

2. Drain the radiator.

3. Disconnect the upper radiator hose at the thermostat cover.

3a. On CVCC models, remove distributor cap, ignition wires and primary wire. Also, loosen the alternator bracket and remove the upper mounting bolt from the cylinder head.

4. Remove the air cleaner case.

5. Disconnect the tube running between the canister and carburetor at the canister.

6. Disconnect the throttle and choke control cables. Label and disconnect all vacuum hoses.

7. Disconnect the heater hose at the intake manifold.

8. Disconnect the wires from both thermoswitches.

9. Disconnect the fuel line.

9a. On CVCC models, disconnect the temperature gauge sending unit wire, idle cut-off solenoid valve, and primary/main cut-off solenoid valve.

10. Disconnect the engine torque rod.

11. Disconnect the exhaust pipe at the exhaust manifold.

12. Remove the valve cover bolts and the valve cover.

Timing belt pivot and adjustment bolts

Closeup of non-CVCC engine crankshaft showing gear removed, with woodruff key remaining

13. Remove the two timing belt upper cover bolts and the cover.

14. Bring No. 1 piston to top dead center. Do this by aligning the notch next to the red notch you use for setting ignition timing, with the index mark on the timing belt cover (1170, 1237 cc) or rear of engine block (CVCC).

15. Loosen, but do not remove, the timing belt adjusting bolt and pivot bolt.

16. On 1170 and 1237 cc models only, remove the camshaft pulley bolt. Do not let the woodruff key fall inside the timing cover. Remove the pulley with a pulley remover (or special tool 07935-6110000).

CAUTION: *Use care when handling the*

timing belt. *Do not use sharp instruments to remove the belt. Do not get oil or grease on the belt. Do not bend or twist the belt more than 90°.*

17. On 1170 and 1237 cc models only, remove the fuel pump and distributor.

18. On 1170 and 1237 cc models only, remove the oil pump gear holder and remove the pump gear and shaft.

19. Loosen and remove the cylinder head bolts in the *reverse* order given in the head bolt tightening sequence diagram. The number one cylinder head bolt is hidden underneath the oil pump.

20. Remove the cylinder head with the carburetor and manifolds attached.

21. Remove the intake and exhaust manifolds from the cylinder head.

NOTE: *After removing the cylinder head, cover the engine with a clean cloth to prevent materials from getting into the cylinders.*

22. To install, reverse the removal procedure, being sure to pay attention to the following points:

    a. Be sure that No. 1 cylinder is at top dead center before positioning the cylinder head in place;

    b. Use a new head gasket and make

Cylinder head bolt removal. The rocker arms have been removed for clarity

Hidden bolt next to oil pump gear (arrow)

sure the head, engine block, and gasket are clean;

c. The cylinder head aligning dowel pins should be in their proper place in the block before installing the cylinder head;

d. Tighten the head bolts according to the diagram. On the 1335 cc and 1487 cc engines, tighten the bolts in two steps: to 22 ft. lbs., then 43 ft. lbs., in sequence each time.

e. After the head bolts have been tightened, install the woodruff key and camshaft pulley (if removed), and tighten the pulley bolt according to specification. On the non-CVCC engine, align the marks on the camshaft pulley so they are parallel with the top of the head and the woodruff key is facing up; On the CVCC engine, the word "up" should be facing upward and the mark on the cam gear should be aligned with the arrow on the cylinder head. See the illustration in the timing belt removal and installation procedure.

f. After installing the pulley (if removed), install the timing belt. Be careful not to disturb the timing position already set when installing the belt.

1342 and 1488cc Civic

1. Disconnect the negative battery cable.
2. Drain the radiator.
3. Remove the air cleaner:
   a. Remove the air cleaner cover and filter.
   b. Disconnect the hot and cold air intake ducts, and remove the air chamber hose.
   c. Remove the 3 bolts holding the air cleaner.
   d. Lift up on the air cleaner housing, then remove the remaining hoses and the air temperature sensor wire.
   e. Remove the air cleaner.
4. Remove the brake booster vacuum tube from the intake manifold.
5. Remove the engine ground wire from the valve cover and disconnect the wires from the fuel cut-off solenoid valve, automatic choke and the thermosensor.
6. Disconnect the fuel lines.
7. Disconnect the spark plug wires from the spark plugs, then remove the distributor assembly.
8. Disconnect the throttle cable from the carburetor.
9. Disconnect the hoses from the charcoal canister, and from the No. 1 control box at the tubing manifold.
10. Disconnect the air jet controller (California and high altitude only).
11. Disconnect the idle control solenoid hoses (w/air conditioning only).
12. Disconnect the upper radiator heater and bypass hoses.

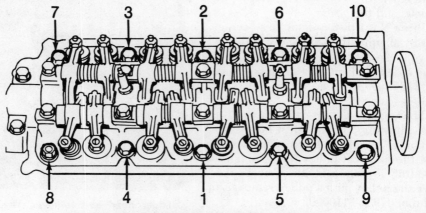

1342 and 1488cc cylinder head torque sequence

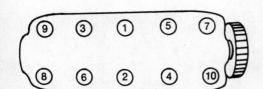

Cylinder head torque sequence for all except the 1342, 1488 and 1829cc

13. Remove the thermostat housing-to-intake manifold hose.

14. Remove the exhaust manifold bracket and manifold bolts, then remove the manifold.

15. Remove the bolts from the intake manifold and bracket.

16. Disconnect the hose from the breather chamber to the intake manifold.

17. Remove the valve and timing belt covers.

18. Loosen the timing belt tensioner adjustment bolt, then remove the belt.

19. Remove the cylinder head bolts in the reverse order given in the head bolt torque sequence.

NOTE: *Unscrew the bolts ⅓ of a turn each time and repeat the sequence to prevent cylinder head warpage.*

20. Carefully remove the cylinder head from the engine.

21. To install reverse the removal procedure, being sure to pay attention to the following points:

   a. Always use a new head gasket and make sure the head, engine block, and gasket are clean.

   b. Be sure the No. 1 cylinder is at top dead center and the camshaft pulley "UP" mark is on the top before positioning the head in place.

   c. The cylinder head dowel pins and oil control jet must be aligned.

   d. Tighten the cylinder head bolts in two progressive steps as shown in the torque sequence diagram. First to 22 ft. lbs. in sequence, then to 43 ft. lbs. in the same sequence.

   e. On the 1342 cc engine torque the valve cover two turns at a time in the sequence shown to 9 ft. lbs.

   f. After installation, check to see that all hoses and wires are installed correctly.

Accord and Prelude 1751 cc

CAUTION: *Cylinder head temperature must be below 100°F.*

1. Disconnect the battery ground cable.

2. Drain the cooling system.

3. Remove the air cleaner, tagging all hoses for installation.

4. Disconnect the wires from the thermosenser temperature gauge sending unit, idle cut-off solenoid valve, primary/main cut-off solenoid valve, and the automatic choke.

5. Disconnect the fuel lines and throttle cable from the carburetor.

6. Tag all emission hoses going to the carburetor then remove them and the carburetor.

7. Disconnect all wires and hoses from the distributor, tagging them for installation, and remove the distributor.

8. Remove all coolant hoses from the head.

9. Disconnect the hot air ducts and head pipe from the head. Loosen the exhaust manifold-to-engine bracket bolts to ease assembly.

10. On cars without A/C, remove the bolt holding the alternator bracket to the head. Loosen the adjustment bolt.

11. On cars with A/C, remove the alternator and bracket from the car.

12. Disconnect the brake booster vacuum hose at the one-way valve.

13. Remove the valve cover and timing bolt upper cover.

14. Loosen the timing belt pivot and adjust bolts and slide the belt off the pulley.

15. Remove the oil pump gear cover and pull the oil pump shaft out of the head.

16. Remove the head bolts in sequence working from the ends, across the head, toward the center. This is the reverse of the tightening sequence.

17. Carefully lift the head from the block.

18. Thoroughly clean the mating surfaces of the head and block.

19. Always use a new gasket.

20. Install the head in reverse order of the removal procedure. Make sure the head dowel pins are aligned. Make sure that the UP mark on the timing belt pulley is at the top. Torque the cylinder head bolts in three equal steps to 43 ft. lb.

Accord and Prelude 1829cc

CAUTION: *Cylinder head temperature must be below 100°F.*

1. Disconnect the battery ground cable.

2. Drain the cooling system.

3. Remove the vacuum hose from the brake booster.

Cleaning the block mating surface of all traces of old gasket material

Cleaned block surface ready for head gasket

Head gasket positioning. Make sure all passages align with holes in the gasket

4. Remove the air intake ducts from the air cleaner case.

5. Remove the secondary ground cable from the valve cover.

6. Remove the air cleaner, tagging all hoses for installation.

7. Disconnect the wires from the automatic choke and the fuel cut-off solenoid valve.

8. Disconnect the throttle cable and the fuel lines.

9. Disconnect the connecter and hoses from the distributor.

10. Disconnect the No. 1 control box hoses from the tubing manifold.

11. On California and high altitude models, disconnect the air jet controller hoses.

12. Disconnect the cooling system hoses at the cylinder head.

13. Remove the power steering pump (on models so equipped) but DO NOT disconnect the pump hoses. Also, remove the hose clamp bolt on the cylinder head.

14. Remove the power steering pump bracket.

15. Disconnect the No. 2 control box connector. Lift the control box from its bracket, and let it hang next to the carburetor (if so equipped).

16. Remove the air chamber, and on models with air conditioning, disconnect the idle boost solenoid hoses.

17. Remove the engine splash guard from under the car (if so equipped).

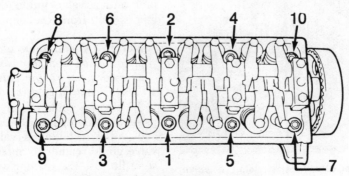

1829cc cylinder head torque sequence

18. Remove the exhaust header pipe and pull it clear of the exhaust manifold.

19. Remove the air cleaner base mount bolts and disconnect the hose from the intake manifold to the breather chamber.

20. Remove the valve cover, upper timing belt cover and then loosen the belt tensioner to remove the belt.

21. Remove the cylinder head bolts and remove the head.

NOTE: *Unscrew the cylinder head bolts ⅓ of a turn in the reverse order of the torque sequence each turn until loose to prevent warpage to the cylinder head.*

22. Installation is the reverse of the removal procedure, taking note of the following items:

　a. Make sure the cylinder head gasket surfaces are clean.

　b. Make sure the "UP" mark on the timing belt pulley is at the top.

　c. Make sure the head dowel pins are aligned.

　d. Adjust the valve timing.

　e. Torque the cylinder head bolts in two steps. Torque all bolts in sequence to 22 ft. lbs., then to 49 ft. lbs. in the final step.

Valves and Valve Guides

REMOVAL AND INSTALLATION

All Models

1. Using a valve spring compressor, remove the valve keepers, retainers, springs, and seats. Then remove the valves.

2. Remove the valve guides with a ham-

With the valve spring compressed, use a small magnet to remove the valve keepers

When the valve keepers are removed, lift off the valve springs

Compressing the valve spring using a valve spring compressor

mer and a valve guide driver. Drive the guides out from the combustion chamber side.

NOTE: *On aluminum alloy heads, an application of heat (approx. 200°F) may be necessary before the valve guides will be "loose" enough to drive out.*

3. Use the guide driver and a hammer to press the valve back into the head.

4. After installing a valve guide, use a valve guide reamer to obtain a proper valve stem fit. Use the reamer with an in-out motion while rotating. For the finished dimen-

Auxiliary valve installation. Always use a new O-ring

sion of the valve guide, check the "Valve Specifications" chart.

NOTE: *Do not forget to install valve guide seals.*

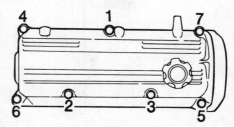

1342cc valve cover torque sequence

Camshaft and Rocker Shafts

REMOVAL AND INSTALLATION

To facilitate installation, make sure that No. 1 piston is at Top Dead Center before removal of camshaft.

1. Follow the "Cylinder Head" removal procedure before attempting to remove the camshaft.

CVCC valve components, including auxiliary valve

Valve installation with head cleaned of all carbon

Rocker arm assembly showing bolts partially removed

Rocker arm assembly—CVCC engine

2. Loosen the camshaft and rocker arm shaft holder bolts in a criss-cross pattern, beginning on the outside holder.

3. Remove the rocker arms, shafts, and holders as an assembly.

4. Lift out the camshaft and right head seal (or tachometer body if equipped).

5. To install, reverse the removal procedure, being sure to install the holder bolts in the reverse order of removal.

NOTE: *Back off valve adjusting screws before installing rockers. Then adjust valves as outlined in Chapter 2.*

Intake Manifold
REMOVAL AND INSTALLATION
Non CVCC Models

1. Drain the radiator.
2. Remove the air cleaner and case.

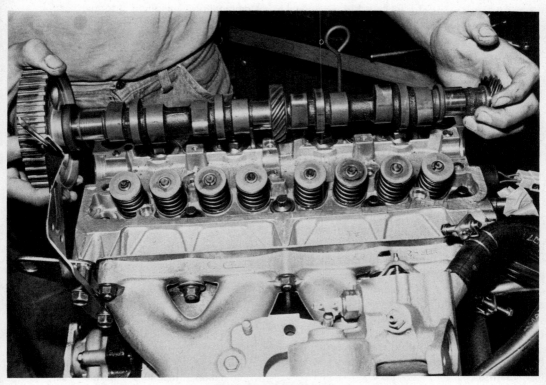

Removing the camshaft

3. Remove the carburetor from the intake manifold (see "Carburetor—Removal and Installation" in Chapter 4).

4. Remove the emission control hoses from the manifold T-joint. One hose leads to the condensation chamber and the other leads to the charcoal canister.

5. Remove the hose connected to the intake manifold directly above the T-joint and underneath the carburetor, leading to the air cleaner check valve (refer to Chapter 4 for diagrams of the various emission control hose connections).

6. Remove the thermo-switch wires from the switches.

7. Remove the solenoid valve located next to the thermo-switch.

8. Remove the six (6) intake manifold attaching nuts in a crisscross pattern, beginning from the center and moving out to both ends. Then remove the manifold.

9. Clean all old gasket material from the manifold and the cylinder head.

10. If the intake manifold is to be replaced, transfer all necessary components to the new manifold.

11. To install, reverse the removal procedure, being sure to observe the following points:

a. Apply a water-resistant sealer to the new intake manifold gasket before positioning it in place;

b. Be sure all hoses are properly connected;

c. Tighten the manifold attaching nuts in the reverse order of removal.

1983 and Later 1342, 1488 and 1829cc CVCC

1. Drain the coolant from the radiator.

2. Remove the air cleaner and case from the carburetor(s).

3. Remove the air valve, EGR valve, air suction valve and air chamber (if so equipped).

4. Label and remove any wires running to the intake manifold.

5. Remove the intake manifold attaching nut in a crisscross pattern, beginning from the center and moving out to both ends. Then remove the manifold.

6. Clean all the old gasket material from the manifold and the cylinder head.

7. If the intake manifold is to be replaced, transfer all the necessary components to the new manifold.

8. To install, reverse the removal procedures, being sure to observe the following points:

a. Always use a new gasket.

b. Tighten the nuts in a crisscross pat-

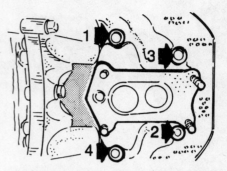

When installing the CVCC combination manifold, tighten the four bolts after the manifolds have been installed to avoid cracking the manifold ears

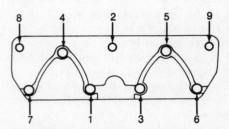

Combination manifold torque sequence—1978–79 1487cc, 1979 1751cc, 1980 1751cc (exc. Calif.), and 1980 1335cc engines

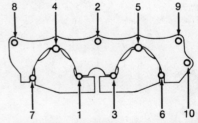

Combination manifold torque sequence—1980–81 1487cc, 1981 1335cc, 1980 1751cc (Calif.), and all 1981 1751cc engines

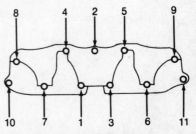

Combination manifold torque sequence—1982–83 1751cc engine

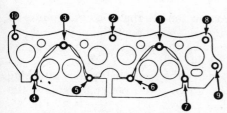

Combination manifold torque sequence—1982–83 1335 and 1487cc engines

tern in 2–3 steps, starting with the inner nuts.

c. Be sure all hoses and wires are correctly connected.

Exhaust Manifold
REMOVAL AND INSTALLATION
Non CVCC Models

CAUTION: *Do not perform this operation on a warm or hot engine.*
1. Remove the front grille.
2. Remove the three (3) exhaust pipe-to-manifold nuts and disconnect the exhaust pipe at the manifold.
2a. On 1975 and later models, disconnect the air injection tubes from the exhaust manifold and remove the air injection manifold.
3. Remove the hot air cover, held by two bolts, from the exhaust manifold.
4. Remove the eight (8) manifold attaching nuts in a crisscross pattern starting from the center, and remove the manifold.
5. To install, reverse the removal procedure. Be sure to use new gaskets and be sure to tighten the manifold bolts in the reverse order of removal, and to the proper tightening torque.

1983 and Later 1342, 1488 and 1829cc Engines

CAUTION: *Do not perform this operation on a warm or hot engine.*
1. Remove the header pipe or catalytic converter to exhaust manifold attaching bolts.
2. Remove the oxygen sensor (if so equipped).
3. Remove the EGR and the air suction tubes (if so equipped).
4. Remove the exhaust manifold shroud.
5. Remove the exhaust manifold bracket bolts.
6. Remove the exhaust attaching nuts in a

crisscross pattern starting from the center, and remove the manifold.
7. To install, reverse the removal procedure. Use new gaskets and tighten the manifold bolts in a crisscross pattern starting from the center.

Intake and Exhaust Manifolds
REMOVAL AND INSTALLATION
CVCC Models

1. Drain the radiator. Disconnect manifold coolant hoses.
2. Remove the air cleaner assembly.
3. Label and disconnect all emission control vacuum hoses and electrical leads.
4. Label and disconnect all emission control vacuum hoses and electrical leads.
5. Remove the carburetor from the intake manifold.
6. Remove the upper heat shield. Loosen, but do not remove the four bolts retaining the intake manifold to the exhaust manifold.
7. Disconnect the exhaust pipe from the exhaust manifold.
8. Remove the nine nuts retaining the intake and exhaust manifolds to the cylinder head. The two manifolds are removed as a unit.
9. Reverse the above procedure to install, using new gaskets. The thick washers used beneath the cylinder head-to-manifold retaining nuts must be installed with the dished (concave), side toward the engine. Torque the bolts in a circular pattern from the center to the ends. Readjust the choke and throttle linkage and bleed the cooling system.

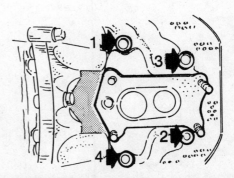

When reinstalling the combination manifold on CVCC models, tighten these four bolts *after* the manifolds have been attached to the engine. You'll crack the manifold ears if you tighten them beforehand

Timing Gear Cover
REMOVAL AND INSTALLATION

1. Align the crankshaft pulley (1170 and 1237 cc), or flywheel pointer (CVCC), at Top Dead Center (TDC).

2. Remove the two bolts which hold the timing belt upper cover and remove the cover.

Engine showing timing belt upper cover removed

The small washers can be removed from behind the tensioner and adjusting bolt to allow removal of the cover. Be sure to reinstall the washers

3. Loosen the alternator and air pump (if so equipped), and remove the pulley belt(s).

4. Remove the three water pump pulley bolts and the water pump pulley.

5. Remove the crankshaft pulley attaching bolt. Use a two-jawed puller to remove the crankshaft pulley.

NOTE: *The crankshaft bolt cannot be reused. It must be replaced every time it is removed.*

6. Remove the timing gear cover retaining bolts and the timing gear cover.

7. To install, reverse the removal procedure. Make sure that the timing guide plates, pulleys and front oil seal are properly installed on the crankshaft end before replacing the cover.

CAUTION: *Be sure not to upset the timing position already set (TDC).*

Timing Belt and Tensioner
REMOVAL AND INSTALLATION

1. Turn the crankshaft pulley until it is at Top Dead Center.

2. Remove the pulley belt, water pump pulley, crankshaft pulley, and timing gear cover. Mark the direction of timing belt rotation.

3. Loosen, *but do not remove*, the tensioner adjusting bolt and pivot bolt.

4. Slide the timing belt off of the camshaft timing gear and the crankshaft pulley gear and remove it from the engine.

5. To remove the camshaft timing gear pulley, first remove the center bolt and then remove the pulley with a pulley remover or a brass hammer. This can be accomplished by simply removing the timing belt upper cover, loosening the tensioner bolts, and sliding the timing belt off of the gear to expose the gear for removal.

NOTE: *If you remove the timing gear with the timing belt cover in place, be sure not to let the woodruff key fall inside the timing cover when removing the gear from the camshaft.*

Inspecting the timing belt

Closeup of the adjustment and pivot bolts. The upper bolt is the pivot bolt, and the lower bolt is the adjustment bolt

On non-CVCC engines, align the marks on the cam gear parallel with the top of the cylinder head

On CVCC engines, when the camshaft pulley is in the correct position, the word "UP" will be facing up and the small mark on the camshaft pulley will be aligned with the arrow on the cylinder head. The marks are just slightly off in this photograph. On the opposite side of the cam gear, there is a small arrow pointing at a small line. This is used by Honda to indicate when the gear has been installed 180 degrees out of time. The marks are not really necessary since then the word "UP" would be pointing down

Frontal view of a non-CVCC engine showing the timing belt correctly installed. Note that the crankshaft key is pointing straight up and the marks on the cam gear are parallel with the top of the cylinder head

Inspect the timing belt. Replace if over 10,000 miles old, if oil soaked (find source of oil leak also), or if worn on leading edges of belt teeth.

6. To install, reverse the removal procedure. Be sure to install the crankshaft pulley and the camshaft timing gear pulley in the top dead center position. (See "Cylinder Head Removal" for further details). On the non-CVCC engine, align the marks on the camshaft timing gear so they are parallel with the top of the cylinder head and the woodruff

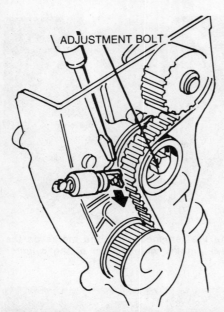

Timing belt tensioner adjustment bolt—
1342 and 1488cc engines

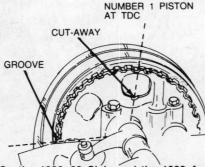

On the 1980–83 Civic and the 1983 Accord, when the No. 1 piston is set at TDC, the cut-away in the pulley is at the top and the groove on the pulley is aligned with the top of the cylinder head.

key is facing up. See the photograph for details on CVCC timing.

When installing the timing belt, do not allow oil to come in contact with the belt. Oil will cause the rubber to swell. Be careful not to bend or twist the belt unnecessarily, since it is made of fiberglass; nor should you use tools having sharp edges when installing or removing the belt. Be sure to install the belt with the arrow facing in the same direction it was facing during removal.

After installing the timing belt, adjust the belt tension by first rotating the crankshaft counterclockwise ¼ turn. Then, retighten the adjusting bolt and finally the tensioner pivot bolt.

CAUTION: *Do not remove the adjusting or pivot bolts, only loosen them. When adjusting, do not use any force other than the adjuster spring. If the belt is too tight, it will result in a shortened belt life.*

Pistons and Connecting Rods
REMOVAL AND INSTALLATION

For removal with the engine out of the car, begin with Step 8.

1. Remove the turn signals (Civic through 1977), grille, and engine hood.
2. Drain the radiator.
3. Drain the engine oil.
4. Raise the front of the car and support it with safety stands.
5. Attach a chain to the clutch cable bracket on the transmission case and raise just enough to take the load off of the center mount.

NOTE: *Do not remove the left engine mount.*

6. Remove the center beam and engine lower mount.
7. Remove the cylinder head (see "Cylinder Head Removal and Installation").
8. Loosen the oil pan bolts and remove

Oil pump removal. There is a bolt hidden under the screen. See the photograph under "Oil Pump Removal"

Mark the pistons for installation if they aren't already marked from the factory

The piston pins must be removed with a press

the oil pan and flywheel dust shield. Loosen the oil pan bolts in a criss-cross pattern beginning with the outside bolt. To remove the oil pan, lightly tap the corners of the oil pan with a mallet. It is not necessary to remove the gasket unless it is damaged.

CAUTION: *Do not pry the oil pan off with the tip of a screwdriver.*

9. Remove the oil passage block and the oil pump assembly.

CAUTION: *As soon as the oil passage block bolts are loosened, the oil in the oil line may flow out.*

NOTE: *Before removing the pistons, check the top of the cylinder bore for carbon build-up or a ridge. Remove the carbon or use a ridge-reamer to remove the ridge before removing the pistons.*

10. Working from the underside of the car, remove the connecting rod bearing caps. Using the wooden handle of a hammer, push the pistons and connecting rods out of the cylinders.

NOTE: *Bearing caps, bearings, and pistons should be marked to indicate their location for reassembly.*

11. When removing the piston rings, be

Piston assembly

sure not to apply excessive force as the rings are made of cast iron and can be easily broken.

NOTE: *A hydraulic press is necessary for removing the piston pin. This is a job best left to the professional, if you need to go this far.*

12. Observe the following points when installing the piston rings:

    a. When installing the three-piece oil

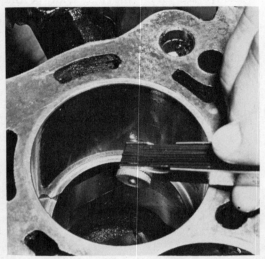

Check the ring end gap before installing the rings on the pistons

Piston ring installation. Tools like this aren't really necessary, as rings can be easily installed by hand

ring, first place the spacer and then the rails in position. The spacer and rail gaps must be staggered 0.787–1.181 in. (2–3 cm);

    b. Install the second and top rings on the piston with their markings facing upward;

    c. After installing all rings on the piston, rotate them to be sure they move smoothly without signs of binding;

    d. The ring gaps must be staggered 120° and must NOT be in the direction of the piston pin boss or at right angles to the pin. The gap of the three-piece oil ring refers to that of the middle spacer.

NOTE: *Pistons and rings are also available in four oversizes, 0.010 in. (0.25 mm), 0.020 in. (0.50 mm), 0.030 in. (0.75 mm), and 0.040 in. (1.00 mm).*

13. Using a ring compressor, install the piston into the cylinder with the skirt protruding about ⅓ of the piston height below the ring compressor. Prior to installation,

Make sure the recess in the cap and recess on the rod are on the same side (Arrows)

Torquing the connecting rod cap

apply a thin coat of oil to the rings and to the cylinder wall.

NOTE: *When installing the piston, the connecting rod oil jet hole or the mark on the piston crown faces the intake manifold.*

14. Using the wooden handle of a hammer, slowly press the piston into the cylinder. Guide the connecting rod so it does not damage the crankshaft journals.

15. Reassemble the remaining components in the reverse order of removal. Install the connecting rod bearing caps so that the recess in the cap and the recess in the rod are on the same side. After tightening the cap bolts, move the rod back and forth on the journal to check for binding.

ENGINE LUBRICATION

Oil Pan

REMOVAL AND INSTALLATION

1. Drain the engine oil.
2. Raise the front of the car and support it with safety stands.
3. Attach a chain to the clutch cable bracket on the transmission case and raise just enough to take the load off the center mount.

NOTE: *Do not remove the left engine mount.*

4. Remove the center beam and engine lower mount.
5. Loosen the oil pan bolts and remove the oil pan flywheel dust shield.

NOTE: *Loosen the bolts in a criss-cross pattern beginning with the outside bolt. To remove the oil pan, lightly tap the corners of the oil pan with a mallet. It is not necessary to remove the gasket unless it is damaged.*

6. To install, reverse the removal procedure. Apply a coat of sealant to the entire mating surface of the cylinder block, except the crankshaft oil seal, before fitting the oil pan.

Rear Main Oil Seal

REPLACEMENT

The rear oil seal on the Honda is installed in the rear main bearing cap. Replacement of the seal requires the removal of the transmission, flywheel and clutch housing, as well as the oil pan. Refer to the appropriate sections for the removal and installation of the above

Driving in the rear main seal using the Honda special tool

components. Both the front and rear main seal are installed after the crankshaft has been torqued, in the event it was removed. Special drivers are used.

Oil Pump

REMOVAL AND INSTALLATION

All except 1342, 1488 and 1829cc CVCC Engines

To remove the oil pump, follow the procedure given for oil pan removal and installa-

Removing the oil pump screen

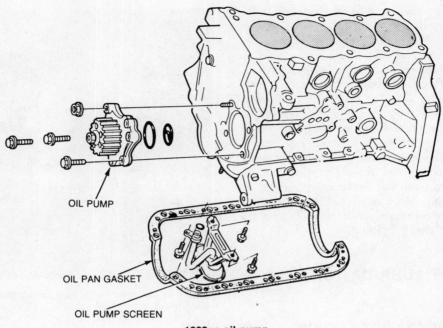

OIL PUMP

OIL PAN GASKET

OIL PUMP SCREEN

1829cc oil pump

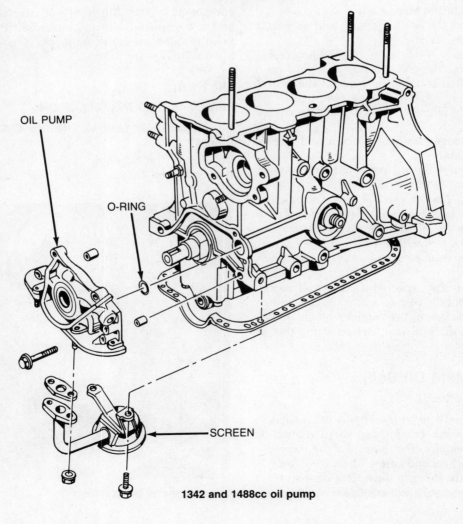

OIL PUMP

O-RING

SCREEN

1342 and 1488cc oil pump

tion. After the oil pan has been dropped, simply unbolt the oil passage block and oil pump assembly from the engine. Remove the oil pump screen to find the last bolt. When installing the pump, torque the bolts to no more than 8 ft. lbs.

CVCC Engines 1342, 1488 and 1829cc

To remove the oil pump, follow the procedure given to remove the timing gear cover. After removing the cover, remove the timing belt and unbolt the oil pump and remove it from the block. When installing the pump, tighten the bolts to 9 ft. lbs. and the nuts to 5 ft. lbs. To remove the oil pump pick-up screen, follow the procedure to remove the oil pan.

OIL PUMP OVERHAUL

1. Check the rotor radial clearance on both the upper and lower rotors. Clearance is 0.006–0.008 in.

Hidden oil pump retaining bolt (arrow)

Torquing the oil pump retaining bolts

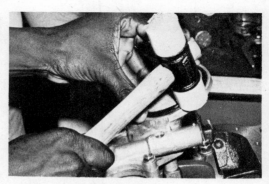
Installing the oil pump screen

2. Check body-to-rotor clearance on both rotors. Clearance is 0.004–0.007 new, with 0.008 in. as the service limit.
3. Check the rotor end play between the rotor face and the gasket surface, gasket installed. End play should be 0.001–0.004 in. new, with a service limit of 0.006 in. Use a straightedge and feeler gauge for this check.
4. If rotors should require replacement, inner and outer rotors on both upper and lower halves, are installed with the punch marks aligned adjacent to one another.

ENGINE COOLING

The Honda employs water-cooling for engine heat dissipation. Air is forced through the radiator by an electric fan which is, in turn, activated by a water temperature sensor screwed into the base of the radiator.

Radiator

REMOVAL AND INSTALLATION

NOTE: *When removing the radiator, take care not to damage the core and fins.*
1. Drain the radiator.
2. Disconnect the thermo-switch wire and the fan motor wire. Remove the fan shroud, if so equipped.
3. Disconnect the upper coolant hose at the upper radiator tank and the lower hose at the water pump connecting pipe.
4. Remove the turn signals (Civic through 1977) and front grille.
5. Detach the radiator mounting bolts and remove the radiator with the fan attached. The fan can be easily unbolted from the back of the radiator.
6. To install, reverse the removal procedure. Bleed the cooling system.

Water Pump

All except 1342 and 1488cc CVCC Engines

REMOVAL AND INSTALLATION

1. Drain the radiator.
2. On 1170 and 1237 cc cars only, loosen the alternator bolts. Move the alternator toward the cylinder block and remove the drive belt.
3. Loosen the pump mounting bolts and remove the pump together with the pulley and the seal rubber.
4. To install, reverse the removal procedure using a new gasket. Bleed the cooling system.

1342 and 1488cc CVCC

1. Drain the radiator.
2. Following the procedures shown under "Timing belt and Tensioner" remove the timing belt from the water pump drive sprocket.
3. Loosen the water pump mounting bolts and remove together with the drive sprocket.
4. To install, reverse the removal procedure using a new O-ring. Bleed the cooling system.

Thermostat

REMOVAL AND INSTALLATION

1. On 1170 and 1237 cc cars, the thermostat is located on the intake manifold, under

Thermostat housing and bleed bolt location—non-CVCC models

the air cleaner nozzle, so you will first have to remove the air cleaner housing. On CVCC cars, it is located at the rear of the distributor housing.
2. Unbolt and remove the thermostat cover and pull the thermostat from the housing.
3. To install, reverse the removal procedure. Always install the spring end of the thermostat toward the engine. Tighten the two cover bolts to 7 ft lbs. Always use a new gasket. Bleed the cooling system.

Thermostat housing and bleed bolt location—CVCC models

Thermostat installation

Emission Controls and Fuel Systems

4

EMISSION CONTROLS

Emission controls on the Honda fall into one of three basic systems: A. Crankcase Emission Control System, B. Exhaust Emission Control System, C. Evaporative Emission Control System.

Crankcase Emission Control System

The Honda's engine is equipped with a "Dual Return System" to prevent crankcase vapor emissions. Blow-by gas is returned to the combustion chamber through the intake manifold and carburetor air cleaner. When the throttle is partially opened, blow-by gas is returned to the intake manifold through breather tubes leading into the tee orifice located on the outside of the intake manifold. When the throttle is opened wide and vacuum in the air cleaner rises, blow-by gas is returned to the intake manifold through an additional passage in the air cleaner case.

Exhaust Emission Control System

1973-74 MODELS

Control of exhaust emissions, hydrocarbon (HC), carbon monoxide (CO), and Oxides of nitrogen (NO^x), is achieved by a combination of engine modifications and special control devices. Improvements to the combustion chamber, intake manifold, valve timing, carburetor, and distributor comprise the engine modifications. These modifications, in conjunction with the special control devices, enable the engine to produce low emission with leaner air-fuel mixtures while maintaining good driveability. The special control devices consist of the following:

    a. Intake air temperature control;

    b. Throttle opener;

    c. Ignition timing retard unit (1973 models only);

    d. Transmission and temperature controlled spark advance (TCS) for the 4-speed transmission;

    e. Temperature controlled spark advance for Hondamatic automatic transmission (1974 models only).

Intake Air Temperature Control

Intake air temperature control is designed to provide the most uniform carburetion possible under various ambient air temperature conditions by maintaining the intake air temperature within a narrow range. When the temperature in the air cleaner is below 100° F (approx.), the air bleed valve, which consists of a bimetallic strip and a rubber seal, remains closed. Intake manifold vacuum is then led to a vacuum motor, located on the snorkel of the air cleaner case, which moves the air control valve door, allowing only preheated air to enter the air cleaner.

When the temperature in the air cleaner becomes higher than approx. 100° F, the air bleed valve opens and the air control valve door returns to the open position allowing only unheated air through the snorkel.

Throttle Opener

When the throttle is closed suddenly at high engine speed, hydrocarbon (HC) emissions increase due to engine misfire caused by an incombustible mixture. The throttle opener is designed to prevent misfiring during de-

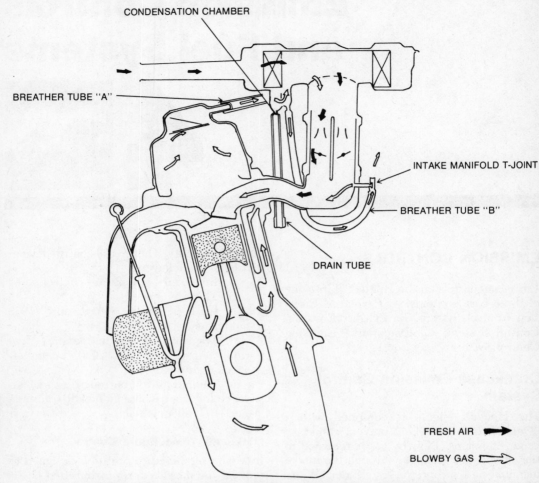

CONDENSATION CHAMBER

BREATHER TUBE "A"

INTAKE MANIFOLD T-JOINT

BREATHER TUBE "B"

DRAIN TUBE

FRESH AIR

BLOWBY GAS

Crankcase ventilation system operation—1170, 1237 cc engines—CVCC similar

celeration by causing the throttle valve to remain slightly open, allowing better mixture control. The control valve is set to allow the passage of vacuum to the throttle opener diaphragm when the engine vacuum is equal to or greater than the control valve preset vacuum (21.6 ± 1.6 in. Hg) during acceleration.

Under running conditions, other than fully closed throttle deceleration, the intake manifold vacuum is less than the control valve set vacuum; therefore the control valve is not actuated. The vacuum remaining in the throttle opener and control valve is returned to atmospheric pressure by the air passage at the valve center.

Ignition Timing Retard Unit

On 1973 models, when the engine is idling, the vacuum produced in the carburetor retarder port is communicated to the spark retard unit and the ignition timing, at idle, is retarded.

TCS System

The transmission and temperature controlled spark advance for 4-speed transmissions is designed to reduce NO^x emissions during normal vehicle operation.

On 1973 models, when the coolant temperature is approximately 120° or higher, and the transmission is in First, Second, or Third gear, the solenoid valve cuts off the vacuum to the spark advance unit, resulting in lower NO^x levels.

On 1974 models, the vacuum is cut off to the spark advance unit regardless of temperature when First, Second, or Third gear is selected. Vacuum advance is restored when Fourth gear is selected.

Temperature Controlled Spark Advance

Temperature controlled spark advance on 1973 cars equipped with Hondamatic transmission is designed to reduce NO^x emissions

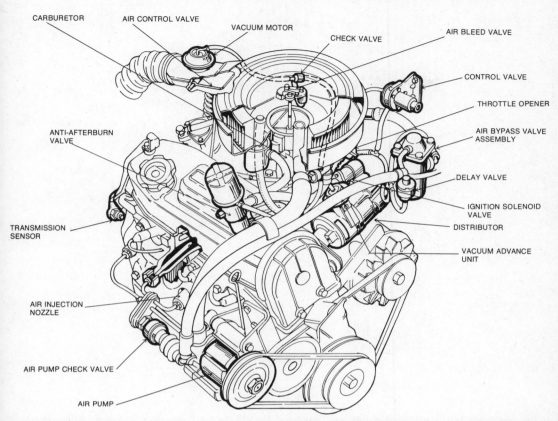

CARBURETOR AIR CONTROL VALVE VACUUM MOTOR CHECK VALVE AIR BLEED VALVE CONTROL VALVE THROTTLE OPENER AIR BYPASS VALVE ASSEMBLY ANTI-AFTERBURN VALVE DELAY VALVE IGNITION SOLENOID VALVE TRANSMISSION SENSOR DISTRIBUTOR VACUUM ADVANCE UNIT AIR INJECTION NOZZLE AIR PUMP CHECK VALVE AIR PUMP

Location of emission control system components—1975 1237 cc AIR models with manual transmission; other years similar

by disconnecting the vacuum to the spark advance unit during normal vehicle operation. When the coolant temperature is approximately 120° or higher, the solenoid valve is energized, cutting off vacuum to the advance unit.

1975–79 1237 CC AIR MODELS

Intake Air Temperature Control

Same as 1973–74 models.

Throttle Opener

Same as 1973–74 models.

Transmission Controlled Spark Advance

Same as 1974 models, with no coolant control override.

Ignition Timing Retard Unit

Same as 1973 models, but is used only on Hondamatic models and has no vacuum advance mechanism.

Air Injection System

Beginning with the 1975 model year, an air injection system is used to control hydrocarbon and carbon monoxide emissions. With this system, a belt-driven air pump delivers filtered air under pressure to injection nozzles located at each exhaust port. Here, the additional oxygen supplied by the vane-type pump reacts with any uncombusted fuel mixture, promoting an afterburning effect in the hot exhaust manifold. To prevent a reverse flow in the air injection manifold when exhaust gas pressure exceeds air supply pressure, a nonreturn check valve is used. To prevent exhaust afterburning or backfiring during deceleration, an anti-afterburn valve delivers air to the intake manifold instead. When manifold vacuum rises above the preset vacuum of the air control valve and/or below that of the air by-pass valve, air pump air is returned to the air cleaner.

1975–82 1487, 1600, 1751 CC MODELS

Intake Air Temperature Control

Same as 1973–74 models.

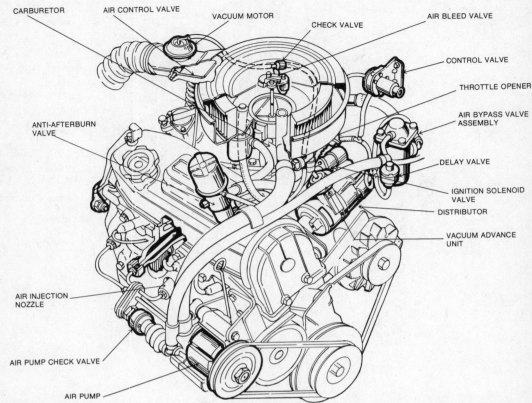

CARBURETOR

AIR CONTROL VALVE

VACUUM MOTOR

CHECK VALVE

AIR BLEED VALVE

CONTROL VALVE

THROTTLE OPENER

AIR BYPASS VALVE ASSEMBLY

ANTI-AFTERBURN VALVE

DELAY VALVE

IGNITION SOLENOID VALVE

DISTRIBUTOR

VACUUM ADVANCE UNIT

AIR INJECTION NOZZLE

AIR PUMP CHECK VALVE

AIR PUMP

Location of emission control system components—1975 1237 cc AIR models with Hondamatic—other years similar

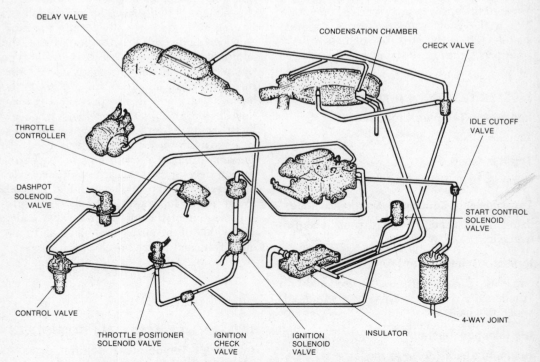

DELAY VALVE

CONDENSATION CHAMBER

CHECK VALVE

IDLE CUTOFF VALVE

THROTTLE CONTROLLER

DASHPOT SOLENOID VALVE

START CONTROL SOLENOID VALVE

CONTROL VALVE

THROTTLE POSITIONER SOLENOID VALVE

IGNITION CHECK VALVE

IGNITION SOLENOID VALVE

INSULATOR

4-WAY JOINT

Emission controls system schematic—Accord with manual transmission

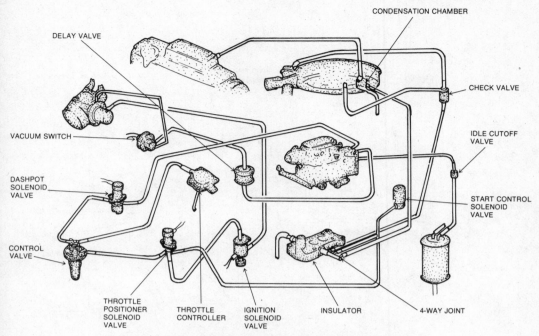

CONDENSATION CHAMBER

DELAY VALVE

CHECK VALVE

VACUUM SWITCH

IDLE CUTOFF VALVE

DASHPOT SOLENOID VALVE

START CONTROL SOLENOID VALVE

CONTROL VALVE

THROTTLE POSITIONER SOLENOID VALVE

THROTTLE CONTROLLER

IGNITION SOLENOID VALVE

INSULATOR

4-WAY JOINT

Emission controls system schematic—Accord with Hondamatic

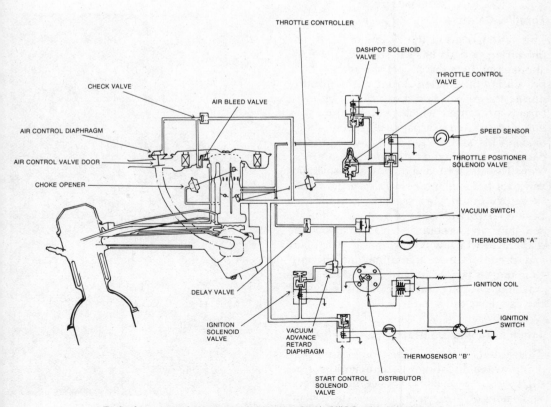

THROTTLE CONTROLLER

DASHPOT SOLENOID VALVE

THROTTLE CONTROL VALVE

CHECK VALVE

AIR BLEED VALVE

SPEED SENSOR

AIR CONTROL DIAPHRAGM

AIR CONTROL VALVE DOOR

THROTTLE POSITIONER SOLENOID VALVE

CHOKE OPENER

VACUUM SWITCH

THERMOSENSOR "A"

IGNITION COIL

DELAY VALVE

IGNITION SOLENOID VALVE

VACUUM ADVANCE RETARD DIAPHRAGM

IGNITION SWITCH

THERMOSENSOR "B"

START CONTROL SOLENOID VALVE

DISTRIBUTOR

Emission control system schematic—Civic CVCC with Hondamatic

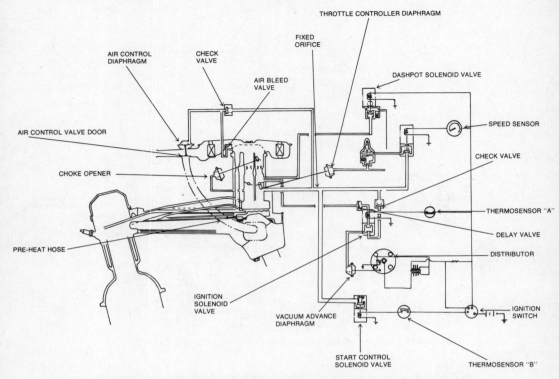

Emission control system schematic—Civic CVCC with manual transmission

Throttle Controls

This system controls the closing of the throttle during periods of gear shifting, deceleration, or anytime the gas pedal is released. In preventing the sudden closing of the throttle during these conditions, an overly rich mixture is prevented which controls excessive emissions of hydrocarbons and carbon monoxide. This system has two main parts; a dashpot system and a throttle positioner system. The dashpot diaphragm and solenoid valve act to dampen or slow down the throttle return time to 1–4 seconds. The throttle positioner part consists of a speed sensor, a solenoid valve, a control valve and an opener diaphragm which will keep the throttle open and predetermined minimum amount any time the gas pedal is released when the car is traveling 15 mph or faster, and closes it when the car slows to 10 mph.

Ignition Timing Controls

This system uses a coolant temperature sensor to switch distributor vacuum ignition timing controls on or off to reduce hydrocarbon and oxides of nitrogen emissions. The coolant switch is calibrated at 149°F for 1487 and

Vacuum delay valve mounted on air cleaner

1600 cc engines and 167°F for 1751 cc engines.

Hot Start Control

This system is designed to prevent an over-rich mixture condition in the intake manifold due to vaporization of residual fuel when starting a hot engine. This reduces hydrocarbon and carbon monoxide emissions.

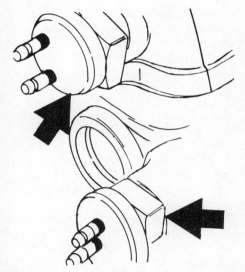

Thermosensors located on engine block. The upper thermosensor energizes a solenoid when the engine is cold, giving vacuum advance. The lower thermosensor is used when the engine is warm (1977 and earlier)

Anti-Afterburn Valve

1979–82 1751 cc engines have an anti-afterburn valve. This unit is used only on models with manual transmission. The valve lets fresh air into the intake manifold when it senses sudden increases in manifold vacuum. The valve responds only to sudden increases in vacuum and the amount of time it stays open is determined by an internal diaphragm which is acted on by the vacuum level.

CVCC Engine Modifications

By far, the most important part of the CVCC engine emission control system is the Compound Vortex Controlled Combustion (CVCC) cylinder head itself. Each cylinder has three valves: a conventional intake and conventional exhaust valve, and a smaller auxiliary intake valve. There are actually *two* combustion chambers per cylinder: a pre-combustion or auxiliary chamber, and the main chamber. During the intake stroke, an extremely lean mixture is drawn into the

main combustion chamber. Simultaneously, a very rich mixture is drawn into the smaller precombustion chamber via the auxiliary intake valve. The spark plug, located in the precombustion chamber, easily ignites the rich pre-mixture, and this combustion spreads out into the main combustion chamber where the lean mixture is ignited. Due to the fact that the volume of the auxiliary chamber is much smaller than the main chamber, the overall mixture is very lean (about 18 parts air to one part fuel). The result is low hydrocarbon emissions due to the slow, stable combustion of the lean mixture in the main chamber; low carbon monoxide emissions due to the excess oxygen available; and low oxides of nitrogen emissions due to the lowered peak combustion temperatures. An added benefit of burning the lean mixture is the excellent gas mileage.

AIR JET CONTROLLER

Used on 1981 and later California and High Altitude models, this system senses atmospheric pressure and regulates carburetor air flow accordingly.

Evaporative Emission Control System

This system prevents gasoline vapors from escaping into the atmosphere from the fuel tank and carburetor and consists of the components listed in the illustration.

Fuel vapor is stored in the expansion chamber, in the fuel tank, and in the vapor line up to the one-way valve. When the vapor pressure becomes higher than the set pressure of the one-way valve, the valve opens and allows vapor into the charcoal canister. While the engine is stopped or idling, the idle cut-off valve in the canister is closed and the vapor is absorbed by the charcoal.

At partially opened throttle, the idle cut-off valve is opened by manifold vacuum. The vapor that was stored in the charcoal canister and in the vapor line is purged into the intake manifold. Any excessive pressure or vacuum which might build up in the fuel tank is relieved by the two-way valve in the filler cap.

Maintenance and Service
COMPONENTS PERTAINING TO EMISSION CONTROLS

The proper control of exhaust emissions depends not only on the primary components of the emission controls mentioned above, but also on such related areas as ignition timing, spark plugs, valve clearance, engine oil, cooling system, etc. Before tackling the primary emission controls, you should determine if the related components are functioning properly, and correct any deficiencies.

CRANKCASE EMISSION CONTROL SYSTEM

1. Squeeze the lower end of the drain tube and drain any oil or water which may have collected.

2. Make sure that the intake manifold T-joint is clear by passing the shank end of a No. 65 (0.035 in. dia.) drill through both ends (orifices) of the joint.

3. Check for any loose, disconnected, or deteriorated tubes and replace if necessary.

EXHAUST EMISSION CONTROL SYSTEM

Intake Air Temperature Control System (Engine Cold)

1. Inspect for loose, disconnected, or deteriorated vacuum hoses and replace as necessary.

2. Remove the air cleaner cover and element.

3. With the transmission in Neutral and the blue distributor disconnected, engage the starter motor for approximately two (2) seconds. Manifold vacuum to the vacuum motor should completely raise the air control valve door. Once opened, the valve door should stay open unless there is a leak in the system.

4. If the valve door does not open, check the intake manifold port by passing a No. 78 (0.016 in. dia.) drill or compressed air through the orifice in the manifold.

5. If the valve door still does not open, proceed to the following steps:

a. Vacuum Motor Test—Disconnect the vacuum line from the vacuum motor inlet pipe. Fully open the air control valve door, block the vacuum motor inlet pipe, then release the door. If the door does not remain open, the vacuum motor is defective. Replace as necessary and repeat Steps 1–3;

b. Air Bleed Valve Test—Unblock the inlet pipe and make sure that the valve door fully closes without sticking or binding. Reconnect the vacuum line to the vacuum motor inlet pipe. Connect a vacuum source (e.g. hand vacuum pump) to the manifold vacuum line (disconnect at the intake manifold fixed orifice) and draw enough vacuum to fully open the valve door. If the valve door closes with the manifold vacuum line plugged (by the vacuum pump), then vacuum is leaking through the air bleed valve. Replace as necessary and repeat Steps 1–3;

CAUTION: *Never force the air bleed valve (bi-metal strip) on or off its valve seat. The bi-metal strip and the valve seat may be damaged.*

c. Check Valve Test—Again draw a vacuum (at the manifold vacuum line) until the valve door opens. Unplug the line by disconnecting the pump from the manifold vacuum line. If the valve door closes, vacuum is leaking past the check valve. Replace as necessary and repeat Steps 1–3.

6. After completing the above steps, replace the air cleaner element and cover and fit a vacuum gauge into the line leading to the vacuum motor.

7. Start the engine and raise the idle to 1500–2000 rpm. As the engine warms, the vacuum gauge reading should drop to zero.

NOTE: *Allow sufficient time for the engine to reach normal operating temperature—when the cooling fan cycles on and off.*

If the reading does not drop to zero before the engine reaches normal operating temperature, the air bleed valve is defective and must be replaced. Repeat Step 3 as a final check.

Temperature and Transmission Controlled Spark Advance (Engine Cold)—All Models

1. Check for loose, disconnected, or deteriorated vacuum hoses and replace as necessary.

2. Check the coolant temperature sensor switch for proper operation with an ohmmeter or 12V light. The switch should normally be open (no continuity across the switch terminals) when the coolant temperature is below approximately 120° F (engine cold). If the switch is closed (continuity across the terminals), replace the switch and repeat the check.

3. On manual transmission models, check the transmission sensor switch. The switch should be open (no continuity across the connections) when Fourth gear is selected, and closed (continuity across the connections) in

Start control solenoid valve

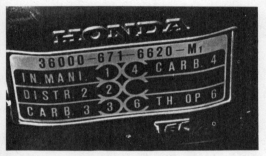

Emission control "black box" for electrical and vacuum hose connections

all other gear positions. Replace if necessary and repeat the check.

4. Remove the spark control vacuum tube, leading between the spark advance/retard unit and the solenoid valve, and connect a vacuum gauge to the now-vacant hole in the solenoid valve, according to the diagram.

5. Start the engine and raise the idle to 2000 rpm. With a cold engine, the vacuum gauge should read approximately 3 in./Hg or more. As the coolant temperature reaches 120° F (and before the radiator fan starts), the vacuum reading should drop to zero. On manual transmission models, vacuum should return when Fourth gear is selected (and the transmission switch is opened). If this is not the case, proceed to the following steps:

NOTE: *If the engine is warm from the previous test, disconnect the coolant temperature switch wires when making the following tests.*

6. If vacuum is not initially available, disconnect the vacuum signal line from the charcoal canister and plug the open end, which will block a possible vacuum leak from the idle cut-off valve of the canister. With the line plugged, again check for vacuum at 2000 rpm. If vacuum is now available, reconnect the vacuum signal line and check the canister for vacuum leaks. (Refer to the "Evaporative Emission Control System" check.) If vacuum is still not available, stop the engine and disconnect the vacuum line from the solenoid valve (the line between the solenoid valve and the manifold T-joint) and insert a vacuum gauge in the line. If vacuum is not available, the vacuum port is blocked. Clear the port with compressed air and repeat the test sequence beginning with Step 3.

7. If vacuum is available in Step 5 after the engine is warm and in all ranges of the automatic transmission and in First, Second, and Third of the manual transmission, stop the engine and check for electrical continuity between the terminals of the coolant temperature sensor:

NOTE: *After completing the following steps, repeat the test procedure beginning with Step 4.*

a. If there is no continuity (and the engine is warm), replace the temperature sensor switch and recheck for continuity;

b. If there is continuity, check the battery voltage to the vacuum solenoid. If no voltage is available (with the ignition switch ON), check the wiring, fuses, and connections;

c. If there is battery voltage and the temperature sensor is operating correctly, check connections and/or replace the solenoid valve.

EVAPORATIVE EMISSION CONTROL SYSTEM (ENGINE AT NORMAL OPERATING TEMPERATURE)

Charcoal Canister

1. Check for loose, disconnected, or deteriorated vacuum hoses and replace where necessary.

2. Pull the free end of the purge air guide tube out of the body frame and plug it securely.

3. Disconnect the fuel vapor line from the charcoal canister and connect a vacuum gauge to the charcoal canister vapor inlet according to the diagram.

4. Start the engine and allow it to idle. Since the vacuum port in the carburetor is

closed off at idle, the vacuum gauge should register no vacuum. If vacuum is available, replace the charcoal canister and recheck for no vacuum. A vacuum reading indicates that the charcoal canister idle cut-off valve is broken or stuck.

5. Open the throttle to 2000 rpm and make sure that the charcoal canister idle cut-off valve is opening by watching the vacuum.

a. Disconnect the vacuum signal line and connect the vacuum gauge to the carburetor T-joint orifice formerly occupied by the signal line. The vacuum reading at 2000 rpm should be greater than 3 in./Hg. If vacuum is now available (with the throttle open), replace the charcoal canister and repeat Steps 4 & 5. If vacuum is still not available, or is below 3 in./Hg, proceed to the next step;

b. If vacuum is less than 3 in./Hg (with the throttle open), the carburetor vacuum port or T-joint might be plugged. Clear the passages with compressed air. If vacuum is now available, repeat Steps 4 & 5. If vacuum is not available, or below 3 in./Hg, the carburetor vacuum port is blocked. Repair or replace as necessary and repeat Steps 4 & 5. If vacuum is *still* not available, proceed to the next step;

c. Plug the solenoid valve vacuum line (the other line to the carburetor T-joint) and recheck for vacuum. If vacuum is now available, the leak is in the advance/retard solenoid valve. Repair or replace as necessary and repeat Steps 4 & 5.

FUEL SYSTEM

1170 and 1237 cc models use a two-barrel downdraft Hitachi carburetor. Fuel pressure is provided by a camshaft-driven mechanical fuel pump. A replaceable fuel filter is located in the engine compartment in-line between the fuel pump and carburetor.

On the 1335, 1487 and 1600 cc CVCC Civic, and Accord, and 1751 cc Accord and Prelude, a Keihin three-barrel carburetor is used. On this carburetor, the primary and secondary venturis deliver a lean air/fuel mixture to the main combustion chamber. Simultaneously, the third or auxiliary venturi which has a complete separate fuel metering circuit, delivers a small (in volume) but very rich air/fuel mixture to the precombustion chamber. Fuel pressure is provided by an electric fuel pump which is actuated when the ignition switch is turned to the "on" position. The electric pump is located under the rear seat beneath a special access plate on sedan and hatchback models, and located under the rear of the car adjacent to the fuel tank on station wagon and Accord models. A replaceable in-line fuel filter located on the inlet side of the electric fuel pump is used on all CVCC models.

Mechanical Fuel Pump
REMOVAL AND INSTALLATION
All Except CVCC

The fuel pump in the Civic is located in back of the engine, underneath the air cleaner snorkel.

1. Remove the air cleaner and cover assembly.

Mechanical fuel pump location. Arrow indicates air hole

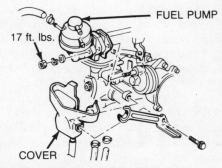

1342 and 1488cc mechanical fuel pump

2. Remove the inlet and outlet fuel lines at the pump.

3. Loosen the pump nuts and remove the pump.

NOTE: *Do not disassemble the pump. Disassembly may cause fuel or oil leakage. If the pump is defective, replace it as an assembly.*

4. To install the fuel pump, reverse the removal procedure.

INSPECTION

1. Check the following items:

    a. Looseness of the pump connector.

    b. Looseness of the upper and lower body and cover screws.

    c. Looseness of the rocker arm pin.

    d. Contamination or clogging of the air hole.

    e. Improper operation of the pump.

2. Check to see if there are signs of oil or fuel around the air hole. If so, the diaphragm is damaged and you must replace the pump.

3. To inspect the pump for operation, first disconnect the fuel line at the carburetor. Connect a fuel pressure gauge to the delivery side of the pump. Start the engine and measure the pump delivery pressure.

4. After measuring, stop the engine and check to see if the gauge drops suddenly. If the gauge drops suddenly and/or the delivery pressure is incorrect, check for a fuel or oil leak from the diaphragm or from the valves.

5. To test for volume, disconnect the fuel line from the carburetor and inset it into a one quart container. Crank the engine for 64

Mechanical Fuel Pump Performance Specifications

Engine rpm	Delivery Pressure (lb/in.^{2})	Vacuum (in. Hg)	Displacement (in.^{3}/ minute)
600	2.56	17.72	27
3,000	2.56	7.87–11.81	43
6,000	2.56	7.87–11.81	46

seconds at 600 rpm, or 40 seconds at 3,000 rpm. The bottle should be half full (1 pint).

Electrical Fuel Pump

REMOVAL AND INSTALLATION

CVCC Models

1. Remove the gas filler cap to relieve any excess pressure in the system.

2. Obtain a pair of clothes pins or other suitable clamps to pinch shut the fuel lines to the pump.

3. Disconnect the negative battery cable.

4. Locate the fuel pump. On sedan and hatchback models, you will first have to remove the rear seat by removing the bolt at the rear center of the bottom cushion and pivoting the seat forward from the rear. The pump and filter are located on the driver's side of the rear seat floor section beneath an access plate retained by four phillips head screws.

On station wagon Accord and Prelude models, you will have to raise the rear of the car, or park it with two wheels up on a curb to obtain access. In all cases, make sure, if you are crawling under the car, that the car is securely supported. *Do not venture beneath the car when it is supported only by the tire changing jack.*

5. Pinch the inlet and outlet fuel lines shut. Loosen the hose clamps. On station wagon models, remove the filter mounting clip on the left-hand side of the bracket. On Prelude models, remove the fuel filter.

6. Disconnect the positive lead wire and ground wire from the pump at their quick disconnect.

7. Remove the two (three on Prelude) fuel pump retaining bolts, taking care not to lose the two spacers and bolt collars.

8. Remove the fuel lines and fuel pump.

NOTE: *The Prelude pump is enclosed in a two-piece housing.*

Checking the fuel pump with a fuel pressure gauge

9. Reverse the above procedure to install. The pump cannot be disassembled and must be replaced if defective. Operating fuel pump pressure is 2–3 psi.

Carburetors

TROUBLESHOOTING

Carburetor problems are among the most difficult internal combustion engine malfunctions to diagnose. If you have a carburetor problem, read the description of carburetor systems in the beginning of the carburetor section of this chapter. Consider which system or combination of systems are in operation when the problem occurs. Some troubleshooting tips are given in the system operation descriptions.

The most reliable way for a nonprofessional to diagnose a bad carburetor is to eliminate all other possible sources of the problem. If you suspect the carburetor is the problem, perform the adjustments given in this chapter. Check the ignition system to ensure that the spark plugs, contact points, and condenser are in good shape and adjusted properly. Check the emission control equipment following the instructions given in the first part of this chapter. Check the ignition timing adjustment. Check all vacuum hoses on the engine for loose connections or splits or breaks. Make sure the carburetor and intake manifold attaching bolts are tightened to the proper torque.

If you do determine that the carburetor is malfunctioning, and the adjustments in this chapter don't help, you have three alternatives: you can take it to a professional mechanic and let him fix it, you can buy a new or rebuilt carburetor to replace the one now on your car, or you can buy a carburetor rebuilding kit and overhaul your carburetor.

Overhaul

All Types

Efficient carburetion depends greatly on careful cleaning and inspection during overhaul since dirt, gum, water, or varnish in or on the carburetor parts are often responsible for poor performance.

Overhaul your carburetor in a clean, dust-free area. Carefully disassemble the carburetor, referring often to the exploded views. Keep all similar and look-alike parts segregated during disassembly and cleaning to

avoid accidental interchange during assembly. Make a note of all jet sizes.

When the carburetor is disassembled, wash all parts (except diaphragms, electric choke units, pump plunger, and any other plastic, leather, fiber, or rubber parts) in clean carburetor solvent. Do not leave parts in the solvent any longer than is necessary to sufficiently loosen the deposits. Excessive cleaning may remove the special finish from the float bowl and choke valve bodies, leaving these parts unfit for service. Rinse all parts in clean solvent and blow them dry with compressed air or allow them to air dry. Wipe clean all cork, plastic, leather, and fiber parts with a clean, lint-free cloth.

Blow out all passages and jets with compressed air and be sure that there are no restrictions or blockages. Never use wire or similar tools to clean jets, fuel passages, or air bleeds. Clean all jets and valves separately to avoid accidental interchange.

Check all parts for wear or damage. If wear or damage is found, replace the defective parts. Especially check the following:

1. Check the float needle and seat for wear. If wear is found, replace the complete assembly.

2. Check the float hinge pin for wear and the float(s) for dents or distortion. Replace the float if fuel has leaked into it.

3. Check the throttle and choke shaft bores for wear or an out-of-round condition. Damage or wear to the throttle arm, shaft, or shaft bore will often require replacement of the throttle body. These parts require a close tolerance of fit; wear may allow air leakage, which could affect starting and idling.

NOTE: *Throttle shafts and bushings are not included in overhaul kits. They can be purchased separately.*

4. Inspect the idle mixture adjusting needles for burrs or grooves. Any such condition requires replacement of the needle, since you will not be able to obtain a satisfactory idle.

5. Test the accelerator pump check valves. They should pass air one way but not the other. Test for proper seating by blowing and sucking on the valve. Replace the valve if necessary. If the valve is satisfactory, wash the valve again to remove breath moisture.

6. Check the bowl cover for warped surfaces with a straightedge.

7. Closely inspect the valves and seats for wear and damage, replacing as necessary.

8. After the carburetor is assembled,

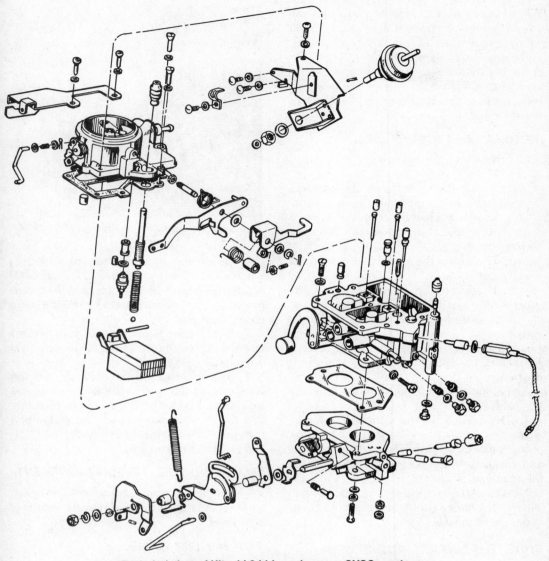

Exploded view of Hitachi 2-bbl used on non-CVCC engines

check the choke valve for freedom of operation.

Carburetor overhaul kits are recommended for each overhaul. These kits contain all gaskets and new parts to replace those that deteriorate most rapidly. Failure to replace all parts supplied with the kit (especially gaskets) can result in poor performance later.

Some carburetor manufacturers supply overhaul kits of three basic types: minor repair; major repair; and gasket kits. Basically, they contain the following:

Minor Repair Kits:
- All gaskets
- Float needle valve
- Volume control screw
- All diaphragms
- Spring for the pump diaphragm

Major Repair Kits:
- All jets and gaskets
- All diaphragms
- Float needle valve
- Volume control screw
- Pump ball valve
- Main jet carrier
- Float
- Complete intermediate rod
- Intermediate pump lever
- Complete injector tube
- Some cover hold-down screws and washers

Gasket Kits:
- All gaskets

After cleaning and checking all components, reassemble the carburetor, using new parts and referring to the exploded view.

When reassembling, make sure that all screws and jets are tight in their seats, but do not overtighten, as the tips will be distorted. Tighten all screws gradually, in rotation. Do not tighten needle vales into their seats; uneven jetting will result. Always use new gaskets. Be sure to adjust the float level when reassembling.

REMOVAL AND INSTALLATION

1. Disconnect the following:
   a. Hot air tube.
   b. Vacuum hose between the one-way valve and the manifold—at the manifold.
   c. Breather chamber (on air cleaner case) to intake manifold at the breather chamber.
   d. Hose from the air cleaner case to the valve cover.
   e. Hose from the carbon canister to the carburetor—at the carburetor.
   f. Throttle opener hose—at the throttle opener.
2. Disconnect the fuel line at the carburetor. Plug the end of the fuel line to prevent dust entry.
3. Disconnect the choke and throttle control cables.
4. Disconnect the fuel shut-off solenoid wires.
5. Remove the carburetor retaining bolts and the carburetor. Leave the insulator on the manifold.
NOTE: *After removing the carburetor, cover the intake manifold parts to keep out foreign materials.*

THROTTLE LINKAGE ADJUSTMENT

1170 and 1237 cc Models

1. Check the gas pedal free-play (the amount of free movement before the throttle cable starts to pull the throttle valve). Adjust the free-play at the throttle cable adjusting nut (near the carburetor) so the pedal has 0.04–0.12 in. (1.0–3.0 mm) freeplay.
2. Make sure that when the accelerator pedal is fully depressed, the primary and secondary throttle valves are opened fully (contact the stops). If the secondary valve does not open fully, adjust by bending the secondary throttle valve connecting rod.

1335, 1342, 1487, 1488, 1600 and 1751 cc CVCC Models

1. Remove the air cleaner assembly to provide access.

Throttle cable adjusting location—CVCC models

2. Check that the cable free-play (deflection) is 0.16–0.40 in. on 1335, 1487 and 1600 cc engines, and 0.18–0.37 in. on 1751 cc engines. This is measured right before the cable enters the throttle shaft bellcrank.
3. If deflection is not to specifications, rotate the cable adjusting nuts in the required direction.
4. As a final check, have a friend press the gas pedal all the way to the floor, while you look down inside the throttle bore checking that the throttle plates reach the wide open throttle (WOT) vertical position.
5. Install the air cleaner.

FLOAT AND FUEL LEVEL ADJUSTMENT

Poor fuel combustion, black sooty exhaust, and fuel overflow are indications of improper float level.

1170 and 1237 cc Models

1. Check the float level by looking at the sight glass on the right of the carburetor. Fuel level should align with the dot on the sight glass. If the level is above or below the dot, the carburetor must be disassembled and the float level set.
NOTE: *Try to check float level with the dot at eye level.*
2. Remove the carburetor from the engine and disconnect the air horn assembly from the carburetor body.
NOTE: *When removing the air horn, do not drop the float pin.*
3. Invert the air horn and raise the float.
4. Now lower the float carefully until the float tang just touches the needle valve stem. The valve stem is spring loaded, so do not allow the float to compress the spring during measurement. Measure the distance be-

tween the float and the air horn flange (without gasket). The distance should be 0.44 in., or 11 mm. Adjust by bending the tang.

5. Raise the float until the float stop contacts the air horn body. Measure the distance between the float tang and the needle valve stem. The distance should be 0.051–0.067 in. (1.3–1.77 mm). Adjust by bending the float stop tang.

6. When the carburetor is installed, recheck the float level by looking into the carburetor float sight glass. Fuel level should be within the range of the dot on the glass.

1335, 1342, 1487, 1488, 1600 and 1751 cc CVCC Models through 1981

Due to the rather unconventional manner in which the Keihin 3-bbl carburetor float level is checked and adjusted, this is one job best left to the dealer, or someone whith Honda tool no. 07501-6570000 for 1487 and 1600 cc engines, or 07501-6950100 for 1751 cc engines (which is a special float level gauge/fuel catch tray/drain bottle assembly not generally available to the public). This carburetor is adjusted while mounted on a running engine. After the auxiliary and the primary/secondary main jet covers are removed, the special float gauge apparatus is installed over the jet aperatures. With the engine running, the float level is checked against a red index line on the gauge. If adjustment proves necessary, there are adjusting screws provided for both the auxiliary and the primary/secondary circuits atop the carburetor.

1982 and later, except 1829cc Prelude

With the car on level ground and at normal operating temperature, check the primary and secondary fuel level inspection windows. If the fuel level is not touching the dot, adjust it by turning the adjusting screws which are located in recessed bosses above the inspection windows.

NOTE: *Do not turn the adjusting screws more than 1 turn every 15 seconds.*

1829cc Prelude

1. Remove the side draft carburetors from the engine and remove the float chambers from the carburetors.

2. Using a float level gauge, measure the float level with the float tip lightly touching the float valve and the float chamber surface tilted about 30° from vertical. The float level should be 16 mm or 0.04 in.

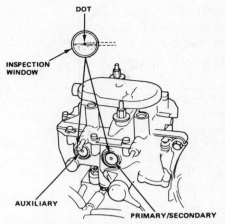

Inspection window showing the fuel level on the 1982 and later models, except 1829cc Prelude

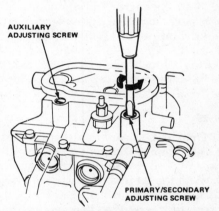

Float level adjustment screw—1982 and later models, except 1829cc Prelude

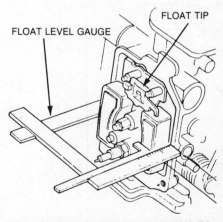

Float level measurement on the dual Keihin sidedraft carburetors—1829cc Prelude

3. To adjust the float level on the sub carburetor, remove the float chamber. Using a float level gauge, measure the float level as described above.

NOTE: *The float level of the sub carburetor cannot be adjusted. If the float level is incorrect the float must be replaced.*

FAST IDLE ADJUSTMENT

During cold engine starting and the engine warm-up period, a specially enriched fuel mixture is required. If the engine fails to run properly or if the engine over-revs with the choke knob pulled out in cold weather, the fast idle system should be checked and adjusted. This is accomplished with the carburetor installed.

1170 and 1237 cc Models

1973

1. Run the engine until it reaches normal operating temperature.

2. With the engine still running, pull the choke knob out to the first detent. The idle speed should rise to 1,500 to 2,000 rpm.

3. If the idle speed is not within this range, adjust by bending the choke rod. (See "Choke Adjustment" section below for further details.)

1974–79

1. Open the primary throttle plate and insert an 0.8 mm (0.032 in.), diameter drill bit between the plate and the bore.

2. With the throttle plate opened 0.8 mm, bend the reference tab so that it is midway between the two scribed lines on the throttle control lever.

1487 and 1600 cc CVCC Models

1976–79

1. Run the engine until it reaches normal operating temperature.

2. Place the choke control knob in its second detent position (two clicks out from the dash). With the coke knob in this position, run the engine for 30 seconds and check that the fast idle speed is 3,000 rpm plus or minus 500 rpm.

3. To adjust, bend the slot in the fast idle adjusting link. Narrow the slot to lower the fast idle, and widen the slot to increase. Make all adjustments in small increments.

1335, 1342, 1487 (1980–82) 1488, 1751 and Accord 1829cc

1. Run the engine to normal operating temperature.

2. Connect a tachometer according to the manufacturer's specifications.

3. Disconnect and plug the hose from the fast idle unloader.

4. Shut the engine off, hold the choke valve closed, and open and close the throttle to engage the fast idle cam.

5. Start the engine, run it for one minute. Fast idle speed should be 2300 to 3300 rpm for manual transmission models and 2200 to 3200 rpm for automatic transmission models.

6. Adjust the idle by turning the fast idle screw.

1829cc Prelude

1. Start the engine and bring it to normal operating temperature. Shut off the engine.

2. Remove the E-clip and flat washer from the thermo-wax valve linkage, then slide the linkage past the fast idle cam.

NOTE: *Be careful not to bend the linkage or the fast idle speed will be changed.*

3. While holding open the throttle, turn the fast idle cam counterclockwise until the fast idle lever is on the third step.

4. Without touching the throttle, start the engine and check the idle speed. The idle speed should be 2,000 rpm. Adjustment of the idle speed can be made by turning the fast idle adjusting screw.

5. Stop the engine and reconnect the thermo-wax valve linkage.

6. Start the engine and check that as the engine warms up, the idle speed decreases.

NOTE: *If the idle speed doesn't drop, clean the linkage along with the carburetor. If the speed still doesn't drop, check for damaged or stuck linkage.*

CHOKE ADJUSTMENT

1170 and 1237 cc Models

The choke valve should be fully open when the choke knob is pushed in, and fully closed with the choke knob pulled out. The choke valve is held in the fully closed position by spring action. Pull the choke knob to the fully closed position and open and close the choke valve by rotating the choke valve shaft. The movement should be free and unrestricted.

If adjustment is required, adjust the cable length by loosening the cable clamp bolt.

PRECISION ADJUSTMENT

1. Using a wire gauge, check the primary throttle valve opening (dimension G1) when the choke valve is fully closed. The opening should be 0.050–0.066 in. (1.28–1.68 mm).

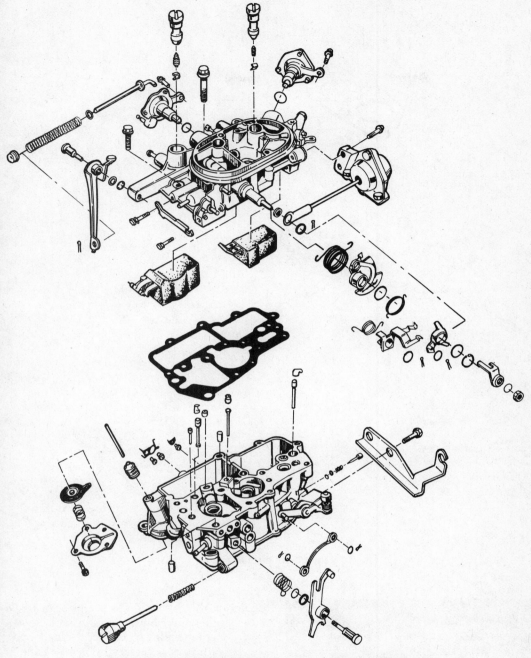

Exploded view of Keihin 3-bbl used on CVCC engines

2. If the opening is out of specification, adjust it by bending the choke rod. After installing, make sure that the highest fast idle speed is 2,500–2,800 rpm while the engine is warm.

NOTE: *When adjusting the fast idle speed, be sure the throttle adjusting screw does not contact the stop.*

1487 and 1600 cc CVCC Models
1976–79

1. Push the choke actuator rod towards its diaphragm, so it does not contact the choke valve linkage.

2. Pull the choke knob out to the first detent (click) position from the dash. With the

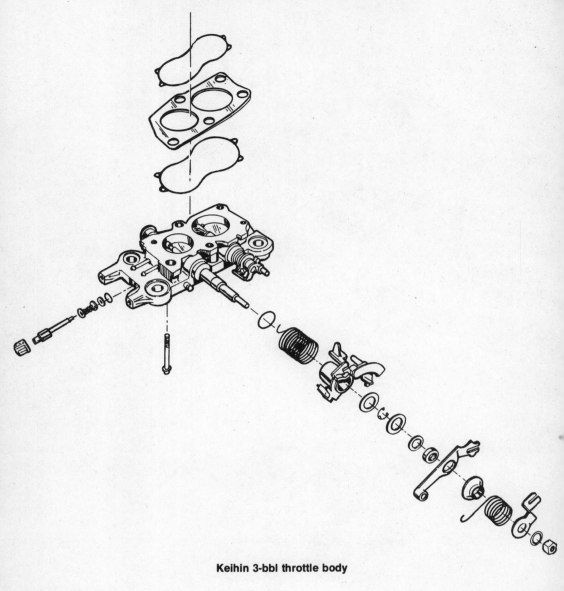

Keihin 3-bbl throttle body

Fast idle adjusting location—CVCC models

knob in this position, check the distance between the choke butterfly valve and the venturi opening with a $3/16$ in. drill (shank end).

3. Adjust as necessary by bending the relief lever adjusting tang with needle nose pliers.

4. Now, pull out the choke knob to its second detent position from the dash. Again, make sure the choke actuator rod does not contact the choke valve linkage.

5. With the choke knob in this position, check that the clearance between the butterfly valve and venturi opening is $1/8$ in. using the shank end of a $1/8$ in. drill.

6. Adjust as necessary by bending the stop tab for the choke butterly linkage.

CHILTON'S
FUEL ECONOMY
& TUNE-UP TIPS

Tune-up • Spark Plug Diagnosis • Emission Controls

Fuel System • Cooling System • Tires and Wheels

General Maintenance

CHILTON'S FUEL ECONOMY & TUNE-UP TIPS

Fuel economy is important to everyone, no matter what kind of vehicle you drive. The maintenance-minded motorist can save both money and fuel using these tips and the periodic maintenance and tune-up procedures in this Repair and Tune-Up Guide.

There are more than 130,000,000 cars and trucks registered for private use in the United States. Each travels an average of 10-12,000 miles per year, and, and in total they consume close to 70 billion gallons of fuel each year. This represents nearly ⅔ of the oil imported by the United States each year. The Federal government's goal is to reduce consumption 10% by 1985. A variety of methods are either already in use or under serious consideration, and they all affect you driving and the cars you will drive. In addition to "down-sizing", the auto industry is using or investigating the use of electronic fuel delivery, electronic engine controls and alternative engines for use in smaller and lighter vehicles, among other alternatives to meet the federally mandated Corporate Average Fuel Economy (CAFE) of 27.5 mpg by 1985. The government, for its part, is considering rationing, mandatory driving curtailments and tax increases on motor vehicle fuel in an effort to reduce consumption. The government's goal of a 10% reduction could be realized — and further government regulation avoided — if every private vehicle could use just 1 less gallon of fuel per week.

How Much Can You Save?

Tests have proven that almost anyone can make at least a 10% reduction in fuel consumption through regular maintenance and tune-ups. When a major manufacturer of spark plugs sur-

TUNE-UP

1. Check the cylinder compression to be sure the engine will really benefit from a tune-up and that it is capable of producing good fuel economy. A tune-up will be wasted on an engine in poor mechanical condition.

2. Replace spark plugs regularly. New spark plugs alone can increase fuel economy 3%.

3. Be sure the spark plugs are the correct type (heat range) for your vehicle. See the Tune-Up Specifications.

Heat range refers to the spark plug's ability to conduct heat away from the firing end. It must conduct the heat away in an even pattern to avoid becoming a source of pre-ignition, yet it must also operate hot enough to burn off conductive deposits that could cause misfiring.

The heat range is usually indicated by a number on the spark plug, part of the manufacturer's designation for each individual spark plug. The numbers in bold-face indicate the heat range in each manufacturer's identification system.

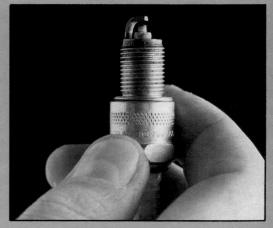

Periodically, check the spark plugs to be sure they are firing efficiently. They are excellent indicators of the internal condition of your engine.

Manufacturer	Typical Designation
AC	R **45** TS
Bosch (old)	WA **145** T30
Bosch (new)	HR **8** Y
Champion	RBL **15** Y
Fram/Autolite	4**15**
Mopar	P-**62** PR
Motorcraft	BRF-**42**
NGK	BP **5** ES-15
Nippondenso	W **16** EP
Prestolite	14GR **5** 2A

On AC, Bosch (new), Champion, Fram/Autolite, Mopar, Motorcraft and Prestolite, a higher number indicates a hotter plug. On Bosch (old), NGK and Nippondenso, a higher number indicates a colder plug.

4. Make sure the spark plugs are properly gapped. See the Tune-Up Specifications in this book.

5. Be sure the spark plugs are firing efficiently. The illustrations on the next 2 pages show you how to "read" the firing end of the spark plug.

6. Check the ignition timing and set it to specifications. Tests show that almost all cars have incorrect ignition timing by more than 2°.

veyed over 6,000 cars nationwide, they found that a tune-up, on cars that needed one, increased fuel economy over 11%. Replacing worn plugs alone, accounted for a 3% increase. The same test also revealed that 8 out of every 10 vehicles will have some maintenance deficiency that will directly affect fuel economy, emissions or performance. Most of this mileage-robbing neglect could be prevented with regular maintenance.

Modern engines require that all of the functioning systems operate properly for maximum efficiency. A malfunction anywhere wastes fuel. You can keep your vehicle running as efficiently and economically as possible, by being aware of your vehicle's operating and performance characteristics. If your vehicle suddenly develops performance or fuel economy problems it could be due to one or more of the following:

PROBLEM	POSSIBLE CAUSE
Engine Idles Rough	Ignition timing, idle mixture, vacuum leak or something amiss in the emission control system.
Hesitates on Acceleration	Dirty carburetor or fuel filter, improper accelerator pump setting, ignition timing or fouled spark plugs.
Starts Hard or Fails to Start	Worn spark plugs, improperly set automatic choke, ice (or water) in fuel system.
Stalls Frequently	Automatic choke improperly adjusted and possible dirty air filter or fuel filter.
Performs Sluggishly	Worn spark plugs, dirty fuel or air filter, ignition timing or automatic choke out of adjustment.

Check spark plug wires on conventional point type ignition for cracks by bending them in a loop around your finger.

Be sure that spark plug wires leading to adjacent cylinders do not run too close together. (Photo courtesy Champion Spark Plug Co.)

7. If your vehicle does not have electronic ignition, check the points, rotor and cap as specified.

8. Check the spark plug wires (used with conventional point-type ignitions) for cracks and burned or broken insulation by bending them in a loop around your finger. Cracked wires decrease fuel efficiency by failing to deliver full voltage to the spark plugs. One misfiring spark plug can cost you as much as 2 mpg.

9. Check the routing of the plug wires. Misfiring can be the result of spark plug leads to adjacent cylinders running parallel to each other and too close together. One wire tends to pick up voltage from the other causing it to fire "out of time".

10. Check all electrical and ignition circuits for voltage drop and resistance.

11. Check the distributor mechanical and/or vacuum advance mechanisms for proper functioning. The vacuum advance can be checked by twisting the distributor plate in the opposite direction of rotation. It should spring back when released.

12. Check and adjust the valve clearance on engines with mechanical lifters. The clearance should be slightly loose rather than too tight.

SPARK PLUG DIAGNOSIS

Normal

APPEARANCE: This plug is typical of one operating normally. The insulator nose varies from a light tan to grayish color with slight electrode wear. The presence of slight deposits is normal on used plugs and will have no adverse effect on engine performance. The spark plug heat range is correct for the engine and the engine is running normally.

CAUSE: Properly running engine.

RECOMMENDATION: Before reinstalling this plug, the electrodes should be cleaned and filed square. Set the gap to specifications. If the plug has been in service for more than 10-12,000 miles, the entire set should probably be replaced with a fresh set of the same heat range.

Oil Deposits

APPEARANCE: The firing end of the plug is covered with a wet, oily coating.

CAUSE: The problem is poor oil control. On high mileage engines, oil is leaking past the rings or valve guides into the combustion chamber. A common cause is also a plugged PCV valve, and a ruptured fuel pump diaphragm can also cause this condition. Oil fouled plugs such as these are often found in new or recently overhauled engines, before normal oil control is achieved, and can be cleaned and reinstalled.

RECOMMENDATION: A hotter spark plug may temporarily relieve the problem, but the engine is probably in need of work.

Incorrect Heat Range

APPEARANCE: The effects of high temperature on a spark plug are indicated by clean white, often blistered insulator. This can also be accompanied by excessive wear of the electrode, and the absence of deposits.

CAUSE: Check for the correct spark plug heat range. A plug which is too hot for the engine can result in overheating. A car operated mostly at high speeds can require a colder plug. Also check ignition timing, cooling system level, fuel mixture and leaking intake manifold.

RECOMMENDATION: If all ignition and engine adjustments are known to be correct, and no other malfunction exists, install spark plugs one heat range colder.

Photos Courtesy Fram Corporation

Carbon Deposits

APPEARANCE: Carbon fouling is easily identified by the presence of dry, soft, black, sooty deposits.

CAUSE: Changing the heat range can often lead to carbon fouling, as can prolonged slow, stop-and-start driving. If the heat range is correct, carbon fouling can be attributed to a rich fuel mixture, sticking choke, clogged air cleaner, worn breaker points, retarded timing or low compression. If only one or two plugs are carbon fouled, check for corroded or cracked wires on the affected plugs. Also look for cracks in the distributor cap between the towers of affected cylinders.

RECOMMENDATION: After the problem is corrected, these plugs can be cleaned and reinstalled if not worn severely.

MMT Fouled

APPEARANCE: Spark plugs fouled by MMT (Methycyclopentadienyl Maganese Tricarbonyl) have reddish, rusty appearance on the insulator and side electrode.

CAUSE: MMT is an anti-knock additive in gasoline used to replace lead. During the combustion process, the MMT leaves a reddish deposit on the insulator and side electrode.

RECOMMENDATION: No engine malfunction is indicated and the deposits will not affect plug performance any more than lead deposits (see Ash Deposits). MMT fouled plugs can be cleaned, regapped and reinstalled.

High Speed Glazing

APPEARANCE: Glazing appears as shiny coating on the plug, either yellow or tan in color.

CAUSE: During hard, fast acceleration, plug temperatures rise suddenly. Deposits from normal combustion have no chance to fluff-off; instead, they melt on the insulator forming an electrically conductive coating which causes misfiring.

RECOMMENDATION: Glazed plugs are not easily cleaned. They should be replaced with a fresh set of plugs of the correct heat range. If the condition recurs, using plugs with a heat range one step colder may cure the problem.

Ash (Lead) Deposits

APPEARANCE: Ash deposits are characterized by light brown or white colored deposits crusted on the side or center electrodes. In some cases it may give the plug a rusty appearance.

CAUSE: Ash deposits are normally derived from oil or fuel additives burned during normal combustion. Normally they are harmless, though excessive amounts can cause misfiring. If deposits are excessive in short mileage, the valve guides may be worn.

RECOMMENDATION: Ash-fouled plugs can be cleaned, gapped and reinstalled.

Detonation

APPEARANCE: Detonation is usually characterized by a broken plug insulator.

CAUSE: A portion of the fuel charge will begin to burn spontaneously, from the increased heat following ignition. The explosion that results applies extreme pressure to engine components, frequently damaging spark plugs and pistons.

Detonation can result by over-advanced ignition timing, inferior gasoline (low octane) lean air/fuel mixture, poor carburetion, engine lugging or an increase in compression ratio due to combustion chamber deposits or engine modification.

RECOMMENDATION: Replace the plugs after correcting the problem.

Photos Courtesy Champion Spark Plug Co.

EMISSION CONTROLS

13. Be aware of the general condition of the emission control system. It contributes to reduced pollution and should be serviced regularly to maintain efficient engine operation.

14. Check all vacuum lines for dried, cracked or brittle conditions. Something as simple as a leaking vacuum hose can cause poor performance and loss of economy.

15. Avoid tampering with the emission control system. Attempting to improve fuel econ-

FUEL SYSTEM

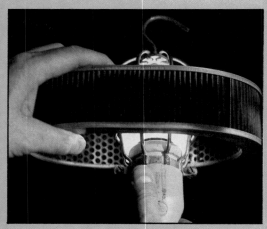

Check the air filter with a light behind it. If you can see light through the filter it can be reused.

Extremely clogged filters should be discarded and replaced with a new one.

18. Replace the air filter regularly. A dirty air filter richens the air/fuel mixture and can increase fuel consumption as much as 10%. Tests show that ⅓ of all vehicles have air filters in need of replacement.

19. Replace the fuel filter at least as often as recommended.

20. Set the idle speed and carburetor mixture to specifications.

21. Check the automatic choke. A sticking or malfunctioning choke wastes gas.

22. During the summer months, adjust the automatic choke for a leaner mixture which will produce faster engine warm-ups.

COOLING SYSTEM

29. Be sure all accessory drive belts are in good condition. Check for cracks or wear.

30. Adjust all accessory drive belts to proper tension.

31. Check all hoses for swollen areas, worn spots, or loose clamps.

32. Check coolant level in the radiator or expansion tank.

33. Be sure the thermostat is operating properly. A stuck thermostat delays engine warm-up and a cold engine uses nearly twice as much fuel as a warm engine.

34. Drain and replace the engine coolant at least as often as recommended. Rust and scale

TIRES & WHEELS

38. Check the tire pressure often with a pencil type gauge. Tests by a major tire manufacturer show that 90% of all vehicles have at least 1 tire improperly inflated. Better mileage can be achieved by over-inflating tires, but never exceed the maximum inflation pressure on the side of the tire.

39. If possible, install radial tires. Radial tires deliver as much as ½ mpg more than bias belted tires.

40. Avoid installing super-wide tires. They only create extra rolling resistance and decrease fuel mileage. Stick to the manufacturer's recommendations.

41. Have the wheels properly balanced.

omy by tampering with emission controls is more likely to worsen fuel economy than improve it. Emission control changes on modern engines are not readily reversible.

16. Clean (or replace) the EGR valve and lines as recommended.

17. Be sure that all vacuum lines and hoses are reconnected properly after working under the hood. An unconnected or misrouted vacuum line can wreak havoc with engine performance.

---

23. Check for fuel leaks at the carburetor, fuel pump, fuel lines and fuel tank. Be sure all lines and connections are tight.

24. Periodically check the tightness of the carburetor and intake manifold attaching nuts and bolts. These are a common place for vacuum leaks to occur.

25. Clean the carburetor periodically and lubricate the linkage.

26. The condition of the tailpipe can be an excellent indicator of proper engine combustion. After a long drive at highway speeds, the inside of the tailpipe should be a light grey in color. Black or soot on the insides indicates an overly rich mixture.

27. Check the fuel pump pressure. The fuel pump may be supplying more fuel than the engine needs.

28. Use the proper grade of gasoline for your engine. Don't try to compensate for knocking or "pinging" by advancing the ignition timing. This practice will only increase plug temperature and the chances of detonation or pre-ignition with relatively little performance gain.

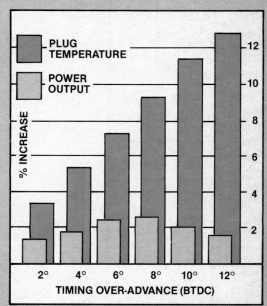

Increasing ignition timing past the specified setting results in a drastic increase in spark plug temperature with increased chance of detonation or preignition. Performance increase is considerably less. (Photo courtesy Champion Spark Plug Co.)

---

that form in the engine should be flushed out to allow the engine to operate at peak efficiency.

35. Clean the radiator of debris that can decrease cooling efficiency.

36. Install a flex-type or electric cooling fan, if you don't have a clutch type fan. Flex fans use curved plastic blades to push more air at low speeds when more cooling is needed; at high speeds the blades flatten out for less resistance. Electric fans only run when the engine temperature reaches a predetermined level.

37. Check the radiator cap for a worn or cracked gasket. If the cap does not seal properly, the cooling system will not function properly.

---

42. Be sure the front end is correctly aligned. A misaligned front end actually has wheels going in differed directions. The increased drag can reduce fuel economy by .3 mpg.

43. Correctly adjust the wheel bearings. Wheel bearings that are adjusted too tight increase rolling resistance.

Check tire pressures regularly with a reliable pocket type gauge. Be sure to check the pressure on a cold tire.

GENERAL MAINTENANCE

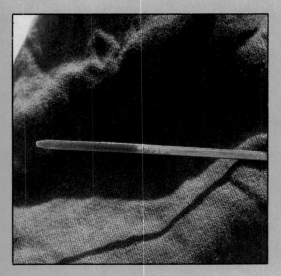

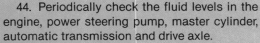

Check the fluid levels (particularly engine oil) on a regular basis. Be sure to check the oil for grit, water or other contamination.

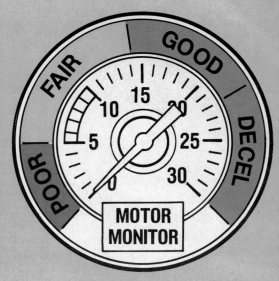

A vacuum gauge is another excellent indicator of internal engine condition and can also be installed in the dash as a mileage indicator.

44. Periodically check the fluid levels in the engine, power steering pump, master cylinder, automatic transmission and drive axle.

45. Change the oil at the recommended interval and change the filter at every oil change. Dirty oil is thick and causes extra friction between moving parts, cutting efficiency and increasing wear. A worn engine requires more frequent tune-ups and gets progressively worse fuel economy. In general, use the lightest viscosity oil for the driving conditions you will encounter.

46. Use the recommended viscosity fluids in the transmission and axle.

47. Be sure the battery is fully charged for fast starts. A slow starting engine wastes fuel.

48. Be sure battery terminals are clean and tight.

49. Check the battery electrolyte level and add distilled water if necessary.

50. Check the exhaust system for crushed pipes, blockages and leaks.

51. Adjust the brakes. Dragging brakes or brakes that are not releasing create increased drag on the engine.

52. Install a vacuum gauge or miles-per-gallon gauge. These gauges visually indicate engine vacuum in the intake manifold. High vacuum = good mileage and low vacuum = poorer mileage. The gauge can also be an excellent indicator of internal engine conditions.

53. Be sure the clutch is properly adjusted. A slipping clutch wastes fuel.

54. Check and periodically lubricate the heat control valve in the exhaust manifold. A sticking or inoperative valve prevents engine warm-up and wastes gas.

55. Keep accurate records to check fuel economy over a period of time. A sudden drop in fuel economy may signal a need for tune-up or other maintenance.

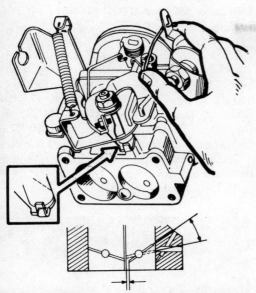

Precision choke adjustment—1170, 1237 cc models

1. Stop tab
2. Relief lever adjusting tang
3. Actuator rod
4. Choke opener diaphragm

Choke adjusting components—CVCC models

1335, 1487 (1980–83) and 1751 cc Models

1. With the engine cold, remove the air cleaner.

2. Open and close the throttle all the way to engage the fast idle cam.

3. The choke plate should close to within ⅛" of the air horn wall.

4. If not, remove the choke cover and inspect the linkage for free movement. Repair or replace parts if necessary.

5. Install the cover and adjust so that the index marks align. Recheck the choke for proper closing clearance. If the clearance is not correct, replace the cap and retest.

CHOKE CABLE ADJUSTMENT
1974–79 1237 cc Models

NOTE: *Perform the adjustment only after the throttle plate opening has been set and referenced, as in the preceding procedure.*

1. Make sure that the choke cable is correctly adjusted.

    a. With the choke knob in, the choke butterfly should be completely open;

    b. Slowly pull out the choke knob and check for slack in the cable. Remove any excessive free-play and recheck for full open when the knob is pushed in.

2. Check the link rod adjustment by pulling the choke knob out to the first detent. The two scribed lines on the throttle control lever should line up on either side of the reference tab. If not, adjust by bending the choke link rod.

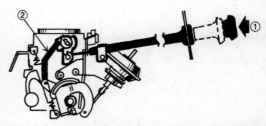

Choke cable adjustment—1974 and later 1237 cc models. Number one is the detent position, and number two is the link adjusting location

1487 and 1600 cc CVCC Models

1. Remove the air cleaner assembly.

2. Push the choke knob all the way in at the dash. Check that the choke butterfly valve (choke plate) is fully open (vertical).

3. Next, have a friend pull out the choke knob while you observe the action of the butterfly valve. When the choke knob is pulled out to the second detent position, the butterfly valve should just close. Then, when the choke knob is pulled all the way out, the butterfly valve should remain in the closed position.

4. To adjust, loosen the choke cable locknut and rotate the adjusting nut so that with the choke knob pushed flush against the dash (open position), the butterfly valve just rests against its positioning stop tab. Tighten the locknut.

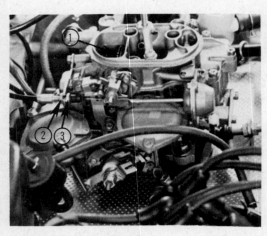

1. Choke butterfly valve   2. Adjusting nut
3. Locknut

Choke cable adjustment—CVCC models

5. If the choke butterfly valve is notchy in operation, or if it does not close properly, check the butterfly valve and shaft for binding. Check also the operation of the return spring.

THROTTLE VALVE OPERATION

1170 and 1237 cc Models

1. Check to see if the throttle valve opens fully when the throttle lever is moved to he fully open position. See if the valve closes fully when the lever is released.
2. Measure the clearance between the primary throttle valve and the chamber wall where the connecting rod begins to open the secondary throttle valve. The clearance should be 0.221–0.237 in. (5.63–6.03 mm).
3. If the clearance is out of specification, adjust by bending the connecting rod.
   NOTE: *After adjusting, operate the throttle lever and check for any sign of binding.*

ACCELERATOR PUMP ADJUSTMENT

1170 and 1237 cc Models

Check the pump for smooth operation. See if fuel squirts out of the pump nozzle by operating the pump lever or the throttle lever. When the pump is operated slowly, fuel must squirt out until the pump comes to the end of its travel. If the pump is defective, check for clogging or a defective piston. Adjust the pump by either repositioning the end of the connecting rod arm in the pump lever, or the arm itself.

1487 and 1600 cc CVCC Models
1976–79

1. Remove the air cleaner assembly.
2. Check that the distance between the tang at the end of the accelerator pump lever and the lever stop at the edge of the throttle body (distance "A") is 0.0311–0.0335 in. through 1977, or 0.57–0.6 in. 1978–79. This corresponds to effective pump lever travel.
3. To adjust, bend the pump lever tang in the required direction.
4. Install the air cleaner.

Accelerating pump travel adjustment—CVCC models. Distance "A" is 0.0311–0.0335 in.

1335, 1487 (1980–83) and 1751 cc Models

1. Remove the air cleaner.
2. Make sure that the pump shaft is moving freely throughout the pump stroke.
3. Check that the pump lever is in contact with the pump shaft.
4. Measure between the bottom end of the pump lever and the lever stop tang. The gap should be $9/16$ to $19/32$ inch through 1980,

or $^{29}/_{64}$ to $^{31}/_{64}$ inch for 1981–82. If not, bend the tang to adjust.

Fuel Tank

REMOVAL AND INSTALLATION

1. Drain the tank by loosening the tank drain bolt.

NOTE: *Catch the fuel in a clean, safe container.*

2. Disconnect the fuel tubes, filler neck connecting tube and the clear vinyl tube.

NOTE: *Disconnect the fuel tubes by removing the clips, taking care not to damage the tubes.*

Filler tube location

3. Disconnect the fuel meter unit wire at its connection.

4. Remove the fuel tank by removing its attaching bolts.

5. To install, reverse the removal procedure. Be sure that all tubes and fuel lines are securely fastened by the clips.

Chassis Electrical

HEATER
REMOVAL AND INSTALLATION
Civic through 1979

NOTE: *These procedures do not apply to cars equipped with air conditioning. On cars equipped with air conditioning, heater removal may differ from the procedures listed below. Only a trained air conditioning specialist should disassemble A/C equipped units. Air conditioning units contain pressurized Freon which can be extremely dangerous (e.g. burns and/or blindness) to the untrained.*

1. Drain the radiator.
2. Disconnect the right and left defroster hoses.
3. Disconnect the inlet and outlet water hoses at the heater assembly.

NOTE: *There will be a coolant leakage when disconnecting the hoses. Catch the coolant in a container to prevent damage to the interior.*

4. Disconnect the following items:
   a. Fre-Rec control cable;
   b. Temperature control rod;
   c. Room/Def. control cable;
   d. Fan motor switch connector;
   e. Upper attaching bolts;
   f. Lower attaching bolts;
   g. Lower bracket.
5. Remove the heater assembly through the passenger side.
6. To install the heater assembly, reverse the removal procedure. Pay attention to the following points:
   a. When installing the heater assembly, do not forget to connect the motor ground wire to the right side of the upper bracket;
   b. Connect the inlet and outlet water hoses SECURELY;

NOTE: *The inlet hose is a straight type, and the outlet hose is an L-type.*
   c. Install the defroster nozzles in the correct position;
   d. Connect the control cables securely. Operate the control valve and lever to check for proper operation;
   e. Be sure to bleed the cooling system (see Chapter 1).

1980 and later

1. Drain the radiator.
2. Remove the dashboard.
3. Disconnect both heater hoses at the firewall and drain the coolant into a container.
4. Remove the heater lower mounting nut on the firewall.
5. Remove the two heater duct retaining clips.
6. Disconnect the control cables from the heater.
7. Remove the heater valve cable cover and remove the heater assembly.
8. Installation is the reverse of removal. Bleed cooling system and make sure cables are properly adjusted.

Accord

1. The heater blower assembly can be removed by removing the glove box, the fresh air control cable, and the three bolts that hold the blower.
2. To remove the heater core, first drain the radiator.
3. Remove the instrument panel (see the instrument panel removal section later in this chapter).
4. Once the instrument panel is removed, remove the hoses from the core.

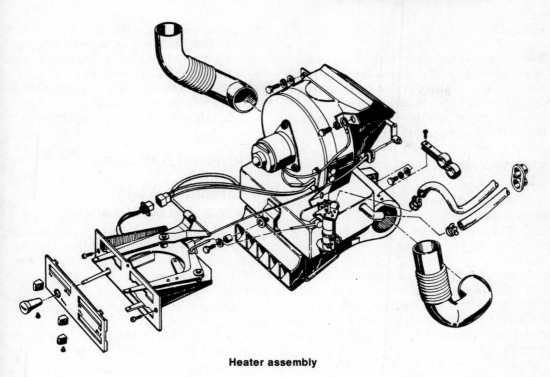

Heater assembly

5. Remove the control cables from their clips.

6. Remove the left and right upper bolts.

7. Remove the lower bolts and remove the heater core.

8. Installation is the reverse of removal. Keep the following points in mind:

   a. Don't interchange the inlet and outlet water hoses.

   b. Make sure all the cables operate correctly.

   c. Bleed the air from the cooling system (see chapter one).

Prelude 1979–82

1. Remove the blower by removing the instrument panel side cover.

2. Remove the glove box and the three blower mounting bolts.

3. Remove the blower from the heater case.

4. Drain the coolant.

5. Remove the lower dash panel.

6. Place a drain pan under the case and disconnect both heater hoses at the core tubes.

7. Remove the heater lower mount nut on the firewall.

8. Disconnect the cable at the water valve.

9. Remove the control cables from the heater case.

10. Remove the upper mount bolts and remove the heater.

NOTE: *Only the 1983 and later Prelude models may have the heater core replaced without removing the heater assembly.*

1983 and later Prelude

1. Drain the cooling system. Remove the heater pipe cover and heater pipe clamps.

2. Remove the heater core retaining plate.

3. Pull the cotter pin out of the hose clamp joint and separate the heater pipes.

NOTE: *Engine coolant will drain from the heater pipes when they are disconnected. Place a drip pan under the pipes to catch the coolant.*

4. When all the coolant has drained from the heater core, remove it from the heater housing.

5. Installation is the reverse of the removal procedure, please note the following:

   a. Replace the hose clamps with new ones.

   b. Turn the cotter pin in the hose clamps tightly to prevent leaking coolant.

   c. Fill the cooling system with coolant and open the bleed bolt until coolant begins to flow from it. Tighten the bolt when all the air has escaped from the system.

RADIO

Never operate the radio without a speaker; severe damage to the output transistors will result. If the speaker must be replaced, use a speaker of the correct impedance (ohms) or else the output transistors will be damaged and require replacement.

REMOVAL AND INSTALLATION
Civic

1. Remove the screw which holds the rear radio bracket to the back tray underneath the dash. Then remove the wing nut which holds the radio to the bracket and remove the bracket.
2. Remove the control knobs, hex nuts, and trim plate from the radio control shafts.
3. Disconnect the antenna and speaker leads, the bullet type radio fuse, and the white lead connected directly over the radio opening.
4. Drop the radio out, bottom first, through the package tray.
5. To install, reverse the removal procedure. When inserting the radio through the package tray, be sure the bottom side is up and the control shafts are facing toward the engine. Otherwise, you will not be able to position the radio properly through its opening in the dash.

Accord and Prelude

1. Remove the two screws which hold the center lower lid and remove the lid.
2. Remove the radio attaching screws found underneath the lid.
3. Remove the radio knobs and the faceplate.
4. Remove the heater fan switch knob and the heater lever knobs.
5. Remove the heater control bezel and the center panel. To do this, remove the three center panel screws and the ash tray. Slide the panel to the left to remove it. Unhook the cigarette lighter leads.
6. Remove the leads which are attached to the radio and remove the radio.
7. Installation is the reverse of removal.

WINDSHIELD WIPERS

Motor and Linkage
REMOVAL AND INSTALLATION

The wiper motor on all models is connected to the engine compartment wall, below the front windshield.

1. Remove the negative (−) cable from the battery.
2. Disconnect the motor leads at the connector.
3. Remove the motor water seal cover clamp, and the seal, from the motor.

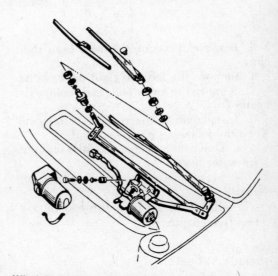

Windshield wiper motor and linkage schematic

Wiper motor location

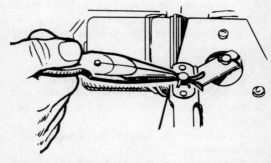

Removing the cotter pin from the motor arm linkage

4. Remove the special nut which holds the wiper arms to the pivot shafts and remove the arms.

5. Remove the left and right pivot nuts and push the pivots down.

6. Remove the three wiper motor mounting bolts and remove the wiper/linkage assembly from the engine compartment.

7. Pull out the motor arm cotter pin and separate the linkage from the motor.

8. Remove the three bracket bolts to remove the motor from its mounting bracket.

9. To install, reverse the removal procedure. Be sure to inspect the linkage and pivots for wear and looseness. When installing the motor, be sure it is in the "automatic stop" position.

INSTRUMENT CLUSTER

REMOVAL AND INSTALLATION
Meter Case Assembly

1. Remove the three meter case mounting wing nuts from the rear of the instrument panel.

2. Disconnect the speedometer and tachometer drive cables at the engine.

3. Pull the meter case away from the

Meter case removed from car

Back of meter case showing wire connection points

panel. Disconnect the meter wires at the connectors.

NOTE: *Be sure to label the wires to avoid confusion during reassembly.*

4. Disconnect the speedometer and tachometer cables at the meter case and remove the case from the car.

5. To install, reverse the removal procedure.

Switch Panel

1. Loosen the four steering wheel column cover screws and remove the upper and lower covers.

2. Remove the four steering column bolts (remove the upper two bolts first) and rest the steering assembly on the floor.

3. Remove the four switch panel screws from the rear of the instrument panel.

4. To release the switch panel, remove the switches in the following manner:

    a. Remove the light switch by prying the cover off the front of the knob. Pinch the retaining tabs together and pull off the knob;

    b. Remove the wiper switch by pushing the knob in and turning counterclockwise. Then remove the retaining nut;

    c. Remove the choke knob by loosening the set screw. Then remove the retaining nut.

5. To install, reverse the removal procedure.

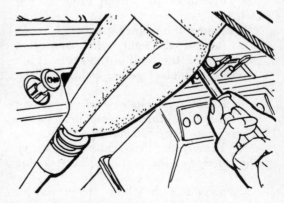

Removing steering column cover

Civic Instrument Panel Assembly (Complete)
THROUGH 1979

1. Loosen the four steering wheel column cover screws and remove the upper and lower covers.

2. Remove the four steering column

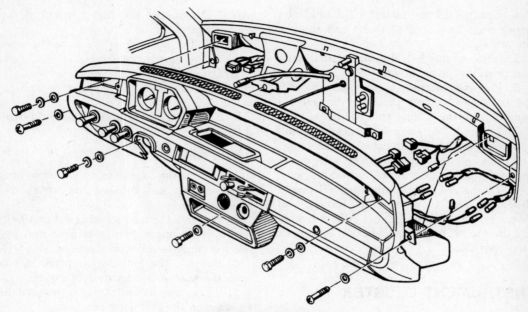

Instrument panel removal

bolts (remove the upper two bolts first) and rest the steering assembly on the floor.

3. Remove the screw on the outside edge of each fresh air vent and pry off the vents with a screwdriver.

4. Disconnect the instrument panel wiring harness from their cabin harnesses by removing the connectors and couplers.

5. Disconnect the speedometer and tachometer cables at the engine.

6. Disconnect the choke cable at the panel.

7. Remove the following switches:

a. Remove the light switch by prying the cover off the front of the knob. Pinch the retaining tabs together and pull off the knob;

b. Remove the wiper switch by pushing the knob in and turning counterclockwise. Then remove the retaining nut;

c. Remove the choke knob by loosening the set screw. Then remove the retaining nut.

8. Disconnect the three heater control cables.

9. Remove the heater fan motor wire connector.

10. Remove the six bolts which attach the panel.

11. Pull the panel out slightly and disconnect the speedometer and tachometer cables at the instruments. Then remove the instrument panel.

12. To install, reverse the removal procedure. Pay attention to the following points:

a. First, connect the speedometer and tachometer cables to the instruments. Then install the panel in place with the center pin in the panel locating hole;

b. Temporarily tighten the bolts which secure the upper, right, and left sides of the instrument panel. Make sure that the wiring harnesses are properly routed.

1980–82

1. On 1980–81 models remove the steering column.

2. On 1982 and later models lower the steering column.

3. On 1980–81 models remove the bulb access panel and remove the two upper mounting screws through the access panel; then the lower mounting bolt and screws.

4. On 1982 and later models, remove the four screws and trim cover.

5. Disconnect the speedometer cable and tachometer cable if so equipped.

6. Disconnect any remaining mount screws and wire connectors and remove the instrument panel.

7. Installation is the reverse of removal.

Accord and Prelude Instrument Panel Assembly (Complete)

1. Remove the instrument cluster as outlined earlier.

2. Remove the speaker grille and then

remove the clock panel and take out the clock.

3. Remove the control knobs and remove the heater control panel from the instrument panel.

4. Remove the three screws which hold the inner panel. The center panel and the heater control assembly are tightened together.

5. Remove the instrument panel left and right side covers, and remove the two bolts on either side.

6. Remove the two bolts in the center of the instrument panel.

7. Remove the bolt behind the clock panel.

8. You should now be able to remove the instrument panel.

9. Installation is the reverse of removal. Remember the following points:

a. Avoid bending the heater lever when installing the dashboard. Make sure the heater levers move freely without binding.

b. Make sure the instrument wiring harnesses aren't pinched.

1984 and later Civic Coupe (CRX)

1. Remove the screws and clips that retain the lower dash panel and remove the panel.

2. Remove the heater lower control knob and the lower panel.

3. Remove the heater control mount screws and the upper screws in the instrument panel.

4. Pull the panel out and disconnect the wire connectors. Remove the instrument panel.

5. Remove the 4 screws, then lift out the gauge assembly so that you can disconnect the wire connectors.

6. Disconnect the speedometer cable, then remove the gauge assembly.

7. To install, reverse the removal procedure.

1984 and later Civic Hatchback and Sedan

1. Remove the upper instrument panel caps and the 4 screws, then remove the panel.

2. Remove the 4 screws retaining the gauge assembly, then lift out the gauge assembly so you can disconnect the wire connectors.

3. Disconnect the speedometer cable and remove the gauge assembly.

4. To install, reverse the removal procedure.

1984 and later Civic Wagon

1. Remove the screws and the dashboard lower panel, this allows access to the four instrument panel retaining bolts.

2. Remove the four instrument panel retaining bolts, raise the panel and disconnect the wire connectors and the speedometer cable. Remove the instrument panel with the gauge assembly.

3. The gauge assembly may be separated from the instrument panel by removing the four screws.

4. To install, reverse the removal procedure.

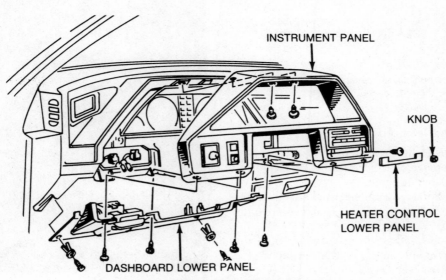

1984 and later CRX instrument panel

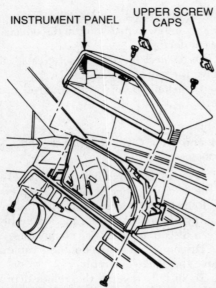

Instrument panel removal—1984 and later Civic Hatchback & Sedan

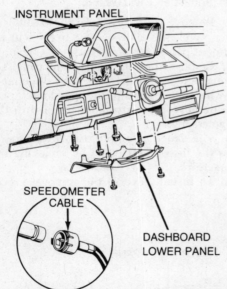

Instrument panel removal—1984 and later Civic Wagon

1982 and later Accord

1. Lower the steering column.
2. Remove the three screws at the top of the instrument panel.
3. Pull the instrument panel out, then disconnect the wire connectors and remove the panel.
4. Remove the four screws that hold the gauge assembly in place, then lift up on the panel so you can reach the wire connectors.
5. Disconnect the wire connectors and the speedometer cable, then remove the gauge assembly.
6. To install, reverse the removal procedure.

1983 and later Prelude

1. Lower the steering column, and remove the lower dashboard panel.
2. Remove the four instrument panel retaining screws.
3. Pull the instrument panel out, and disconnect the wire connectors. Remove the panel.
4. Remove the two screws retaining the gauge assembly, then lift out the assembly and remove the wire connectors and speedometer cable.
5. Installation is the reverse of the removal procedure.

HEADLIGHTS

REMOVAL AND INSTALLATION

1. Remove the retaining ring screws and remove the ring. Do not touch the headlight adjustment screws.
2. While holding the connector plug at the rear of the bulb, pull the headlight out of the housing. It may be necessary to work the bulb back and forth a few times to break it loose from the connector.

Retaining screw location

Removing the lower retaining screw

Light Bulb Specifications

Measurements given in watts except as noted

Headlights	50/40
Front Turn Signal/Parking Lights	32/3 cp
Side Marker Lights—front and rear	4 cp
Gauge Indicator Lights	1
Interior Light	5
Rear Turn/Stop/Taillight	32/32/3 cp
Back-up Lights	32 cp
License Plate Lights	4 cp

cp candle-power

Since each fuse protects more than one circuit, detection of a fuse blowout is an easy task of elimination.

Removing the headlight connector

Main circuit fusible link location

3. Insert the replacement bulb into the connector and install the retaining ring and screws.

FUSES AND FUSIBLE LINKS

All models are equipped with a 45 amp fusible link connected between the starter relay and the main wiring harness of the car.

The fuse box is located below the glove compartment, on the right bulkhead on Civic models. The Accord is equipped with a fuse tray which swings down from the instrument panel. It contains 8 fuses, some of which are rated at 10 amps and others at 15 amps. The rating and function of each fuse is posted inside the fuse box cap for quick reference.

Fuses can be replaced or removed simply by pulling them out of their retaining clips.

Civic fuse box location

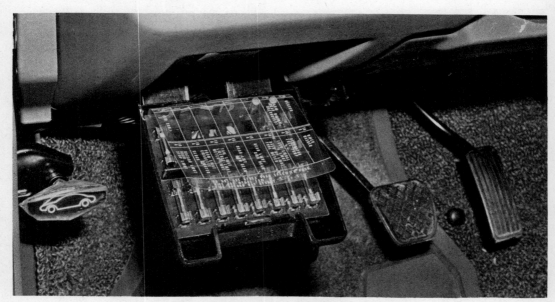

Accord and Prelude fuse box

WIRING DIAGRAMS

Wiring diagrams have been left out of this book. As cars have become more complex and available with longer and longer option lists, wiring diagrams have grown in size and complexity also. It has become virtually impossible to provide a readable reproduction in a reasonable number of pages.

Clutch and Transaxle

6

MANUAL TRANSAXLE

The Honda utilizes a transaxle arrangement where the transmission and the differential are contained within the same housing. Power is transmitted from the engine to the transmission, and in turn, to the differential. The front drive axle halfshafts transfer the power from the differential to the front wheels.

The Civic utilizes a standard design 4-speed, fully-synchronized transmission. The transmission is located on the right end of the engine, along with the differential. A similar 5-speed is used on Civic and Accord CVCC models.

A simple two-speed, semi-automatic transmission, Hondamatic, is also available. As in all automatic transmissions, power is transmitted from the engine to the transmission through a fluid coupling known as a torque converter. Forward gears are selected simply by moving the shift lever to the proper position—D1 (low speed range) or D2 (high speed range). The gears are engaged through the use of a complex clutch system in each gear range.

REMOVAL AND INSTALLATION
Four and Five-Speed Except 1980 and Later Prelude and Civic

1. Drain the transmission.
2. Raise the front of the car and support it with safety stands.
3. Remove the front wheels.
4. Disconnect the battery ground cable at the battery and the transmission case.
5. Remove the starter motor positive battery cable and the solenoid wire. Then remove the starter.

6. Disconnect the following cables and wires (see the "Engine Removal" section in Chapter 3 for the location of the various connections):
   a. Clutch cable at the release arm;
   b. Back-up light switch wires;
   c. TCS (Transmission Controlled Spark) switch wires (see "Emissions Controls" section in Chapter 4);
   d. Speedometer cable.
CAUTION: *When removing the speedometer cable from the transmission, it is not necessary to remove the entire cable holder. Remove the end boot (gear holder seal), the cable retaining clip and then pull the cable out of the holder. In no way should you disturb the holder, unless it is absolutely necessary. For further details, see "Engine Removal" section in Chapter 3.*

7. Disconnect the left and right lower ball joints at the knuckle, using a ball joint remover. See Chapter 8 for ball joint removal.
8. Pull on the brake disc and remove the left and right driveshafts from the differential case.
9. Drive out the gearshift rod pin (8 mm) with a drift and disconnect the rod at the transmission case.
10. Disconnect the gearshift extension at the clutch housing.
11. Screw in the engine hanger bolts (see the "Engine Removal" section in Chapter 3), to the engine torque rod bolt hold and to the hole just to the left of the distributor. Hook a chain onto the bolts and lift the engine just enough to take the load off the engine mounts.
12. After making sure that the engine is properly supported, remove the two center

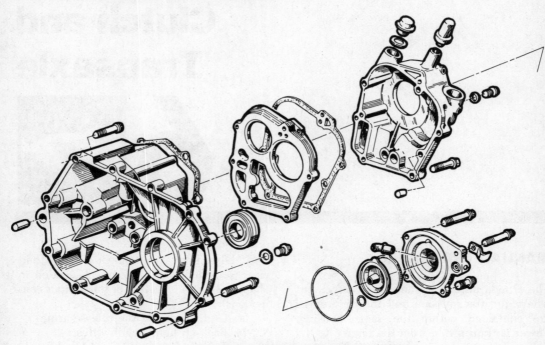

Five speed transmission housing and related parts

Driving out the gearshift rod pin

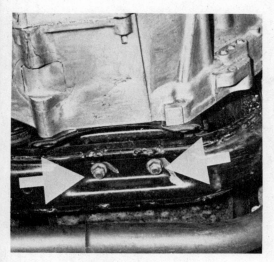

Center engine mount nuts (arrows)

beam-to-lower engine mount nuts. Next, remove the center beam, followed by the lower engine mount.

13. Reinstall the center beam (without mount) and lower the engine until it rests on the beam.

14. Place a jack under the transmission and loosen the 4 attaching bolts. Using the jack to support the transmission, slide it away from the engine and lower the jack until the transmission clears the car.

15. To install, reverse the removal procedure. Be sure to pay attention to the following points:

a. Tighten all mounting nuts and bolts to their specified torque (see the "Engine Removal" section in Chapter 3);

b. Use a new shift rod pin;

c. After installing the driveshafts, attempt to move the inner joint housing in and out of the differential housing. If it moves easily, the driveshaft end clips should be replaced;

d. Make sure that the control cables and wires are properly connected;

e. Be sure the transmission is refilled to the proper level.

1980 and later Prelude and Civic

1. Disconnect the battery ground.

2. Unlock the steering and place the transmission in neutral.

3. Disconnect the following wires in the engine compartment:

a. battery positive cable

b. black/white wire from the solenoid

c. temperature gauge sending unit wire

d. ignition timing thermosensor wire

e. back-up light switch

f. distributor wiring

4. Unclip and remove the speedometer cable at the transmission. Do not disassemble the speedometer gear holder!

5. Remove the clutch slave cylinder with the hydraulic line attached.

6. Remove the side and top starter mounting bolts.

7. Raise and support the car.

8. Drain the transmission.

9. Remove the splash shields from the underside.

10. Remove the stabilizer bar.

11. Disconnect the left and right lower ball joints and tie rod ends, using a ball joint remover.

12. Turn the right steering knuckle out as far as it will go. Place a heavy screwdriver against the inboard CV joint, pry the right axle out of the transmission about ½ inch. This will force the spring clip out of the groove inside the differential gear splines. Pull it out the rest of the way. Repeat this procedure on the other side.

13. Disconnect the shift lever torque rod from the clutch housing.

14. Remove the bolt from the shift rod clevis.

15. Raise the transmission jack securely against the transmission to take up the weight.

16. Remove the engine torque rods and brackets.

17. Remove the remaining starter mounting bolt and take out the starter.

18. Remove the remaining transmission mounting bolts and the upper bolt from the engine damper bracket.

19. Start backing the transmission away from the engine and remove the two lower damper bolts.

20. Pull the transmission clear of the engine and lower the jack.

21. To ease installation, fabricate two 14 mm diameter dowel pins and install them in the clutch housing.

22. Raise the transmission and slide it onto the dowels. Slide the transmission into position aligning the mainshaft splines with the clutch plate.

23. Attach the damper lower bolts when the positioning allows. Tighten both bolts until the clutch housing is seated against the block.

24. Install two lower mounting bolts and torque them to 33 ft. lb.

25. Install the front and rear torque rod brackets. Torque the front torque rod bolts to 54 ft. lb., the front bracket bolts to 33 ft. lb., the rear torque rod bolts to 54 ft. lb. and the rear bracket bolts to 47 ft. lb.

26. Remove the transmission jack.

27. Install the starter and torque the mounting bolts to 33 ft. lb.

28. Turn the right steering knuckle out far enough to fit the end into the transmission. Use new 26 mm spring clips on both axles. Repeat procedure for the other side.

CAUTION: *Make sure that the axles bottom fully so that you feel the spring clip engage the differential.*

29. Install the lower ball joints. Torque the nuts to 32 ft. lb.

30. Install the tie rods. Torque the nuts to 32 ft. lb.

31. Connect the shift linkage.

32. Connect the shift lever torque rod to the clutch housing and torque the bolt to 7 ft. lb.

33. Install the stabilizer bar.

34. Install the lower shields.

35. Install the front wheels and torque the lugs to 108 ft. lb.

36. Install the remaining starter bolts and torque to 33 ft. lb.

37. Install the clutch slave cylinder.

38. Install the speedometer cable using a new O-ring coated with clean engine oil.

39. Connect all engine compartment wiring.

40. Fill the transmission with SAE 10W-40 engine oil.

Halfshaft

(DRIVESHAFT) REMOVAL AND INSTALLATION

The front driveshaft assembly consists of a sub-axle shaft and a driveshaft with two universal joints.

A constant velocity ball joint is used for both universal joints, which are factory-packed with special grease and enclosed in sealed rubber boots. The outer joint cannot be disassembled except for removal of the boot.

1. Remove the hubcap from the front wheel and then remove the center cap.

2. Pull out the 4 mm cotter pin and loosen, but do not remove, the spindle nut.

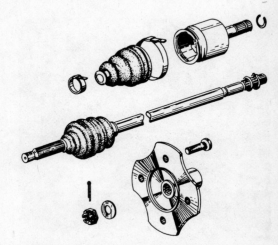

Exploded view of driveshaft and related parts

3. Raise the front of the car and support it with safety stands.

4. Remove the wheel lug nuts and then the wheel.

5. Remove the spindle nut.

6. Drain the transmission.

7. Remove the lower arm ball joints at the knuckle by using a ball joint remover.

CAUTION: *On 1984 and later Civic models, make sure that a floor jack is positioned securely under the lower control arm, at the ball joint. Otherwise, the lower control arm may "jump" suddenly away from the steering knuckle as the ball joint is removed.*

On 1983 and later Prelude models, remove the damper fork bolt and damper locking bolt. Remove the damper fork.

8. To remove the driveshaft, hold the knuckle and pull it toward you. Then slide the driveshaft out of the knuckle. Pry the CV joint out about ½ in. Pull the inboard joint side of the driveshaft out of the differential case.

9. To install, reverse the removal procedure. If either the inboard or outboard joint boot bands have been removed for inspection or disassembly of the joint (only the inboard joint can be disassembled), be sure to repack the joint with a sufficient amount of bearing grease.

CAUTION: *Make sure the CV joint sub-axle bottoms so that the spring clip may hold the sub-axle securely in the transmission.*

SHIFTER ADJUSTMENT

No external adjustment is needed or possible. However, you should check the linkage bushings for looseness and wear and replace if necessary.

CLUTCH

The clutch is a system of parts which, when engaged, connects the engine to the transmission. When the clutch is disengaged (clutch pedal pushed in), the turning motion of the engine crankshaft is separated from the transmission. Since the engine does not produce enough torque at idle to turn the rear wheels and start the car in motion, it is necessary to gradually connect the engine to the rest of the drive train to prevent the engine from stalling on acceleration. It is also much easier to shift the gears within a manual transmission when engine power is disconnected from the transmission.

The clutch unit is run directly off the flywheel. In this case, the pressure plate forces the friction disc onto the flywheel and power is then transmitted to the transmission. By depressing the clutch pedal, you allow the clutch disc to move away from the flywheel, thus isolating the engine power from the rest of the drive train.

REMOVAL AND INSTALLATION

1. Follow the transaxle removal procedure, previously given in this chapter. Matchmark the flywheel and clutch for reassembly.
2. Hold the flywheel ring gear with a large screwdriver or other fabricated tool (see illustration), remove the retaining bolts and remove the pressure plate and clutch disc.

NOTE: *Loosen the retaining bolts two turns at a time in a circular pattern. Removing one bolt while the rest are tight may warp the diaphragm spring.*

3. The flywheel can now be removed, if it needs repairing or replacing.
4. To separate the pressure plate from the diaphragm spring, remove the 4 retracting clips.
5. To remove the release, or throw-out, bearing, first straighten the locking tab and remove the 8 mm bolt, followed by the release shaft and release arm with the bearing attached.

NOTE: *It is recommended that the release bearing be removed after the release arm has been removed from the casing. Trying to remove or install the bearing with the*

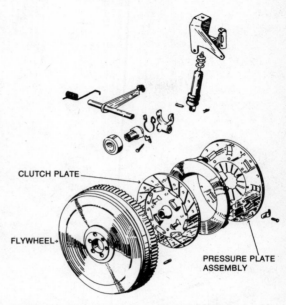

CLUTCH PLATE

FLYWHEEL

PRESSURE PLATE ASSEMBLY

Civic CVCC clutch, flywheel, and related parts

Clutch disc

Pressure plate

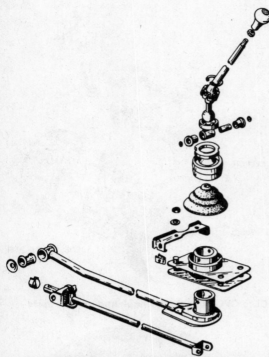

Exploded view of gearshift mechanism and related parts

release arm in the case, will damage the retaining clip.

6. If a new release bearing is to be installed, separate the bearing from the holder, using a bearing drift.

7. To assemble and install the clutch, reverse the removal procedure. Be sure to pay attention to the following points:

a. Make sure that the flywheel and the end of the crankshaft are clean before assembling;

b. When installing the pressure plate, align the mark on the outer edge of the flywheel with the alignment mark on the pressure plate. Failure to align these marks will result in imbalance;

c. When tightening the pressure plate bolts, use a pilot shaft to center the friction disc. The pilot shaft can be bought at any large auto supply store or fabricated from a wooden dowel. After centering the disc, tighten the bolts two turns at a time, in a circular pattern to avoid warping the diaphragm spring;

d. When installing the release shaft and arm, place a lock tab washer under the retaining bolt;

e. When installing the transmission, make sure that the mainshaft is properly aligned with the disc spline and the align-

ing pins are in place, before tightening the case bolts.

PEDAL HEIGHT ADJUSTMENT

Civic

1976–79

Check the clutch pedal height and if necessary, adjust the upper stop, so that the clutch and brake pedals rest at approximately the same height from the floor. First, be sure that the brake pedal free-play is properly adjusted.

1980 AND LATER

The pedal height should be 1³⁄₁₆ in. minimum from the floor.

Accord and Prelude

1. Pedal height should be 184 mm (7.24 in.) measured from the front of the pedal to the floorboard (mat removed).

2. Adjust by turning the pedal stop bolt in or out until height is correct. Tighten the locknut after adjustment.

FREE PLAY ADJUSTMENT

Civic

Adjust the clutch release lever so that it has 0.12–0.16 in. (3–4 mm) through 1980, or ⁷⁄₁₆–⁹⁄₁₆ in. (4.4–5.4 mm) 1981 and later of play when you move the clutch release lever at the transmission with your hand. This adjustment is made at the outer cable housing adjuster, near the release lever on non-CVCC models. Less than ⅛ in. of free-play may lead to clutch slippage, while more than ⅛ in. clearance may cause difficult shifting.

Accord slave cylinder (arrow)

CAUTION: *Make sure that the upper and lower adjusting nuts are tightened after adjustment.*

On CVCC models, the free-play adjustment is made on the cable at the firewall. Remove the C-clip and then rotate the threaded control cable housing until there is 0.12–0.16 in. free-play at the release lever. On Accord and Prelude models through 1981, adjustment is made at the slave cylinder. Simply loosen the lock nut and turn the adjusting nut until the correct free play is obtained. Free play should be $5/64$–$7/64$ in. at the release lever. On 1982 and later Accord and Prelude, adjustment is made on the cable at the firewall. Remove the C-clip and rotate the threaded control cable until $1/5$–$1/4$ in. exists at the clutch release lever.

Clutch Master Cylinder
REMOVAL AND INSTALLATION
Accord and Prelude

1. The clutch master cylinder is located on the firewall.
2. After locating the master cylinder, remove the hydraulic line to the slave cylinder. Either plug the port to prevent fluid escaping, or remove the brake fluid from the reservoir prior to this step.
3. Remove the pin which attaches the master cylinder rod to the clutch pedal arm. The rod is located under the instrument panel.
4. Remove the two bolts which retain the master cylinder to the firewall or the power booster.
5. Remove the master cylinder.
6. Installation is the reverse of removal.

OVERHAUL

1. Remove the snap ring which retains the stopper plate.
2. Once the snap ring is removed, use compressed air to remove the piston assembly. Note the order of all components. The piston assembly is in two parts—the piston itself and the spring assembly.
3. Check the inside of the cylinder bore for rust, pitting, or scratching. Light scores or scratches can be removed with a brake cylinder hone. If the bore won't clean up with a few passes of the hone, the entire cylinder will have to be replaced.
4. Replace the interior components with

Closeup of Accord and Prelude slave cylinder showing locknut and adjusting nut

new ones. Overhaul kits will simply be two pieces—a new piston and a new spring assembly. Reassemble them in the correct order. Coat the inside of the cylinder with brake fluid before installing the parts.
5. Install the cylinder and bleed the system.

Clutch Slave Cylinder
REMOVAL AND INSTALLATION

The slave cylinder is retained by two bolts. To remove the cylinder, simply disconnect the hydraulic line, remove the return spring and remove the bolts. Installation is the reverse of removal. Bleed the system after installation.

OVERHAUL

1. There is little you can do to the slave cylinder other than replace the piston and seal inside the cylinder.
2. Blow the piston out of the cylinder with compressed air. The seal will probably come out with it.
3. Once the piston and seal are removed, check the inside of the cylinder bore for pitting, rust or scratching. The bore can be honed, but it's probably not worth the effort. A new slave cylinder would make more sense.

AUTOMATIC TRANSAXLE

Shift Lever

INSPECTION

1. Pull up fully on the parking brake lever and run the engine at idle speed, while depressing the brake pedal.

CAUTION: *Be sure to check continually for car movement.*

2. By moving the shift selector lever slowly forward and backward from the "N" position, make sure that the distance between the "N" and the points where the D clutch is engaged for the "2" and "R" positions are the same. The D clutch engaging point is just before the slight response is felt. The reverse gears will make a noise when the clutch engages. If the distances are not the same, then adjustment is necessary.

ADJUSTMENT—2 SPEED

1. Remove the center console retaining screws, and pull away the console to expose the shift control cable and turnbuckle.

2. Adjust the length of the control cable by turning the turnbuckle, located at the front bottom of the shift lever assembly.

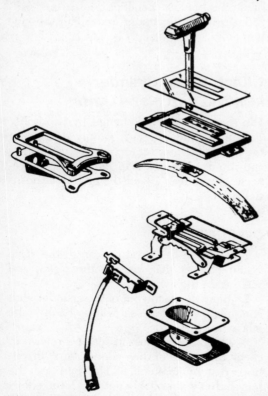

Exploded view of automatic transmission shift lever control

After adjustment, the cable and turnbuckle should twist toward the left (driver's) side of the car when shifted toward the "2" position and toward the right-side when shifted into the R position.

ADJUSTMENT—3 SPEED

1. Remove the shift console.

2. Shift to reverse and remove the lock-pin from the cable adjuster.

3. With the lock-pin removed, the hole in the adjuster, from which the lock-pin was removed, should be perfectly aligned with the corresponding hole in the shift cable.

4. If they are not perfectly aligned, turn the adjusting nuts as required.

5. Install the lock-pin.

NOTE: *If there is any binding on the lock-pin as it is installed, there is some misalignment. Check and adjust as required!*

REMOVAL AND INSTALLATION

The automatic transmission is removed in the same basic manner as the manual transmission (refer to Manual Transmission Removal and Installation). The following exceptions should be noted during automatic transmission removal and installation.

1. Remove the center console and control rod pin.

2. Remove the front floor center mat and control cable bracket nuts.

3. Jack and support the front of the car.

4. Remove the two selector lever bracket nuts at front side.

5. Loosen the bolts securing the control cable holder and support beam and disconnect the control cable.

6. Disconnect the transmission cooler lines at the transmission.

7. Remove the transmission together with the engine. Remove the engine mounts and torque converter case cover.

8. Remove the starter motor and separate the transmission from the engine.

9. Installation of the automatic transmission is the reverse of removal. Close attention should be paid to the following points.

10. Be sure that the stator hub is correctly located and moves smoothly. The stator shaft can be used for this purpose.

11. Align the stator, stator shaft, main shaft and torque converter turbine serrations.

12. After installation of the engine-transmission unit in car, make all required adjustments.

Suspension and Steering

7

FRONT SUSPENSION

All models except 1983 and later Prelude and 1984 and later Civic use a MacPherson strut type front suspension. Each steering knuckle is suspended by a lower control arm at the bottom and a combined coil spring/shock absorber unit at the top. A front stabilizer bar, mounted between each lower control arm and the body, doubles as a locating rod for the suspension. Caster and camber are not adjustable and are fixed by the location of the strut assemblies in their respective sheet metal towers.

The 1983 and later Prelude uses a completely redesigned front suspension. A dou-ble wishbone system, the lower wishbone consists of a forged transverse link with a locating stabilizer bar. The lower end of the shock absorber has a fork shape to allow the driveshaft to pass through it. The upper arm is located in the wheel well and is twist mounted, angled forward from its inner mount, to clear the shock absorber.

The 1984 and later Civic models also use a redesigned front suspension. This change was made to lower the hood line, thus making the car more aero-dynamic. The new suspension consists of two independent torsion bars and front shock absorbers similar to a front strut assembly, but without a spring. Both lower forged radius arms are connected with a stabilizer bar.

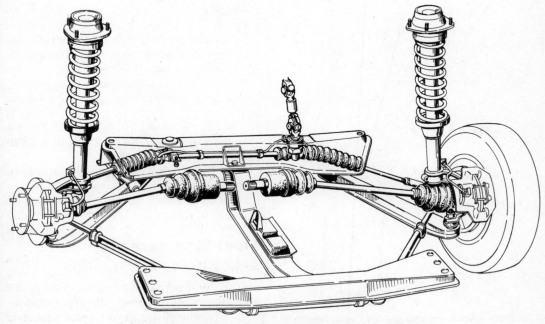

Assembled view of front suspension and steering assemblies

Shock Absorbers

REMOVAL AND INSTALLATION

1983 and Later Prelude

1. Raise the front of the car and support on jackstands. Remove the front wheels.
2. Remove the shock absorber locking bolt.
3. Remove the shock fork bolt and remove the shock fork.
4. Remove the shock absorber assembly.
NOTE: *For spring and shock absorber disassembly procedures, please refer to "Strut Overhaul" in the Unit Repair section.*
5. Installation is the reverse of the removal procedure, taking note of the following:

    a. Align the shock absorber aligning tab with the slot in the shock absorber fork.

    b. The mounting base bolt should be tightened with the weight of the car placed on the shock.

    c. Torque the upper mounting bolts to 29 ft. lbs., the shock locking bolt to 32 ft. lbs. and the shock fork bolt to 47 ft. lbs.

1984 and Later Civic Models

1. Raise the front of the car and support on jackstands. Remove the front wheels.
2. Remove the brake hose clamp bolt.

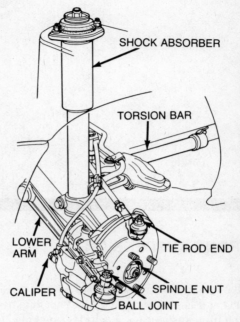

Front suspension—1984 and later Civic

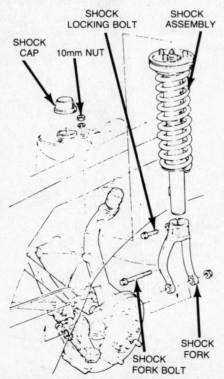

Front shock mounting—1983 and later Prelude

3. Place a floor jack beneath the lower control arm to support it.
4. Remove the lower shock retaining bolt from the steering knuckle, then slowly lower the jack.

CAUTION: *Be sure the jack is positioned securely beneath the lower control arm at the ball joint. Otherwise, the tension from the torsion bar may cause the lower control arm to suddenly "jump" away from the shock absorber as the pinch bolt is removed.*

5. Compress the shock absorber by hand, then remove the two upper lock nuts and remove from the car.
6. Installation is the reverse of the removal procedure, taking note of the following:

    a. Use new self locking nuts on the top of the shock assembly and torque to 28 ft. lbs.

    b. Tighten the lower pinch bolt to 47 ft. lbs.

    c. Install and tighten the brake hose clamp to 16 ft. lbs.

Front Strut Assembly

REMOVAL AND INSTALLATION

1. Raise the front of the car and support it with safety stands. Remove the front wheels.
2. Disconnect the brake pipe at the strut and remove the brake hose retaining clip.

3. Loosen the bolt on the knuckle that retains the lower end of the shock absorber. Push down firmly while tapping it with a hammer until the knuckle is free of the strut.

4. Remove the three nuts retaining the upper end of the strut and remove the strut from the car.

5. To install, reverse the removal procedure. Be sure to properly match the mating surface of the strut and the knuckle notch.

Upper strut removal points

Front strut

Lower strut retaining bolt (arrow)

DISASSEMBLY

1. Disassemble the strut according to the procedure given in the rear strut disassembly section.

2. Remove the rubber cover and remove the center retaining nuts.

3. Slowly release the compressor and remove the spring.

4. Remove the upper mounting cap, washers, thrust plates, bearings and bushing.

NOTE: *Before discarding any parts, check a parts list to determine which parts are available as replacements.*

5. To reassemble, first pull the strut shaft all the way out, hold it in this position and slide the rubber bumper down the shaft to the strut body. This should hold the shaft in the extended position.

6. Install the spring and its top plate. Make sure the spring seats properly.

7. Install the partially assembled strut in the compressor. Compress the strut until the shaft protrudes through the top plate about 1 in.

8. Now install the bushings, thrust plates, top mounting cap washers and retaining nuts in the reverse order of removal.

9. Once the retaining nut is installed, release the tension on the compressor and loosen the thumbscrew on the bottom plate. Separate the bottom plates and remove the compressor.

INSPECTION

1. Check for wear or damage to bushings and needle bearings.

2. Check for oil leaks from the struts.

3. Check all rubber parts for wear or damage.

4. Bounce the car to check shock absorbing effectiveness. The car should continue to bounce for no more than two cycles.

Torsion Bar Assembly

REMOVAL AND INSTALLATION

1984 and Later Civic Models

1. Raise the front of the car and support on jackstands.

2. Remove the height adjusting nut and the torque tube holder.

3. Remove the 33mm circlip.

4. Remove the torsion bar cap, then remove the torsion bar clip by tapping the bar out of the torque tube.

NOTE: *The torsion bar will slide easier if you move the lower arm up and down.*

5. Tap the torsion bar backward, out of the torque tube and remove the torque tube.

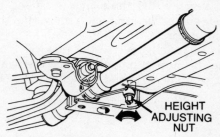

Torsion bar adjustment—1984 and later Civic

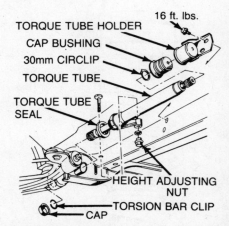

Torsion bar assembly—1984 and later Civic

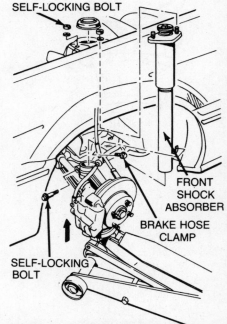

Front shock mounting—1984 and later Civic

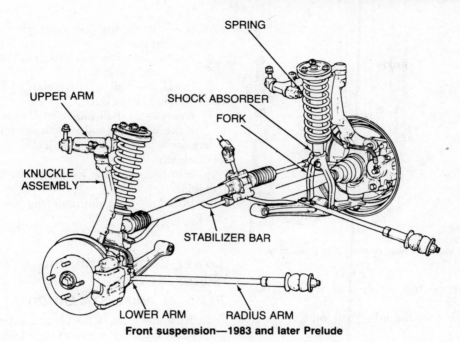

SPRING

UPPER ARM

SHOCK ABSORBER

FORK

KNUCKLE
ASSEMBLY

STABILIZER BAR

LOWER ARM   RADIUS ARM

Front suspension—1983 and later Prelude

6. Install a new seal onto the torque tube. Coat the torque tube seal and torque with grease, then install them on the rear beam.

7. Grease the ends of the torsion bar and insert into the torque tube from the back.

8. Align the projection on the torque tube splines with the cutout in the torsion bar splines and insert the torsion bar approximately (10mm) 0.394 in.

NOTE: *The torsion bar will slide easier if the lower arm is moved up and down.*

9. Install the torsion bar clip and cap, then install the 30mm circlip and the torque tube cap.

NOTE: *Push the torsion bar to the front so there is no clearance between the torque tube and the 30mm circlip.*

10. Coat the cap bushing with grease and install it on the torque tube. Install the torque tube holder.

11. Temporarily tighten the height adjusting nut.

12. Remove the jackstands and lower the car to the ground. Adjust the torsion bar spring height.

TORSION BAR ADJUSTMENT

1. Measure the torsion bar spring height between the ground and the highest point of the wheel arch.
   - COUPE(CRX) 25.35 + or − 0.20 in.
   - HATCHBACK 25.43 + or − 0.20 in.
   - SEDAN 25.63 + or − 0.20 in.
   - WAGON 25.55 + or − 0.20 in.

2. If the spring height does not meet the specifications above, make the following adjustment.

   a. Raise the front wheels off the ground.

   b. Adjust the spring height by turning the height adjusting nut. Tightening the nut raises the height, and loosening the nut lowers the height.

NOTE: *The height varies 0.20 in. per turn of the adjusting nut.*

Lower the front wheels to the ground, then bounce the car up and down several times and recheck the spring height to see if it is within specifications.

Lower Ball Joints
INSPECTION

Check ball joint play as follows:

   a. Raise the front of the car and support it with safety stands;

   b. Clamp a dial indicator onto the lower control arm and place the indicator tip on the knuckle, near the ball joint;

   c. Place a pry bar between the lower control arm and the knuckle. Replace the ball joint if the play exceeds 0.020 in.

LUBRICATION

1. Remove the screw plug from the bottom of the ball joint and install a grease nipple.

2. Lubricate the ball joint with NLGI No. 2 multipurpose type grease.

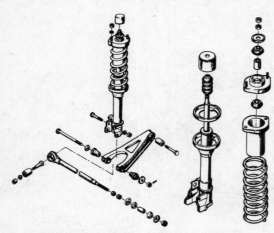

Exploded view of lower control arm assembly

3. Remove the nipple and reinstall the screw plug.

4. Repeat for the other ball joint.

REMOVAL AND INSTALLATION
All except 1983–84 Prelude

1. Raise the car and support it with safety stands.

2. Remove the front wheel.

3. Pull out the cotter pin holding the ball joint castle nut and remove the nut.

4. Remove the ball joint from the knuckle using a ball joint remover. This is done by hitting the end of the long wedge, thus forcing the ball joint down and out.

5. To install, reverse the removal procedure. Tighten the ball joint nut to 29–35 ft lbs of torque. Be sure to grease the ball joint.

1983 and Later Prelude

NOTE: *This procedure is performed after the removal of the steering knuckle and requires the use of the following special tools or their equivalent: Honda part no. 07965-SB00100 Ball Joint Remover/Installer, 07965-SB00200 Ball Joint Removal Base, 07965-SB00300 Ball Joint Installation Base, and 07974-SA50700 Clip Guide Tool.*

1. Pry the snap-ring off and remove the boot.

2. Pry the snap-ring out of the groove in the ball joint.

3. Install the ball joint removal tool with the large end facing out and tighten the ball joint nut.

4. Position the ball joint removal tool base on the ball joint and set the assembly in a large vise. Press the ball joint out of the steering knuckle.

5. Position the new ball joint into the hole of the steering knuckle.

6. Install the ball joint installer tool with the small end facing out.

7. Position the ball joint installation base tool on the ball joint and set the assembly in a large vise. Press the ball joint into the steering knuckle.

8. Seat the snap-ring in the groove of the ball joint.

9. Install the boot and snap-ring using the clip guide tool.

Lower Control Arm and Stabilizer Bar
REMOVAL AND INSTALLATION

1. Raise the front of the car and support it with safety stands. Remove the front wheels.

2. Disconnect the lower arm ball joint as described above. Be careful not to damage the seal.

3. Remove the stabilizer bar retaining brackets, starting with the center brackets.

4. Remove the lower arm pivot bolt.

5. Disconnect the radius rod and remove the lower arm.

6. To install, reverse the removal procedure. Be sure to tighten the components to their proper torque.

Radius Arm
REMOVAL AND INSTALLATION
1984 and Later Civic Models Only

1. Raise the front of the car off the ground and support on jackstands. Remove the front wheels.

2. Place a floor jack beneath the lower control arm, then remove the ball joint cotter pin and nut.

CAUTION: *Be sure to place the jack securely beneath the lower control arm at the ball joint. Otherwise, the tension from the torsion bar may cause the arm to suddenly "jump" away from the steering knuckle as the ball joint is removed.*

3. Using a ball joint remover, remove the ball joint from the steering knuckle.

4. Remove the radius arm locking nuts and the stabilizer locking nut, then separate the radius arm from the stabilizer bar.

5. Remove the lower arm bolts and re-

Torque Specifications

Part(s)	Torque (ft. lbs.)
Lower ball joint retaining nut	
Civic	22–29
Accord and Prelude	33
Lower control arm-to-body mount bolts	
Civic	25–36
Accord and Prelude	40
Front radius rod-to-knuckle bolt	40
Rear radius rod-to-carrier bolt	40–54
Rear radius rod-to-body bolt	40
Front stabilizer mount bolts	5–9
Strut center nut (front and rear)	40–50
Strut to body retaining bolts (front and rear)	16
Front strut-to-knuckle retaining bolt	36–43
Rear strut-to-carrier mount bolts	26–35
Rear strut-to-control arm bolt	36–47

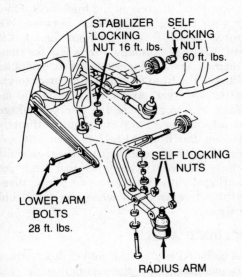

STABILIZER SELF
LOCKING LOCKING
NUT 16 ft. lbs. NUT
60 ft. lbs.

SELF LOCKING
NUTS

LOWER ARM
BOLTS
28 ft. lbs.

RADIUS ARM

Radius arm—1984 and later Civic

move the radius arm by pulling it down and then forward.

6. Installation is the reverse of the removal procedure. Tighten all the rubber bushings and dampered parts only after the car is placed back on the ground.

Steering Knuckles

REMOVAL AND INSTALLATION

1. Raise the front of the car and support it with safety stands. Remove the front wheel.

2. Remove the spindle nut cotter pin and the spindle nut.

3. Remove the two bolts retaining the brake caliper and remove the caliper from the knuckle. Do not let the caliper hang by the brake hose, support it with a length of wire.

NOTE: *In case it is necessary to remove the disc, hub, bearings and/or outer dust seal, use Steps 4 and 5 given below. You will need a hydraulic press for this (see Chapter 9). If this is unnecessary, omit Steps 4 and 5.*

4. Install a hub puller attachment against the hub with the lug nuts.

5. Attach a slide hammer in the center hole of the attachment and pull out the hub, with the disc attached, from the knuckle.

6. Remove the tie-rod from the knuckle using the ball joint remover. Use care not to damage the ball joint seals.

7. Remove the lower arm from the knuckle using the ball joint remover.

8. Loosen the lockbolt which retains the strut in the knuckle. Tap the top of the knuckle with a hammer and slide it off the shock.

9. Remove the knuckle and hub, if still attached, by sliding the driveshaft out of the hub.

10. To install, reverse the removal procedure. If the hub was removed, refer to Chapter 9 (Brake Disc Removal), for procedures with the dydraulic press. Be sure to visually check the knuckle for visible signs of wear or damage and to check the condition of the inner bearing dust seals.

Wheel Alignment

Front wheel alignment (also known as front end geometry) is the position of the front wheels relative to each other and to the vehicle. Correct alignment must be maintained to provide safe, accurate steering, vehicle stability, and minimum tire wear. The factors which determine wheel alignment are interdependent. Therefore, when one of the factors is adjusted, the others must be adjusted to compensate.

CASTER ANGLE

Caster angle is the number of degrees that a line, drawn through the center of the upper and lower ball joints and viewed from the side, can be tilted forward or backward. Positive caster means that the top of the upper ball joint is tilted toward the rear of the car, and negative caster means that it is tilted toward the front. A car with a slightly positive caster setting will have its lower ball joint pivot slightly ahead of the tire's center.

This will assist the directional stability of the car by causing a drag at the bottom center of the wheel when it turns, thereby resisting the turn and tending to hold the wheel steady in whatever direction the car is pointed. Therefore, the car is less susceptible to crosswinds and road surface deviations. A car with too much (positive) caster will be hard to steer and shimmy at low speeds. A car with insufficient (negative) caster may tend to be unstable at high speeds and may respond erratically when the brakes are applied.

CAMBER ANGLE

Camber angle is the number of degrees that the wheel itself is tilted from a vertical line when viewed from the front. Positive camber means that the top of the wheel is slanted away from the car, while negative camber means that it is tilted toward the car. Ordinarily, a car will have a slight positive camber when unloaded. Then, when the car is loaded and rolling down the road, the wheels will just about be vertical. If you started with no camber at all, then loading the car would produce a negative camber. Excessive camber (either positive or negative) will produce rapid tire wear, since one side of the tire will be more heavily loaded than the other side.

STEERING AXIS INCLINATION

Steering axis inclination is the number of degrees that a line drawn through the upper and lower ball joints and viewed from the front, is tilted to the left or the right. This, in combination with caster, is responsible for the directional stability and self-centering of the steering. As the steering knuckle swings from lock to lock, the spindle generates an arc, causing the car to be raised when it is turned from the straight-ahead position. The reason the car body must rise is straightforward: since the wheel is in contact with the ground, it cannot move down. However, when it is swung away from the straight-ahead position, it must move either up or down (due to the arc generated by the steering knuckle). Not being able to move down, it must move up. Then, the weight of the car acts against this lift, and attempts to return the spindle to the straight-ahead position when the steering wheel is released.

TOE-IN

Toe-in is the difference (in inches) between the front and the rear of the front tires. On a car with toe-in, the distance between the front wheels is less at the front than at the rear. Toe-in is normally only a few fractions of an inch, and is necessary to ensure parallel rolling of the front wheels and to prevent excessive tire wear. As the car is driven at increasingly faster speeds, the steering linkage has a tendency to expand slightly, thereby allowing the front wheels to turn out and away from each other. Therefore, initially setting the front wheels so that they are pointing slightly inward (toe-in), allows them to turn straight ahead when the car is underway.

INCLUDED ANGLE

The included angle is the sum of the steering axis inclination and the camber angle. Included angle determines the point of inter-

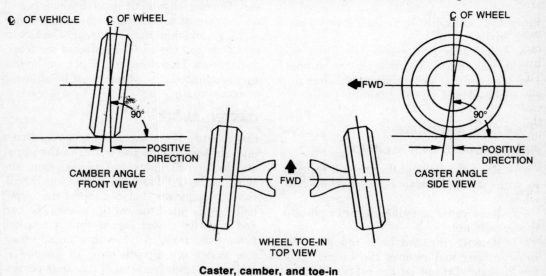

Caster, camber, and toe-in

section of the wheel and the steering axis center lines. This is important because this determines, in turn, whether the wheel will toe out or toe in. When the point of intersection is below the road surface, the wheel will toe out. When the intersection point is above the road surface, the wheel tends to toe in.

TOE-OUT (DURING TURNS)

The steering is designed so that the inner wheel turns more sharply toward the center of the turn than the outer wheel turns. This compensates for the fact that the inner wheel actually travels a shorter distance during the turn. Designing the steering in this manner avoids having the front wheels fight each other, thus improving tire life and aiding stability. Where toe-out is to be checked, angles are given for the inner and outer wheel relative to travel in a straight line. Thus, in a left-hand turn, the left (inner) wheel might be 24° from straight ahead, and the right (outer) wheel 20° from straight ahead. For a right turn, the figures would be reversed.

CASTER AND CAMBER ADJUSTMENT

Caster and camber cannot be adjusted on any Honda except the 1983–84 Prelude. If caster, camber or kingpin angle is incorrect or front end parts are damaged or worn, they must be replaced.

1983 and Later Prelude

NOTE: *Wheel alignment adjustments must be performed in the following order: camber, caster and then toe-in.*

The camber adjustment can be made by loosening the two nuts on the upper control arm and sliding the ball joint until the camber meets specifications. The caster adjustment can be made by loosening the 16mm nuts on the front beam radius rods and then turning the locknut to make the adjustment. Turning the nut clockwise decreases the caster and turning it counterclockwise increases the caster. After adjusting to specifications, hold the nylon locknut and lightly tighten the adjuster. Tighten the 16mm nut to 58 ft. lbs., then tighten the locknut to 32 ft. lbs. while holding the 16mm nut.

TOE-IN ADJUSTMENT

Toe-in (or toe-out) can be adjusted on all Hondas by loosening the locknuts at each end of the tie-rods. To increase toe-out, turn the right tie-rod in the direction of forward wheel rotation and turn the left tie-rod in the

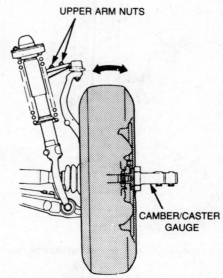

Camber adjustment—1983 and later Prelude

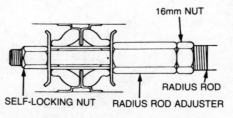

Caster adjustment—1983 and later Prelude

opposite direction. Turn both tie-rods an equal amount until toe-out becomes 0.039 in. (1 mm).

REAR SUSPENSION

All Civic sedan and hatchback models utilize an independent MacPherson strut arrangement for each rear wheel. Each suspension unit consits of a combined coil spring/shock absorber strut, a lower control arm, and a radius rod.

Station wagon models use a more conventional leaf spring rear supension with a solid rear axle. The springs are three-leaf, semi-elliptic types located longitudinally with a pair of telescopic shock absorbers to control rebound. The solid axle and leaf springs allow for a greater load carrying capacity for the wagon over the sedan.

Strut Assembly
REMOVAL AND INSTALLATION

1. Raise the rear of the car and support it with safety stands.

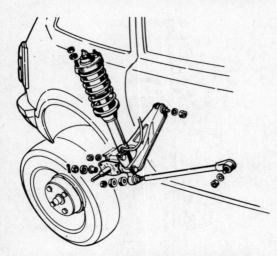

Rear suspension—sedan and hatchback models

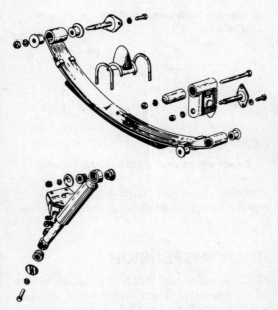

Exploded view of rear suspension—station wagon models

2. Remove the rear wheel.

3. Disconnect the brake line at the shock absorber. Remove the retaining clip and separate the brake hose from the shock absorber.

4. Disconnect the parking brake cable at the backing plate lever.

5. Remove the lower strut retaining bolt and hub carrier pivot bolt. To remove the pivot bolt, you first have to remove the castle nut and its cotter pin.

6. Remove the two upper strut retaining nuts and remove the strut from the car.

7. To install, reverse the removal proce-

dure. Be sure to install the top of the strut in the body first. After installation, bleed the brake lines (see Chapter 9).

DISASSEMBLY

1. Use a coil spring compressor to disassemble the strut. When assembling the compressor onto the strut, the long studs should be installed so that they are flush with the bottom plate and also flush with the retaining nut on the top end. The adjustable plate in the center cup should be screwed all the way in.

2. Insert the strut in the compressor and compress the strut about 2 in. Then remove the center retaining nut.

3. Loosen the compressor and remove the strut.

4. Remove the top plate, rubber protector, spring and rubber bumper.

5. To assemble, reverse the removal procedure after checking the shock for oil leaks and all rubber parts for damage, wear or deterioration.

Rear control arm

Wheel Alignment Specifications

Year	Model	Caster Range (deg)	Caster Preferred Setting (deg)	Camber Range (deg)	Camber Preferred Setting (deg)	Toe-In (in.)	Steering Axis Inclination (deg)
'73–'79	Civic—all exc. Station Wagon	¼P–1¼ ①	¾ ②	0–1P	½P	3/64 ③	9 5/16
'73–'79	Civic Station Wagon	0–1P	½P	0–1P	½P	3/64 ④	9 5/16
'80–'81	Civic—all exc. Station Wagon	¾P–2¾P	1¾P	1N–1P	0	0	12 5/16
'80–'81	Civic Station Wagon	0–2P	1P	1N–1P	0	0	12 5/16
'82–'83	Civic—all exc. Station Wagon	1½P–3½P	2½P	1N–1P	0	0	12 11/32
'82–'83	Civic Station Wagon	5/16P–2 5/16P	1 5/16P	1N–1P	0	0	12 11/32
'84–'85	Civic—all exc. Station Wagon	1 5/16P–3 5/16P	2 5/16P	1N–1P	0	0	12 13/16
'84–'85	Civic Station Wagon	1⅛P–3⅛P	2⅛P	1N–1P	0	0	12
'76–'78	Accord	1P–3P	2P	¼N–1¾P	¾P	3/64	12 3/16
'79–'80	Accord	¾P–1¾P	1¼P	0–1P	½P	1/32	12 3/16
'81	Accord	11/16P–2 11/16P	1 11/16	11/16N–1 5/16P	5/16	3/64	12½
'82–'85	Accord	7/16P–2 7/16	1 7/16	1N–1P	0	0	12½
'79–'82	Prelude	½P–2½P	1½P	1N–1P	0	0	12 13/16
'83–'85	Prelude	1N–1P	0	1N–1P	0	0	6 13/16

P—Positive
N—Negative
① '73–'78 CVCC 0–1P
② '73–'78 CVCC ½P
③ '73–'78 CVCC 1/32
④ '73–'78 CVCC Wagon 1/32

Rear Control Arm

REMOVAL AND INSTALLATION

All Except Wagon

1. Remove the control arm outboard and inboard pivot bolts.
2. Pull the inboard side of the arm down until it clears the body.
3. Slide the arm towards the center of the car until it is free of the hub carrier.
4. To install, reverse the removal procedure. Be sure to check the bushings at each end of the controfl arm and the control arm for damage and wear.

Civic rear suspension showing toe-in adjustment point (arrow)

Leaf Spring
REMOVAL AND INSTALLATION
Station Wagon Only

1. Raise the rear of the car and support it on stands placed on the frame. Remove the wheels.

2. Remove the shock absorber lower mounting bolt.

3. Remove the nuts from the U-bolt and remove the U-bolts, bump rubber, and clamp bracket.

4. Unbolt the front and rear spring shackle bolts, remove the bolts, and remove the spring.

5. To install, first position the spring on the axle and install the front and rear shackle bolts. Apply a soapy water solution to the bushings to ease installation. Do not tighten the shackle nuts yet.

6. Install the U-bolts, spring clamp bracket and bump rubber loosely on the axle and spring.

7. Install the wheels and lower the car. Tighten the front and rear shackle bolts to 33 ft. lbs. Also tighten the U-bolt nuts to 33 ft. lbs., after the shackle bolts have been tightened.

8. Install the shock absorber to the lower mount. Tighten to 33 ft. lbs.

Shock Absorbers
REMOVAL AND INSTALLATION
Station Wagon Only

1. It is not necessary to jack the car or remove the wheels unless you require working clearance. Unbolt the upper mounting nut and lower bolt and remove the shock absorber. Note the position of the washers and lock washers upon removal.

2. Installation is the reverse. Be sure the

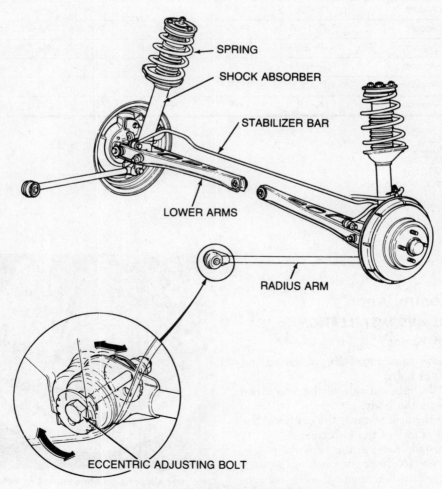

SPRING

SHOCK ABSORBER

STABILIZER BAR

LOWER ARMS

RADIUS ARM

ECCENTRIC ADJUSTING BOLT

1983 and later Accord and Prelude rear suspension

washers and lock washers are installed correctly. Tighten the upper mount to 44 ft. lbs. and the lower mount to 33 ft. lbs.

REAR WHEEL ALIGNMENT

Toe-in is adjustable on the rear wheels of all models except the station wagon. On the Civic, toe-in is adjusted by means of a threaded radius rod. On the Accord and Prelude a cam-type adjuster is used.

Rear toe-in adjustment point on Accord (arrow)

STEERING

All Hondas are equipped with rack and pinion steering. Movement of the steering wheel is transmitted through the linkage to the input shaft, which in turn is connected to the pinion gear. The pinion gear engages the rack, and rotation of the pinion, transmitted from the input shaft, causes the rack to move laterally.

Steering Wheel
REMOVAL AND INSTALLATION

1. Remove the steering wheel pad by lifting it off.
2. Remove the steering wheel retaining nut. Gently hit the backside of each of the steering wheel spokes with equal force from the palms of your hands.
   CAUTION: *Avoid hitting the wheel or the shaft with excessive force. Damage to the shaft could result.*
3. Installation is the reverse of the removal procedure. Be sure to tighten the steering wheel nut to 26–36 ft. lb.

Combination Switch
REMOVAL AND INSTALLATION

1. Remove the steering wheel.
2. Disconnect the column wiring harness and coupler.
   CAUTION: *Be careful not to damage the steering column or shaft.*
3. Remove the upper and lower column covers.
4. On models so equipped, remove the cruise control slip ring.
5. Remove the turn signal cancelling sleeve.
6. On later models, remove the switch retaining screws, then remove the switch.
7. Loosen the screw on the turn signal switch cam nut and lightly tap its head to permit the cam nut to loosen. Then remove the turn signal switch assembly and the steering shaft upper bushing.
8. To assemble and install, reverse the above procedure. When installing the turn signal switch assembly, engage the locating tab on the switch with the notch in the steering column. The steering shaft upper bushing should be installed with the flat side facing the upper side of the column. The

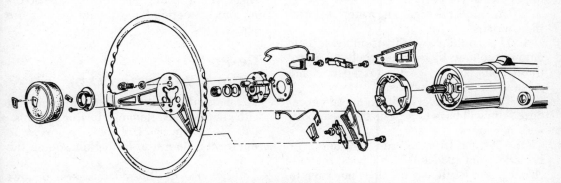

Exploded view of steering wheel and related parts

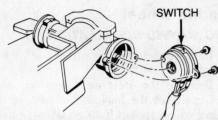

Ignition switch removal—1982 and later Accord, 1984 and later Civic and 1983 and later Prelude.

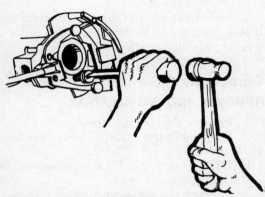

Loosening the turn signal cam nut screw

alignment notch for the turn signal switch will be centered on the flat side of the bushing.

NOTE: *On earlier models, if the cam nut has been removed, be sure to install it with the small end up.*

Ignition Switch

REMOVAL AND INSTALLATION

1. Remove the steering shaft hanger retaining bolts and lower the steering shaft from the instrument panel to expose the ignition switch.

2. Remove the steering column housing upper and lower covers.

3. Disconnect the ignition switch wiring at the couplers.

4. The ignition switch assembly is held onto the column by two shear bolts. Remove these bolts, using a drill, to separate and remove the ignition switch.

5. To install, reverse the removal procedure. You will have to replace the shear bolts with new ones.

On 1982 and later Accords, 1983 and later Preludes, and 1984 and later Civics, the mechanical part of the switch does not have to be removed to replace the electrical part. To

remove the electrical part or base of the switch proceed as follows:

1. Remove the steering column lower cover.

2. Disconnect the electrical connector at the switch.

3. Insert the key and turn it to lock position.

4. Remove the two switch retaining screws, then remove the switch (base) from the rest of the switch.

Steering Gear

TESTING

1. Remove the dust seal ellows retaining bands and slide the dust seals off the left and right side of the gearbox housing.

2. Turn the front wheels full left and, using your hand, attempt to move the steering rack in an up-down direction.

3. Repeat with the wheel turned full right.

4. If any movement is felt, the steering gearbox must be adjusted.

ADJUSTMENT

1. Make sure that the rack is well lubricated.

2. Loosen the rack guide adjusting locknut.

3. Tighten the adjusting screw just to the point where the front wheels cannot be turned by hand.

4. Back off the adjusting screw 45 degrees and hold it in that position while adjusting the locknut.

5. Recheck the play, and then move the wheels lock-to-lock, to make sure that the rack moves freely.

6. Check the steering force by first raising the front wheels and then placing them in a straight-ahead position. Turn the steering wheel with a spring scale to check the steering force. Steering force should be no more than 3.3 lbs.

Tie-Rods

REMOVAL AND INSTALLATION

1. Raise the front of the car and support it with safety stands. Remove the front wheels.

2. Use a special ball joint remover. To remove the tie-rod from the knuckle on the Civic:

3. Remove the tie-rod dust seal bellows clamps and move the rubber bellows on the

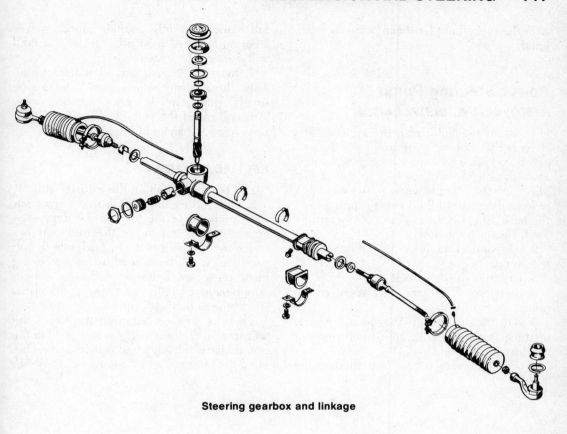

Steering gearbox and linkage

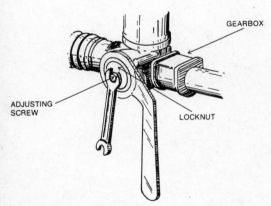

GEARBOX

ADJUSTING
SCREW

LOCKNUT

Steering gearbox adjustment

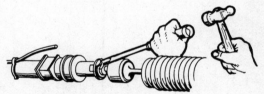

Tie-rod lockwasher removal

tie-rod and rack joints. On the Civic, you first
have to disconnect the air tube at the dust
seal joint.

4. Straighten the tie-rod lockwasher tabs
at the tie-rod-to-rack joint and remove the
tie-rod by turning it with a wrench.

5. To install, reverse the removal procedure. Always use a new tie-rod lockwasher
during reassembly. Fit the locating lugs into
the slots on the rack and bend the outer edge
of the washer over the flat part of the rod,

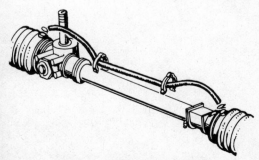

Separate the air tube from the dust seal bellows

Steering Torque Specifications
(ft. lbs.)

Tie-rod end locknut	29.0–35.0
Tie-rod ball joint nut	29.0–25.0
Bask guide locknut	29.0–36.0
Steering wheel retaining nut(s)	22.0–33.0

after the tie-rod nut has been properly tightened.

Power Steering Pump
REMOVAL AND INSTALLATION

1. Drain the fluid from the system: Disconnect the cooler return hose from the reservoir and place the end in a large container. Start the engine and allow it to run at fast idle. Turn the steering wheel from lock to lock several times, until fluid stops running from the hose. Shut off the engine and discard the fluid. Reattach the hose.

2. Disconnect the inlet and outlet hoses at the pump.

3. Remove the drive belt.

4. Remove the bolts and remove the pump.

5. To install, install the pump on its mounts, install the belt, adjust belt tension, and install the fluid hoses.

6. Fill the reservoir with fresh fluid, to the full mark. Use only genuine Honda power steering fluid; ATF or other brands of fluid will damage the system.

7. Start the engine and allow to fast idle. Turn the steering wheel from side to side several times, lightly contacting the stops. This will bleed the system of air. Check the reservoir level and add fluid if necessary.

BELT ADJUSTMENT

1. Loosen the bolt on the adjuster arm.

2. Move the pump toward or away from the engine, until the belt can be depressed approximately $9/16$ in. at the midpoint between the two pulleys under moderate thumb pressure. If the tension adjustment is being made on a new belt, the deflection should only be about $7/16$ in., to allow for the initial stretching of the belt.

There is a raised bump on the top of the adjusting arm. If the belt has stretched to the point where the adjustment bolt is at or beyond the bump, the belt should be replaced.

BRAKE SYSTEM

Understanding the Brakes
HYDRAULIC SYSTEM

The brake pedal operates a hydraulic system that is used for 2 reasons. First, fluid under pressure can be carried to all parts of the car by small hoses or metal lines without taking up a lot of room or causing routing problems. Second, the hydraulic fluid offers a great mechanical advantage—little foot pressure is required on the pedal, but a great deal of pressure is generated at the wheels.

The brake pedal is linked to a piston in the brake master cylinder, which is filled with hydraulic brake fluid. The master cylinder consists of a cylinder, containing a small piston, and a fluid reservoir.

Modern master cylinders are actually 2 separate cylinders. These systems are called a dual circuit, because the front cylinder is connected to the front brakes and the rear cylinder to the rear brakes. (Some cars are connected diagonally.) The 2 cylinders are actually separated, allowing for emergency stopping power should one part of the system fail.

The entire hydraulic system from the master cylinder to the wheels is full of hydraulic brake fluid. When the brake pedal is depressed, the pistons in the master cylinder are forced to move, exerting tremendous force on the fluid in the lines. The fluid has nowhere to go, and forces the wheel cylinder piston (drum brakes) or caliper pistons (disc brakes) to exert pressure on the brake shoes or pads. The resulting friction between the brake shoe and wheel drum or the brake pad and disc slows the car down and eventually stops it.

Also attached to the brake pedal is a switch which lights the brake lights as the pedal is depressed. The lights stay on until the brake pedal is released and returns to its normal position.

Each wheel cylinder in a drum brake system contains 2 pistons, one at either end, which push outward in opposite directions. In disc brake systems, the wheel cylinders are part of the caliper (there can be as many as 4 or as few as 1). Whether disc or drum type, all pistons use some type of rubber seal to prevent leakage around the piston, and a rubber dust boot seals the outer ends of the wheel cylinders against dirt and moisture.

When the brake pedal is released, a spring pushes the master cylinder pistons back to their normal position. Check valves in the master cylinder piston allow fluid to flow toward the wheel cylinders or calipers as the piston returns. Then as the brake shoe return springs pull the brake shoes back to the released position, excess fluid returns to the

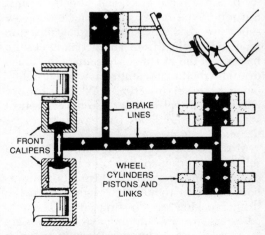

Hydraulic system schematic

master cylinder through compensating ports, which have been uncovered as the pistons move back. Any fluid that has leaked from the system will also be replaced through the compensating ports.

All dual circuit brake systems use a switch to activate a light, warning of brake failure. The switch is located in a valve mounted near the master cylinder. A piston in the valve receives pressure on each end from the front and rear brake circuits. When the pressures are balanced, the piston remains stationary, but when one circuit has a leak, greater pressure during the application of the brakes will force the piston to one side or the other, closing the switch and activating the warning light.

Disc brake systems also have a metering valve to prevent the front disc brakes from engaging before the rear brakes have contacted the drums. This ensures that the front brakes will not normally be used alone to stop the car. Approportioning valve is also used to limit pressure to the rear brakes to prevent rear wheel lock-up during hard braking.

DRUM BRAKES

Drum brakes use two brake shoes mounted on a stationary backing plate. These shoes are positioned inside a circular cast iron drum which rotates with the wheel assembly. The shoes are held in place by springs; this allows them to slide toward the drums (when they are applied) while keeping the linings and drums in alignment. The shoes are actuated by a wheel cylinder which is usually mounted at the top of the backing plate. When the brakes are applied, hydraulic pressure forces the wheel cylinder's two actuating links outward. Since these links bear directly against the top of the brake shoes, the tops of the shoes are then forced outward against the inner side of the drum. This action forces the bottoms of the two shoes to contact the brake drum by rotating the entire assembly slightly (known as servo action). When pressure within the wheel cylinder is relieved, return springs pull the shoes back away from the drum.

Most modern drum brakes are designed to self-adjust during application when the vehicle is moving in reverse. This motion causes both shoes to rotate very slightly with the drum, rocking an adjusting lever. The self-adjusters are only intended to compensate for normal wear. Although the adjustment is "automatic," there is a definite method to actuate the self-adjuster, which is done during normal driving. Driving the car in reverse and applying the brakes usually activates the automatic adjusters. If the brake pedal was low, you should be able to feel an increase in the height of the brake pedal.

DISC BRAKES

Instead of the traditional expanding brakes that press outward against a circular drum, disc brake systems utilize a cast iron disc with brake pads positioned on either side of it. Braking effect is achieved in a manner similar to the way you would squeeze a spinning disc between your fingers. The disc (rotor) is a one-piece casting with cooling fins between the two braking surfaces. This enables air to circulate between the braking surfaces making them less sensitive to heat buildup and more resistant to fade. Dirt and water do not affect braking action since contaminants are thrown off by the centrifugal action of the rotor or scraped off by the pads. Also, the equal clamping action of the two brake pads tends to ensure uniform, straightline stops. All disc brakes are inherently self-adjusting.

There are three general types of disc brake:

1) A fixed caliper, four-piston type.
2) A floating caliper, single piston type.
3) A sliding caliper, single piston type.

The fixed caliper design uses two pistons mounted on either side of the rotor (in each side of the caliper). The caliper is mounted rigidly and does not move.

The sliding and floating designs are quite similar and often considered as one. The pad on the inside of the rotor is moved into contact with the rotor by hydraulic force. The caliper, which is not held in a fixed position, moves slightly, bringing the outside pad into contact with the rotor. There are various methods of attaching floating calipers; some pivot at the bottom or top, and some slide on mounting bolts.

POWER BRAKE BOOSTERS

Power brakes operate just as standard brake systems except in the actuation of the master cylinder pistons. A vacuum diaphragm is located behind the master cylinder and assists the driver in applying the brakes, reducing both the effort and travel he must put into moving the brake pedal.

The vacuum diaphragm housing is connected to the intake manifold by a vacuum hose. A check valve at the point where the hose enters the diaphragm housing, ensures that during periods of low manifold vacuum brake assist vacuum will not be lost.

Depressing the brake pedal closes off the vacuum source and allows atmospheric pressure to enter on one side of the diaphragm. This causes the master cylinder pistons to move and apply the brakes. When the brake pedal is released, vacuum is applied to both sides of the diaphragm, and return springs return the diaphragm and master cylinder pistons to the released position. If the vacuum fails, the brake pedal rod will butt against the end of the master cylinder actuating rod, and direct mechanical application will occur as the pedal is depressed.

The hydraulic and mechanical problems that apply to conventional brake systems also apply to power brakes.

Honda uses a dual hydraulic system, with the brakes connected diagonally. In other words, the right front and left rear brakes are on the same hydraulic line and the left front and right rear are on the other line. This has the added advantage of front disc emergency braking, should either of the hydraulic systems fail. The diagonal rear brake serves to counteract the sway from single front disc braking.

A leading/trailing drum brake is used for the rear brakes, with disc brakes for the front. All Hondas are equipped with a brake warning light, which is activated when a defect in the brake system occurs.

Adjustments
BRAKE PEDAL FREE-PLAY

Free-play is the distance the pedal travels from the stop (brake light switch) until the pushrod actuates the master cylinder.

To check free-play, first measure the distance (with the carpet removed) from the floor to the brake pedal. Then disconnect the return spring and again measure the distance from the floor to the brake pedal. The difference between the two measurements is the pedal free-play. The specified free-play is 0.04–0.20 in. Free-play adjustment is made by loosening the locknut on the brake light switch and rotating the switch body until the specified clearance is obtained.

CAUTION: *If there is no free-play, the master cylinder pistons will not return to their stops. This can block the compensating ports, which will prevent the brake*

pads and linings from returning fully when the pedal is released. This will result in rapid brake burn-up. Free-play provides a safety factor against normal rubber swell and expansion or deflection of body parts and pedal linkage.

REAR DRUM BRAKE ADJUSTMENT

1. Block the front wheels, release the parking brake and raise the rear of the car, supporting it with safety stands.
2. Depress the brake pedal two or three times and release.
3. The adjuster is located on the inboard side, underneath the control arm. Turn the adjuster clockwise until the wheel no longer turns.
4. Back off the adjuster two (2) clicks and turn the wheel to see if the brake shoes are dragging. If they are dragging, back off the adjuster one more click.

Drum brake adjustment

FRONT DISC BRAKES

Front disc brakes require no adjustment, as hydraulic pressure maintains the proper brake pad-to-disc contact at all times.

NOTE: *Because of this, the brake fluid level should be checked regularly (see Chapter 1).*

HYDRAULIC SYSTEM

The hydraulic system is composed of the master cylinder and brake booster, the brake lines, the brake pressure differential valve(s), and the wheel cylinders (drum brakes) and calipers (disc brakes).

The master cylinder serves as a brake fluid reservoir and (along with the booster) as a hydraulic pump. Brake fluid is stored in the two sections of the master cylinder. Each section corresponds to each part of the dual braking system. This tandem master cylinder is required by Federal law as a safety device.

When the brake pedal is depressed, it moves a piston mounted in the bottom of the master cylinder. The movement of this piston creates hydraulic pressure in the master cylinder. This pressure is carried to the wheel cylinders or the calipers by brake lines, passing through the pressure differential or proportioning valve.

When the hydraulic pressure reaches the wheels, after the pedal has been depressed, it enters the wheel cylinders or calipers. Here it comes into contact with a piston or pistons. The hydraulic pressure causes the piston(s) to move, which moves the brake shoes or pads (disc brakes), causing them to come into contact with the drums or rotors (disc brakes). Friction between the brake shoes and the drums causes the car to slow down. There is a relationship between the amount of pressure that is applied to the brake pedal and the amount of force which moves the brake shoes against the drums. Therefore, the harder the brake pedal is depressed, the quicker the car will stop.

Since a hydraulic system is one which operates on fluids, air is a natural enemy of the brake system. Air in the hydraulic system retards the passage of hydraulic pressure from the master cylinder to the wheels. Anytime a hydraulic component below the master cylinder is opened or removed, the system must be bled of air to ensure proper operation. Air trapped in the hydraulic system can also cause the brake warning light to come on, even though the system has not failed. This is especially true after repairs have been performed on the system.

Master Cylinder

REMOVAL AND INSTALLATION

Before removing the master cylinder, cover the body surfaces with fender covers and rags to prevent damage to painted surfaces by brake fluid.

1. Disconnect the brake lines at the master cylinder.

2. Remove the master cylinder-to-vacuum booster attaching bolts and remove the master cylinder from the car.

3. To install, reverse the removal procedure. Before operating the car, you must bleed the brake system (see below).

DISASSEMBLY AND OVERHAUL

1. Remove the fluid reservoir caps and floats, and drain the reservoirs.

2. Loosen the retaining clamps and remove the reservoirs.

3. Remove the primary piston stop bolt.

4. Remove the piston retaining clip and washer, and remove the primary piston.

5. Wrap a rag around the end of the master cylinder, so that it blocks the bore. Hold your finger over the stop bolt hole and direct a small amount of compressed air into the primary outlet. This should slide the primary piston to the end of the master cylinder bore, so that it can be removed.

6. Remove the two union caps, washers, check valves and springs.

Disassembled master cylinder

Closeup of master cylinder stop bolt

Removing retaining clip

Piston removal

c. Tighten the union cap and stop bolts securely.

BLEEDING

When it is necessary to flush the brake hydraulic system because of parts replacement or fluid contamination, the following procedure should be observed:

1. Loosen the wheel cylinder bleeder screw. Drain the brake fluid by pumping the brake pedal. Pump the pedal until all of the old fluid has been pumped out and replaced by new fluid.

2. The flushing procedure should be performed in the following sequence:

    a. Bleed the left front brake;
    b. Bleed the right rear brake;
    c. Bleed the right front brake;
    d. Bleed the left rear brake.

3. Bleed the back of the master cylinder before the front, through the two bleed valves. Fasten one end of a plastic tube onto the bleed valve and immerse the other end in a clear jar filled with brake fluid. When air bubbles cease to emerge from the end of the tubing, the bleeding is completed. Be sure to keep the fluid reservoir filled at all times during the bleeding process so air does not enter the system.

CAUTION: *Brake fluid is adversely affected by contamination from dirt, au-*

7. For overhaul, check the following:

    a. Clogged orifices in the pistons and cylinder;

    b. Damage to the reservoir attaching surface;

    c. Damage to the check valves;

    d. Wear or damage to the piston cups;

    e. The clearance between the master cylinder bore and the pistons. The clearance should be 0.0008–0.0050 in.

8. Assembly of the master cylinder is the reverse of the disassembly procedures. Be sure to check the following:

    a. The check valves and piston cups should be replaced when the master cylinder is assembled, regardless of their condition;

    b. Apply a thin coat of brake fluid to the pistons before installing. When installing the pistons, push in while rotating to prevent damage to the piston cups;

Closeup of front bleeder

Bleeding the rear brakes

tomative petroleum products and water.
Contaminants can plug parts of the hydraulic system, causing rapid wear or
swelling of rubber parts and lower the boil-
ing point of the fluid. *KEEP FLUID
CLEAN.*

Vacuum Booster

INSPECTION

A preliminary check of the vacuum booster
can be made as follows:

    a. Depress the brake pedal several
times using normal pressure. Make sure
that the pedal height does not vary;

    b. Hold the pedal in the depressed po-
sition and start the engine. The pedal
should drop slightly;

    c. Hold the pedal in the above position
and stop the engine. The pedal should stay
in the depressed position for approximately 30 seconds;

    d. If the pedal does not drop when the
engine is started or rises after the engine is
stopped, the booster is not functioning
properly.

REMOVAL AND INSTALLATION

    1. Disconnect the vacuum hose at the
booster.

    2. Disconnect the brake lines at the mas-
ter cylinder.

    3. Remove the brake pedal-to-booster link
pin and the four nuts retaining the booster.
The pushrod and nuts are located inside the
car on the passenger side, under the dashboard.

    4. Remove the booster with the master
cylinder attached.

    5. To install, reverse the removal proce-
dure. Don't forget to bleed the brake system
before operating the car.

FRONT DISC BRAKES

The major components of the disc brake system are the brake pads, the caliper, and the
rotor (disc). The caliper is similar in function
to the wheel cylinder used with drum brakes,
and the rotor is similar to the brake drum
used in drum brakes.

    The major difference between drum
brakes and disc brakes is that with drum
brakes, the wheel cylinder forces the brake
shoes *out* against the brake drum to stop the
car, while with disc brakes, the caliper forces
the brake pads *inward* to squeeze the rotor
and stop the car. The biggest advantage of
disc brakes over drum brakes is that the caliper and brake pads enclose only a small portion of the rotor, leaving the rest of it exposed
to outside air. This aids in rapid heat dissipation, reducing brake fade, and throws off
water fast, too.

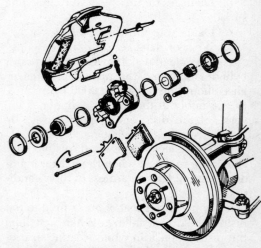

Exploded view of the disc brake components

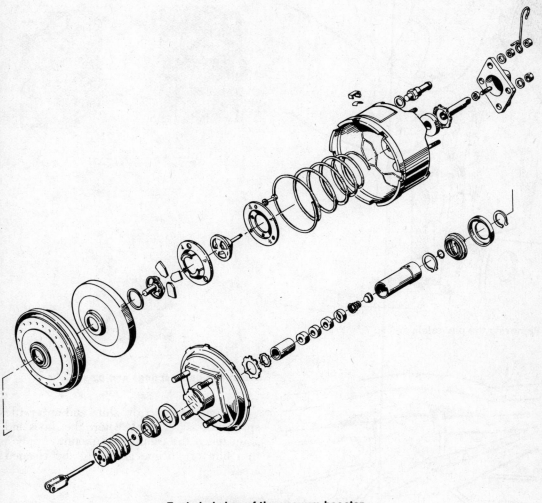

Exploded view of the vacuum booster

Disc Brake Pads

REMOVAL AND INSTALLATION

1973–78 Models

1. After removing the wheel, remove the pad retaining clip which is fitted in the holes of the pad retaining pins.

2. Remove the two retaining pins and fitting springs with pliers. When removing them, care must be taken to prevent the springs from flying apart.

3. The front brake pad can be removed, together with the shim, after removing the springs and pins. If the pads are difficult to remove, open the bleeder valve and move the caliper in the direction of the piston. The pads will become loose and can be easily removed.

NOTE: *After the pads are removed, the brake pedal must not be touched.*

The disc pads should be replaced when approximately 0.08 in. lining thickness remains (thickness of lining material only).

To provide space for installing the pad, loosen the bleed valve and push the inner piston back into the cylinder. Also push back the outer piston by applying pressure to the caliper. After providing space for the pads, close the bleed valve and insert the pad. Insert a shim behind each pad with the arrow on the shim pointing up. Incorrect installation of the shims can cause squealing brakes.

1979–84 Models

1. Raise and support the car. Remove the wheels.

2. Remove the lower caliper support pin and pivot the caliper up and away from the rotor.

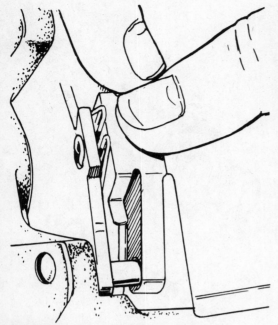

Removing the pad retaining clip

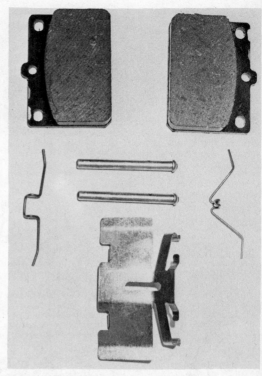

Disc brake pads, springs and pins

3. Remove the pads, shim and anti-rattle spring. Clean all points where the shoes and shim touch the caliper and mount. Apply a thin film of silicone grease to the cleaned areas.

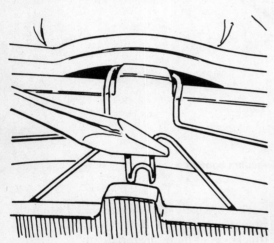

Removing the retaining pin springs

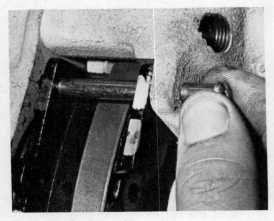

Retaining pin removal

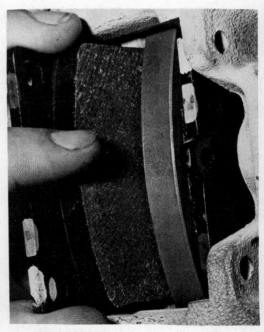

Removing the pads

Closeup showing retaining pins

Caliper housing removal

To install, reverse the removal procedure. Be sure to inspect all parts before installing and bleed the brake system before operating the car.

INSPECTION AND OVERHAUL

NOTE: *Wash all parts in brake fluid. Do not use cleaning solvent or gasoline.*

1. Remove the inner and outer pad springs and pin clips. Then remove the pins and pads.

NOTE: *The springs are different, so note the location and method of installation before removing.*

2. Push the yoke toward the rear (inboard side) of the cylinder, until it is free to separate the yoke from the cylinder. You may

4. Place the anti-rattle springs in position.

5. Install the pads with the shim against the outside shoe.

6. Loosen the bleed screw slightly and push in the caliper piston to allow mounting of the caliper over the rotor. Tighten the bleed screw.

7. Pivot the caliper down over the rotor and install the lower support pin. Tighten the pin to 13 ft. lb.

Disc Brake Calipers

REMOVAL AND INSTALLATION

All Models

1. Raise the front of the car and support it with safety stands. Remove the front wheels.

2. Loosen the brake line at the wheel cylinder.

3. The caliper housing is mounted to the knuckle with two bolts located behind the cylinder. Remove these bolts and the caliper.

Retaining ring removal

Piston removal

Piston seal

Note the discoloration in the caliper. If it cannot
be cleaned up easily, it will have to be replaced

have to tap lightly with a plastic hammer
(where the mounting bolts are located) to
remove the cylinder. Exercise extreme care
to avoid damaging the cylinder body. If only
the cylinder body moves, without the outer
piston, a gentle tap on the piston should
loosen it.

3. To dismantle the cylinder, first remove
the retaining rings at both ends of the cylinder with a screwdriver, being careful not to
damage the rubber boot.

4. Both pistons can be removed from the
cylinder body either by pushing through one
end with a wooden rod or by blowing compressed air into the cylinder inlet port.

NOTE: *If the wheel cylinder pistons are removed for any reason, the piston seals
must be replaced.*

5. Remove the piston seals, installed on
the inside of the cylinder at both ends, with a
screwdriver.

6. Inspect the caliper operation. If the lining wear differs greatly between the inner
and outer pads, the caliper may be unable to
move properly due to rust and dirt on the
sliding surfaces. Clean the sliding part of the
caliper and apply brake grease.

NOTE: *All brake parts are critical items. If
there is any question as to the service-
ability of any brake part—replace it.*

7. Check the piston-to-cylinder clearance.
The specified clearance is 0.0008–0.005 in.
Also check the pistons and cylinder bore for
scuffing and scratching.

8. Check the dust covers, retaining rings,
nylon retainers and all other parts for wear or
damage.

9. To reassemble the caliper, reverse the
removal procedure. Bleed the brake system.

Installing piston in caliper

Brake Disc
REMOVAL AND INSTALLATION

NOTE: *The following procedure for the brake disc removal necessitates the use of a hydraulic press. You will have to go to a machine or auto shop equipped with a press. Do not attempt this procedure without a press.*

1. Raise the front of the car and support it with safety stands. Remove the front wheels.
2. Remove the center spindle nuts.
3. Remove the caliper assembly. Do not let the caliper assembly hang by the brake hose.
4. Use a slide hammer with a hub puller attachment, or a conventional hub puller, to extract the hub with the disc attached.
5. Remove the four bolts and separate the hub and disc.
6. Remove the knuckle from the car (see Chapter 8).
7. Remove the wheel bearings from the knuckle (see below).

NOTE: *If, for any reason, the hub is removed, the front wheel bearings must be replaced.*

8. To install the disc, you have to use a hydraulic press for both the bearings and the

Checking disc runout

hub. After installing the bearings (see below), install the front hub using the special base (tool no. 07965-6340300) and drifts (tool no. 07965-6340100 and 07965-6340200). Position the hub with the knuckle underneath on the base and press it down through the base.

INSPECTION

1. The brake disc develops circular scores after long or even short usage when there is frequent braking. Excessive scoring not only causes a squealing brake, but also shortens the service life of the brake pads. However, light scoring of the disc surface, not exceeding 0.015 in. in depth, will result from normal use and is not detrimental to brake operation.

NOTE: *Differences in the left and right disc surfaces can result in uneven braking.*

2. Disc run-out is the movement of the disc from side-to-side. Place a dial indicator in the middle of the pad wear area and turn the disc, while checking the indicator. If disc run-out exceeds 0.006 in., replace the disc.
3. Disc parallelism is the measurement of variations in disc thickness at several locations on the disc circumference. To measure parallelism, place a mark on the disc and measure the disc thickness with a micrometer. Repeat this measurement at eight (8) equal increments on the circumference of the disc. If the measurements vary more than 0.0028 in., replace the disc.

NOTE: *Only the outer portion of the disc can be checked while installed on the car. If the installed parallelism check is within specifications, but you have reason to suspect that parallelism is the problem, then remove the disc and repeat the check using the center of pad wear for a checking point.*

Wheel Bearings
REMOVAL AND INSTALLATION

NOTE: *The following procedure for the Honda wheel bearing removal and installation necessitates the use of an hydraulic press. You will have to go to a machine or auto shop equipped with a press. Do not attempt this procedure without a press.*

1. Raise the front of the car and support it with safety stands. Remove the front wheel.
2. Remove the caliper assembly from the

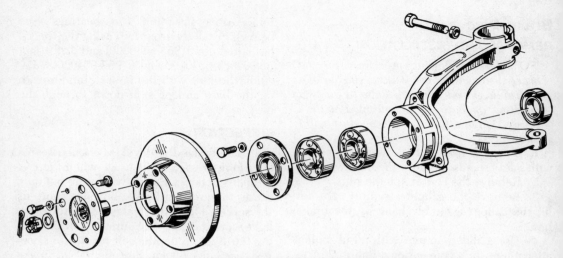

Exploded view of front wheel bearings, rotor, and related parts

brake disc and separate the tie-rod ball joint and lower ball joint from the knuckle (see Chapter 8).

3. Loosen the lockbolt which retains the front strut in the knuckle. Tap the top of the knuckle with a hammer and slide it off the shock. Remove the knuckle and hub by sliding the driveshaft out of the hub.

4. Remove the wheel bearing dust cover on the inboard side of the knuckle.

5. Remove the four bolts which hold the brake disc onto the hub. Remove the splashguard by removing the three retaining screws.

6. Remove the outer bearing retainer.

7. Remove the wheel bearings by supporting the knuckle in a hydraulic press, using two support plates (or special tool no. 07965-6340300). Make sure that the plates do not overlap the outer bearing race. Now use a proper sized driver (or tool no. 07947-6340400) and handle (tool no. 07949-6110000) to remove the bearings.

NOTE: *Whenever the wheel bearings are removed, always replace with a new set of bearings and outer dust seal.*

8. Pack each bearing with grease before installing (see below).

9. To install the bearings, press them into the knuckle using the same support plates as above, plus the installing base (tool no. 07965-634040). Use the same driver and handle you used to remove the bearing.

NOTE: *The front wheel bearings are the angular contact type. It is important that they be installed with the manufacturer's markings facing inward.*

10. Use the press to install the front hub (see above).

11. The rest of installation is the reverse of the removal procedure.

CLEANING AND REPACKING

1. Clean all old grease from the driveshafts spindles on the car.

2. Remove all old grease from the hub and knuckle and thoroughly dry and wipe clean all components.

3. When fitting new bearings, you must pack them with wheel bearing grease. To do this, place a glob of grease in your left palm, then, holding one of the bearings in your right hand, drag the face of the bearing heavily through the grease. This must be done to work as much grease as possible through the ball bearings and the cage. Turn the bearing and continue to pull it through the grease, until the grease is thoroughly packed between the bearing balls and the cage, all around the bearing. Repeat this operation until all of the bearings are packed with grease.

4. Pack the inside of the rotor and knuckle hub with a moderate amount of grease. Do not overload the hub with grease.

5. Apply a small amount of grease to the spindle and to the lip of the inner seal before installing.

6. To install the bearings, check the above procedures.

7. See Chapter 1 for adjustment and spindle nut torque.

REAR DRUM BRAKES

All Hondas employ a leading/trailing type of drum brake, in which there are two curved brake shoes supported by an anchor plate and wheel cylinder. When the brake pedal is depressed and hydraulic pressure is delivered to the wheel cylinder, the wheel cylinder expands to force the shoes against the drum.

Friction between the brake shoes and the drum causes the car to slow down and stop. When the brake pedal is released, the brake shoe return springs move the brakes away from the drum. If the lining on the brakes becomes contaminated or if the lining or drum becomes grooved, the engagement of the brakes and drum will become very harsh, causing the brakes to lock up and/or squeal. If the brake shoes on one wheel contact the drum before the same action occurs in the other wheels, the brakes will pull to one side when applied.

Brake Drums

REMOVAL AND INSTALLATION

All Models

1. Raise the rear of the car and support it with safety stands. Remove the rear wheels. Make sure that the parking brake is *off*.

2. Remove the bearing cap and the castle nut.

3. Pull off the rear brake drum. If the drum is difficult to remove, use a brake drum

Bearing cap removal on the Civic

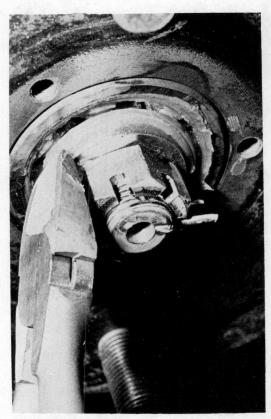

Cotter pin removal

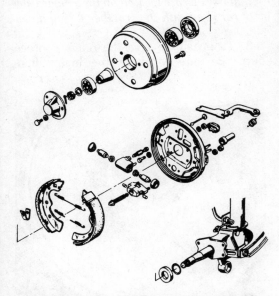

Exploded view of rear drum brake assembly— Civic sedan and hatchback

puller, or a front hub puller and slide hammer.

4. To install, reverse the removal procedures.

Tighten the rear hub nut to 83 ft lbs on 1973–79 Civics. On the Accord, Prelude and

Castle nut removal

Bearing cap removal on the Accord and Prelude

Removing the rear drum with a slide hammer

1980 and later Civics which have a tapered roller bearing, use the following procedure:

1. Tighten the hub nut to 18 ft lbs.
2. Rotate the drum by hand several times and then loosen the nut.
3. Torque the nut to 3.6 ft lbs.
4. If the spindle nut is not aligned with the hole in spindle, tighten the nut just enough to align the nut and the hole.
5. Insert the cotter pin holder and a new cotter pin.

INSPECTION

Check the drum for cracks and the inner surface of the shoe for excessive wear and damage. The inner diameter (I.D.) of the drum should be no more than specifications, nor should the drum be more than 0.004 in. out-of-round.

Brake Shoes

REMOVAL AND INSTALLATION

All Models

1. Remove the brake drum (see above).
2. Remove the tension pin clips and the two brake return springs. Then remove the shoes. If you are installing new shoes, back off the adjusters.

CAUTION: *The upper and lower brake shoe return springs on the sedan are different and should not be interchanged. The upper spring is designed so that the spring coils are located on the outboard side of the shoe, while the lower spring is designed so that its coils are located on the inboard side of the shoe with the crossbar facing downward.*

3. To install, reverse the removal procedure. Be sure to check the brake lining

Inspecting the drum for cracks

Rear brake shoes

Closeup of brake shoe retaining clip

Torquing the rear hub nut on the Civic

thickness before assembly. If the thickness is less than 0.08 in., replace the lining.

Wheel Cylinders

REMOVAL AND INSTALLATION

All Models

1. Remove the brake drum and shoes (see above).

Disassembled wheel cylinder

2. Disconnect the parking brake cable and brake lines at the backing plate. Be sure to have a drip pan to catch the brake fluid.

3. Remove the two wheel cylinder retaining nuts on the inboard side of the backing plate and remove the wheel cylinder.

4. To install, reverse the removal procedure. When assembling, apply a thin coat of grease to the grooves of the wheel cylinder piston and the sliding surfaces of the backing plate.

OVERHAUL

Remove the wheel cylinder dust seals from the grooves to permit the removal of the cylinder pistons.

Wash all parts in fresh brake fluid and check the cylinder bore and pistons for scratches and other damage, replacing where necessary. Check the clearance between the piston and the cylinder bore, by taking the difference between the piston diameter and the bore diameter. The specified clearance is 0.0008–0.004 in.

When assembling the wheel cylinder, apply a coat of brake fluid to the pistons, piston cups and cylinder walls.

HANDBRAKE (PARKING BRAKE)

The parking brake is a mechanical type which applies braking force to the rear wheels, through the rear brake shoes. The cable, which is attached to the tail end of the parking brake lever, extends to the equalizer and to the right and left rear brakes. When the lever is pulled, the cable becomes taut, pulling both the right and left parking brake arms fitted to the brake shoes.

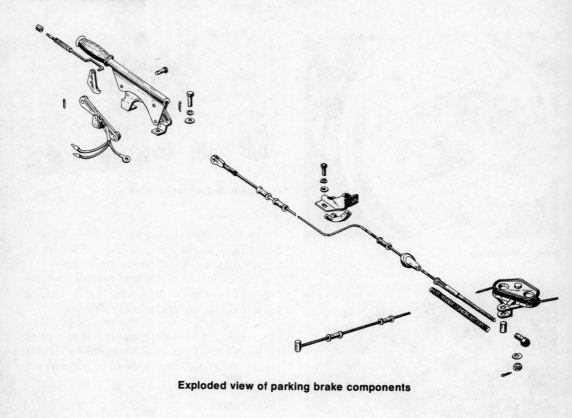

Exploded view of parking brake components

Brake Specifications

(All measurements given are in in. unless noted)

Year	Model	Lug Nut Torque (ft. lbs.)	Brake Disc		Brake Drum		Minimum Lining Thickness	
			Minimum Thickness	Maximum Run-Out	Inner Diameter	Max. Machine O/S	Front	Rear
'73–'83	Civic Sedan, Hatchback, (Wagon '80–'83)	51–65	0.354 ①	0.006	7.087 ⑥	7.126 ⑦	0.063	0.079
'73–'79	Civic Wagon	51–65	0.449	0.006	7.874	7.93	0.300	0.08
'76–'82	Accord, Prelude	51–65 ⑧	0.433 ③	0.006	7.087 ④	7.126 ⑤	0.039 ②	0.079
'83	Accord	80	0.60	0.006	7.87	7.91	0.063	0.079
'83	Prelude	80	0.59	0.004	7.87	7.91	0.118	0.079
'84–'85	Civic	80	0.59 ⑨	0.006	7.09 ⑥	7.13 ⑦	0.120	0.080
'84–'85	Accord	80	0.67	0.006	7.87	7.91	0.120	0.080
'84–'85	Prelude	80	0.67 ⑩	0.004	N.A.	N.A.	0.120	0.060

N.A. Not applicable
① '81–'83—0.394 exc. '83 1500—0.60
　'80 Wagon—0.394
② 0.063—'80–'82
③ '80—0.4126, '81—0.4134, '82—0.60
④ '82—7.87
⑤ '82—7.91
⑥ Wagon—7.87
⑦ Wagon—7.91
⑧ Prelude: 80
⑨ Civic: 1300 CRX 0.35, 1300 Hatchback 0.39
⑩ Rear disc: 0.31

CABLE REMOVAL AND INSTALLATION

1. Remove the adjusting nut from the equalizer mounted on the rear axle or in the console (on '82–84 Accord and '83–84 Prelude and '84 Civic) and separate the cable from the equalizer.

2. Set the parking brake to a fully released position and remove the cotter pin from the side of the brake lever.

3. After removing the cotter pin, pull out the pin which connects the cable and the lever.

4. Detach the cable from the guides at the front and right side of the fuel tank and remove the cable.

5. To install, reverse the removal procedure, making sure that grease is applied to the cable and the guides.

ADJUSTMENT

Inspect the following items:

a. Check the ratchet for wear;

b. Check the cables for wear or damage and the cable guide and equalizer for looseness;

c. Check the equalizer cable where it contacts the equalizer and apply grease if necessary;

d. Check the rear brake adjustment.

The rear wheels should be locked when the handbrake lever is pulled 1 to 5 notches on the ratchet for 1973–78 cars and 3 to 7 notches on the ratchet for 1979–84 cars. Adjustment is made by lifting the lever one notch and turning the nut located at the equalizer, between the lower control arms or console.

Troubleshooting

This section is designed to aid in the quick, accurate diagnosis of automotive problems. While automotive repairs can be made by many people, accurate troubleshooting is a rare skill for the amateur and professional alike.

In its simplest state, troubleshooting is an exercise in logic. It is essential to realize that an automobile is really composed of a series of systems. Some of these systems are interrelated; others are not. Automobiles operate within a framework of logical rules and physical laws, and the key to troubleshooting is a good understanding of all the automotive systems.

This section breaks the car or truck down into its component systems, allowing the problem to be isolated. The charts and diagnostic road maps list the most common problems and the most probable causes of trouble. Obviously it would be impossible to list every possible problem that could happen along with every possible cause, but it will locate MOST problems and eliminate a lot of unnecessary guesswork. The systematic format will locate problems within a given system, but, because many automotive systems are interrelated, the solution to your particular problem may be found in a number of systems on the car or truck.

USING THE TROUBLESHOOTING CHARTS

This book contains all of the specific information that the average do-it-yourself mechanic needs to repair and maintain his or her car or truck. The troubleshooting charts are designed to be used in conjunction with the specific procedures and information in the text. For instance, troubleshooting a point-type ignition system is fairly standard for all models, but you may be directed to the text to find procedures for troubleshooting an individual type of electronic ignition. You will also have to refer to the specification charts throughout the book for specifications applicable to your car or truck.

TOOLS AND EQUIPMENT

The tools illustrated in Chapter 1 (plus two more diagnostic pieces) will be adequate to troubleshoot most problems. The two other tools needed are a voltmeter and an ohmmeter. These can be purchased separately or in combination, known as a VOM meter.

In the event that other tools are required, they will be noted in the procedures.

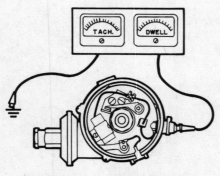

Tach-dwell hooked-up to distributor

Troubleshooting Engine Problems

See Chapters 2, 3, 4 for more information and service procedures.

Index to Systems

System	To Test	Group
Battery	Engine need not be running	1
Starting system	Engine need not be running	2
Primary electrical system	Engine need not be running	3
Secondary electrical system	Engine need not be running	4
Fuel system	Engine need not be running	5
Engine compression	Engine need not be running	6
Engine vacuum	Engine must be running	7
Secondary electrical system	Engine must be running	8
Valve train	Engine must be running	9
Exhaust system	Engine must be running	10
Cooling system	Engine must be running	11
Engine lubrication	Engine must be running	12

Index to Problems

Problem: Symptom	Begin at Specific Diagnosis, Number ____
Engine Won't Start:	
Starter doesn't turn	1.1, 2.1
Starter turns, engine doesn't	2.1
Starter turns engine very slowly	1.1, 2.4
Starter turns engine normally	3.1, 4.1
Starter turns engine very quickly	6.1
Engine fires intermittently	4.1
Engine fires consistently	5.1, 6.1
Engine Runs Poorly:	
Hard starting	3.1, 4.1, 5.1, 8.1
Rough idle	4.1, 5.1, 8.1
Stalling	3.1, 4.1, 5.1, 8.1
Engine dies at high speeds	4.1, 5.1
Hesitation (on acceleration from standing stop)	5.1, 8.1
Poor pickup	4.1, 5.1, 8.1
Lack of power	3.1, 4.1, 5.1, 8.1
Backfire through the carburetor	4.1, 8.1, 9.1
Backfire through the exhaust	4.1, 8.1, 9.1
Blue exhaust gases	6.1, 7.1
Black exhaust gases	5.1
Running on (after the ignition is shut off)	3.1, 8.1
Susceptible to moisture	4.1
Engine misfires under load	4.1, 7.1, 8.4, 9.1
Engine misfires at speed	4.1, 8.4
Engine misfires at idle	3.1, 4.1, 5.1, 7.1, 8.4

Sample Section

Test and Procedure	Results and Indications	Proceed to
4.1—Check for spark: Hold each spark plug wire approximately ¼″ from ground with gloves or a heavy, dry rag. Crank the engine and observe the spark.	→ If no spark is evident:	→ 4.2
	→ If spark is good in some cases:	→ 4.3
	→ If spark is good in all cases:	→ 4.6

Specific Diagnosis

This section is arranged so that following each test, instructions are given to proceed to another, until a problem is diagnosed.

Section 1—Battery

Test and Procedure	Results and Indications	Proceed to
1.1—Inspect the battery visually for case condition (corrosion, cracks) and water level.	If case is cracked, replace battery:	**1.4**
	If the case is intact, remove corrosion with a solution of baking soda and water (**CAUTION**: *do not get the solution into the battery*), and fill with water:	**1.2**

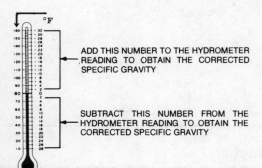

DIRT ON TOP OF BATTERY   PLUGGED VENT

CORROSION

LOOSE CABLE OR POSTS

CRACKS

LOW WATER LEVEL   **Inspect the battery case**

1.2—Check the battery cable connections: Insert a screwdriver between the battery post and the cable clamp. Turn the headlights on high beam, and observe them as the screwdriver is gently twisted to ensure good metal to metal contact.	If the lights brighten, remove and clean the clamp and post; coat the post with petroleum jelly, install and tighten the clamp:	**1.4**
	If no improvement is noted:	**1.3**

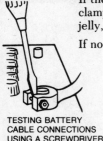

TESTING BATTERY CABLE CONNECTIONS USING A SCREWDRIVER

1.3—Test the state of charge of the battery using an individual cell tester or hydrometer.	If indicated, charge the battery. **NOTE:** *If no obvious reason exists for the low state of charge (i.e., battery age, prolonged storage), proceed to:*	**1.4**

ADD THIS NUMBER TO THE HYDROMETER READING TO OBTAIN THE CORRECTED SPECIFIC GRAVITY

SUBTRACT THIS NUMBER FROM THE HYDROMETER READING TO OBTAIN THE CORRECTED SPECIFIC GRAVITY

Specific Gravity (@ 80° F.)

Minimum	Battery Charge
1.260	100% Charged
1.230	75% Charged
1.200	50% Charged
1.170	25% Charged
1.140	Very Little Power Left
1.110	Completely Discharged

The effects of temperature on battery specific gravity (left) and amount of battery charge in relation to specific gravity (right)

1.4—Visually inspect battery cables for cracking, bad connection to ground, or bad connection to starter.	If necessary, tighten connections or replace the cables:	
		2.1

Section 2—Starting System
See Chapter 3 for service procedures

Test and Procedure	Results and Indications	Proceed to

Note: Tests in Group 2 are performed with coil high tension lead disconnected to prevent accidental starting.

Test and Procedure	Results and Indications	Proceed to
2.1—Test the starter motor and solenoid: Connect a jumper from the battery post of the solenoid (or relay) to the starter post of the solenoid (or relay).	If starter turns the engine normally:	**2.2**
	If the starter buzzes, or turns the engine very slowly:	**2.4**
	If no response, replace the solenoid (or relay).	**3.1**
	If the starter turns, but the engine doesn't, ensure that the flywheel ring gear is intact. If the gear is undamaged, replace the starter drive.	**3.1**
2.2—Determine whether ignition override switches are functioning properly (clutch start switch, neutral safety switch), by connecting a jumper across the switch(es), and turning the ignition switch to "start".	If starter operates, adjust or replace switch:	**3.1**
	If the starter doesn't operate:	**2.3**
2.3—Check the ignition switch "start" position: Connect a 12V test lamp or voltmeter between the starter post of the solenoid (or relay) and ground. Turn the ignition switch to the "start" position, and jiggle the key.	If the lamp doesn't light or the meter needle doesn't move when the switch is turned, check the ignition switch for loose connections, cracked insulation, or broken wires. Repair or replace as necessary:	**3.1**
	If the lamp flickers or needle moves when the key is jiggled, replace the ignition switch.	**3.3**

Checking the ignition switch "start" position

STARTER RELAY (IF EQUIPPED)

Test and Procedure	Results and Indications	Proceed to
2.4—Remove and bench test the starter, according to specifications in the engine electrical section.	If the starter does not meet specifications, repair or replace as needed:	**3.1**
	If the starter is operating properly:	**2.5**
2.5—Determine whether the engine can turn freely: Remove the spark plugs, and check for water in the cylinders. Check for water on the dipstick, or oil in the radiator. Attempt to turn the engine using an 18″ flex drive and socket on the crankshaft pulley nut or bolt.	If the engine will turn freely only with the spark plugs out, and hydrostatic lock (water in the cylinders) is ruled out, check valve timing:	**9.2**
	If engine will not turn freely, and it is known that the clutch and transmission are free, the engine must be disassembled for further evaluation:	**Chapter 3**

Section 3—Primary Electrical System

Test and Procedure	Results and Indications	Proceed to
3.1—Check the ignition switch "on" position: Connect a jumper wire between the distributor side of the coil and ground, and a 12V test lamp between the switch side of the coil and ground. Remove the high tension lead from the coil. Turn the ignition switch on and jiggle the key.	If the lamp lights:	**3.2**
	If the lamp flickers when the key is jiggled, replace the ignition switch:	**3.3**
	If the lamp doesn't light, check for loose or open connections. If none are found, remove the ignition switch and check for continuity. If the switch is faulty, replace it:	**3.3**

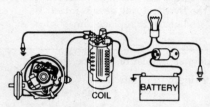

Checking the ignition switch "on" position

3.2—Check the ballast resistor or resistance wire for an open circuit, using an ohmmeter. See Chapter 3 for specific tests.	Replace the resistor or resistance wire if the resistance is zero. **NOTE: *Some ignition systems have no ballast resistor.***	**3.3**

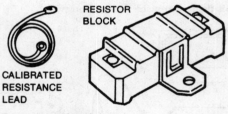

Two types of resistors

3.3—On point-type ignition systems, visually inspect the breaker points for burning, pitting or excessive wear. Gray coloring of the point contact surfaces is normal. Rotate the crankshaft until the contact heel rests on a high point of the distributor cam and adjust the point gap to specifications. On electronic ignition models, remove the distributor cap and visually inspect the armature. Ensure that the armature pin is in place, and that the armature is on tight and rotates when the engine is cranked. Make sure there are no cracks, chips or rounded edges on the armature.	If the breaker points are intact, clean the contact surfaces with fine emery cloth, and adjust the point gap to specifications. If the points are worn, replace them. On electronic systems, replace any parts which appear defective. If condition persists:	**3.4**

Test and Procedure	Results and Indications	Proceed to
3.4—On point-type ignition systems, connect a dwell-meter between the distributor primary lead and ground. Crank the engine and observe the point dwell angle. On electronic ignition systems, conduct a stator (magnetic pickup assembly) test. See Chapter 3.	On point-type systems, adjust the dwell angle if necessary. **NOTE:** *Increasing the point gap decreases the dwell angle and vice-versa.*	**3.6**
	If the dwell meter shows little or no reading;	**3.5**
	On electronic ignition systems, if the stator is bad, replace the stator. If the stator is good, proceed to the other tests in Chapter 3.	

WIDE GAP   NARROW GAP

CLOSE   OPEN

NORMAL DWELL

SMALL DWELL

INSUFFICIENT DWELL

LARGE DWELL

EXCESSIVE DWELL

Dwell is a function of point gap

3.5—On the point-type ignition systems, check the condenser for short: connect an ohmeter across the condenser body and the pigtail lead.	If any reading other than infinite is noted, replace the condenser	**3.6**

OHMMETER

Checking the condenser for short

3.6—Test the coil primary resistance: On point-type ignition systems, connect an ohmmeter across the coil primary terminals, and read the resistance on the low scale. Note whether an external ballast resistor or resistance wire is used. On electronic ignition systems, test the coil primary resistance as in Chapter 3.	Point-type ignition coils utilizing ballast resistors or resistance wires should have approximately 1.0 ohms resistance. Coils with internal resistors should have approximately 4.0 ohms resistance. If values far from the above are noted, replace the coil.	**4.1**

Check the coil primary resistance

Section 4—Secondary Electrical System
See Chapters 2–3 for service procedures

Test and Procedure	Results and Indications	Proceed to
4.1—Check for spark: Hold each spark plug wire approximately ¼" from ground with gloves or a heavy, dry rag. Crank the engine, and observe the spark.	If no spark is evident:	**4.2**
	If spark is good in some cylinders:	**4.3**
	If spark is good in all cylinders:	**4.6**

Check for spark at the plugs

Test and Procedure	Results and Indications	Proceed to
4.2—Check for spark at the coil high tension lead: Remove the coil high tension lead from the distributor and position it approximately ¼" from ground. Crank the engine and observe spark. **CAUTION:** *This test should not be performed on engines equipped with electronic ignition.*	If the spark is good and consistent:	**4.3**
	If the spark is good but intermittent, test the primary electrical system starting at 3.3:	**3.3**
	If the spark is weak or non-existent, replace the coil high tension lead, clean and tighten all connections and retest. If no improvement is noted:	**4.4**
4.3—Visually inspect the distributor cap and rotor for burned or corroded contacts, cracks, carbon tracks, or moisture. Also check the fit of the rotor on the distributor shaft (where applicable).	If moisture is present, dry thoroughly, and retest per 4.1:	**4.1**
	If burned or excessively corroded contacts, cracks, or carbon tracks are noted, replace the defective part(s) and retest per 4.1:	**4.1**
	If the rotor and cap appear intact, or are only slightly corroded, clean the contacts thoroughly (including the cap towers and spark plug wire ends) and retest per 4.1:	
	If the spark is good in all cases:	**4.6**
	If the spark is poor in all cases:	**4.5**

CORRODED OR LOOSE WIRE

EXCESSIVE WEAR OF BUTTON

HIGH RESISTANCE CARBON

ROTOR TIP BURNED AWAY

Inspect the distributor cap and rotor

Test and Procedure	Results and Indications	Proceed to

4.4—Check the coil secondary resistance: On point-type systems connect an ohmmeter across the distributor side of the coil and the coil tower. Read the resistance on the high scale of the ohmmeter. On electronic ignition systems, see Chapter 3 for specific tests.

The resistance of a satisfactory coil should be between 4,000 and 10,000 ohms. If resistance is considerably higher (i.e., 40,000 ohms) replace the coil and retest per 4.1. **NOTE:** *This does not apply to high performance coils.*

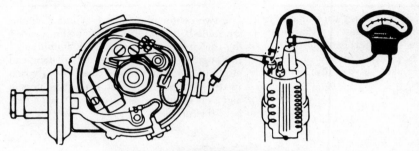

Testing the coil secondary resistance

4.5—Visually inspect the spark plug wires for cracking or brittleness. Ensure that no two wires are positioned so as to cause induction firing (adjacent and parallel). Remove each wire, one by one, and check resistance with an ohmmeter.

Replace any cracked or brittle wires. If any of the wires are defective, replace the entire set. Replace any wires with excessive resistance (over $8000\,\Omega$ per foot for suppression wire), and separate any wires that might cause induction firing.

4.6

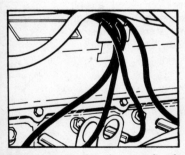

Misfiring can be the result of spark plug leads to adjacent, consecutively firing cylinders running parallel and too close together

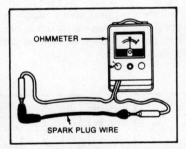

On point-type ignition systems, check the spark plug wires as shown. On electronic ignitions, do not remove the wire from the distributor cap terminal; instead, test through the cap

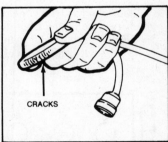

Spark plug wires can be checked visually by bending them in a loop over your finger. This will reveal any cracks, burned or broken insulation. Any wire with cracked insulation should be replaced

4.6—Remove the spark plugs, noting the cylinders from which they were removed, and evaluate according to the color photos in the middle of this book.

See following.

See following.

Test and Procedure	Results and Indications	Proceed to
4.7—Examine the location of all the plugs.	The following diagrams illustrate some of the conditions that the location of plugs will reveal.	**4.8**

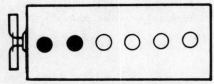

Two adjacent plugs are fouled in a 6-cylinder engine, 4-cylinder engine or either bank of a V-8. This is probably due to a blown head gasket between the two cylinders

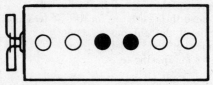

The two center plugs in a 6-cylinder engine are fouled. Raw fuel may be "boiled" out of the carburetor into the intake manifold after the engine is shut-off. Stop-start driving can also foul the center plugs, due to overly rich mixture. Proper float level, a new float needle and seat or use of an insulating spacer may help this problem

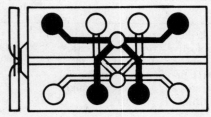

An unbalanced carburetor is indicated. Following the fuel flow on this particular design shows that the cylinders fed by the right-hand barrel are fouled from overly rich mixture, while the cylinders fed by the left-hand barrel are normal

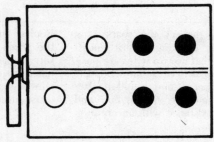

If the four rear plugs are overheated, a cooling system problem is suggested. A thorough cleaning of the cooling system may restore coolant circulation and cure the problem

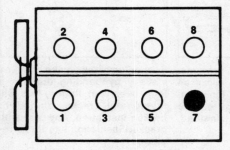

Finding one plug overheated may indicate an intake manifold leak near the affected cylinder. If the overheated plug is the second of two adjacent, consecutively firing plugs, it could be the result of ignition cross-firing. Separating the leads to these two plugs will eliminate cross-fire

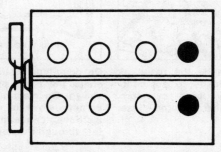

Occasionally, the two rear plugs in large, lightly used V-8's will become oil fouled. High oil consumption and smoky exhaust may also be noticed. It is probably due to plugged oil drain holes in the rear of the cylinder head, causing oil to be sucked in around the valve stems. This usually occurs in the rear cylinders first, because the engine slants that way

Test and Procedure	Results and Indications	Proceed to
4.8—Determine the static ignition timing. Using the crankshaft pulley timing marks as a guide, locate top dead center on the compression stroke of the number one cylinder.	The rotor should be pointing toward the No. 1 tower in the distributor cap, and, on electronic ignitions, the armature spoke for that cylinder should be lined up with the stator.	**4.8**
4.9—Check coil polarity: Connect a voltmeter negative lead to the coil high tension lead, and the positive lead to ground (**NOTE: *Reverse the hook-up for positive ground systems*). Crank the engine momentarily. **Checking coil polarity**	If the voltmeter reads up-scale, the polarity is correct: If the voltmeter reads down-scale, reverse the coil polarity (switch the primary leads):	**5.1** **5.1**

Section 5—Fuel System
See Chapter 4 for service procedures

Test and Procedure	Results and Indications	Proceed to
5.1—Determine that the air filter is functioning efficiently: Hold paper elements up to a strong light, and attempt to see light through the filter.	Clean permanent air filters in solvent (or manufacturer's recommendation), and allow to dry. Replace paper elements through which light cannot be seen:	**5.2**
5.2—Determine whether a flooding condition exists: Flooding is identified by a strong gasoline odor, and excessive gasoline present in the throttle bore(s) of the carburetor.	If flooding is not evident: If flooding is evident, permit the gasoline to dry for a few moments and restart. If flooding doesn't recur: If flooding is persistent:	**5.3** **5.7** **5.5**

If the engine floods repeatedly, check the choke butterfly flap

| **5.3**—Check that fuel is reaching the carburetor: Detach the fuel line at the carburetor inlet. Hold the end of the line in a cup (not styrofoam), and crank the engine. | If fuel flows smoothly: If fuel doesn't flow (**NOTE: *Make sure that there is fuel in the tank*), or flows erratically: | **5.7** **5.4** |

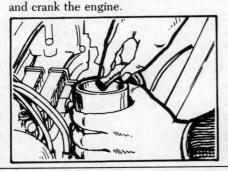

Check the fuel pump by disconnecting the output line (fuel pump-to-carburetor) at the carburetor and operating the starter briefly

Test and Procedure	Results and Indications	Proceed to
5.4—Test the fuel pump: Disconnect all fuel lines from the fuel pump. Hold a finger over the input fitting, crank the engine (with electric pump, turn the ignition or pump on); and feel for suction.	If suction is evident, blow out the fuel line to the tank with low pressure compressed air until bubbling is heard from the fuel filler neck. Also blow out the carburetor fuel line (both ends disconnected):	5.7
	If no suction is evident, replace or repair the fuel pump: **NOTE:** *Repeated oil fouling of the spark plugs, or a no-start condition, could be the result of a ruptured vacuum booster pump diaphragm, through which oil or gasoline is being drawn into the intake manifold (where applicable).*	5.7
5.5—Occasionally, small specks of dirt will clog the small jets and orifices in the carburetor. With the engine cold, hold a flat piece of wood or similar material over the carburetor, where possible, and crank the engine.	If the engine starts, but runs roughly the engine is probably not run enough. If the engine won't start:	5.9
5.6—Check the needle and seat: Tap the carburetor in the area of the needle and seat.	If flooding stops, a gasoline additive (e.g., Gumout) will often cure the problem:	5.7
	If flooding continues, check the fuel pump for excessive pressure at the carburetor (according to specifications). If the pressure is normal, the needle and seat must be removed and checked, and/or the float level adjusted:	5.7
5.7—Test the accelerator pump by looking into the throttle bores while operating the throttle.	If the accelerator pump appears to be operating normally:	5.8
	If the accelerator pump is not operating, the pump must be reconditioned. Where possible, service the pump with the carburetor(s) installed on the engine. If necessary, remove the carburetor. Prior to removal:	5.8

Check for gas at the carburetor by looking down the carburetor throat while someone moves the accelerator

Test and Procedure	Results and Indications	Proceed to
5.8—Determine whether the carburetor main fuel system is functioning: Spray a commercial starting fluid into the carburetor while attempting to start the engine.	If the engine starts, runs for a few seconds, and dies:	5.9
	If the engine doesn't start:	6.1

CHILTON'S
AUTO BODY
REPAIR TIPS

Tools and Materials • Step-by-Step Illustrated Procedures
How To Repair Dents, Scratches and Rust Holes
Spray Painting and Refinishing Tips

With a little practice, basic body repair procedures can be mastered by any do-it-yourself mechanic. The step-by-step repairs shown here can be applied to almost any type of auto body repair.

TOOLS & MATERIALS

You may already have basic tools, such as hammers and electric drills. Other tools unique to body repair — body hammers, grinding attachments, sanding blocks, dent puller, half-round plastic file and plastic spreaders — are relatively inexpensive and can be obtained wherever auto parts or auto body repair parts are sold. Portable air compressors and paint spray guns can be purchased or rented.

Auto Body Repair Kits

The best and most often used products are available to the do-it-yourselfer in kit form, from major manufacturers of auto body repair products. The same manufacturers also merchandise the individual products for use by pros.

Kits are available to make a wide variety of repairs, including holes, dents and scratches and fiberglass, and offer the advantage of buying the materials you'll need for the job. There is little waste or chance of materials going bad from not being used. Many kits may also contain basic body-working tools such as body files, sanding blocks and spreaders. Check the contents of the kit before buying your tools.

BODY REPAIR TIPS

Safety

Many of the products associated with auto body repair and refinishing contain toxic chemicals. Read all labels before opening containers and store them in a safe place and manner.

• Wear eye protection (safety goggles) when using power tools or when performing any operation that involves the removal of any type of material.

• Wear lung protection (disposable mask or respirator) when grinding, sanding or painting.

Sanding

1 Sand off paint before using a dent puller. When using a non-adhesive sanding disc, cover the back of the disc with an overlapping layer or two of masking tape and trim the edges. The disc will last considerably longer.

2 Use the circular motion of the sanding disc to grind *into* the edge of the repair. Grinding or sanding away from the jagged edge will only tear the sandpaper.

3 Use the palm of your hand flat on the panel to detect high and low spots. Do not use your fingertips. Slide your hand slowly back and forth.

WORKING WITH BODY FILLER

Mixing The Filler

Cleanliness and proper mixing and application are extremely important. Use a clean piece of plastic or glass or a disposable artist's palette to mix body filler.

1 Allow plenty of time and follow directions. No useful purpose will be served by adding more hardener to make it cure (set-up) faster. Less hardener means more curing time, but the mixture dries harder; more hardener means less curing time but a softer mixture.

2 Both the hardener and the filler should be thoroughly kneaded or stirred before mixing. Hardener should be a solid paste and dispense like thin toothpaste. Body filler should be smooth, and free of lumps or thick spots.

Getting the proper amount of hardener in the filler is the trickiest part of repairing the filler. Use the same amount of hardener in cold or warm weather. For contour filler (thick coats), a bead of hardener twice the diameter of the filler is about right. There's about a 5% margin on either side, but, if in doubt use less hardener.

3 Mix the body filler and hardener by wiping across the mixing surface, picking the mixture up and wiping it again. Colder weather requires longer mixing times. Do not mix in a circular motion; this will trap air bubbles which will become holes in the cured filler.

Applying The Filler

1 For best results, filler should not be applied over ¼″ thick.

Apply the filler in several coats. Build it up to above the level of the repair surface so that it can be sanded or grated down.

The first coat of filler must be pressed on with a firm wiping motion.

Apply the filler in one direction only. Working the filler back and forth will either pull it off the metal or trap air bubbles.

REPAIRING DENTS

Before you start, take a few minutes to study the damaged area. Try to visualize the shape of the panel before it was damaged. If the damage is on the left fender, look at the right fender and use it as a guide. If there is access to the panel from behind, you can reshape it with a body hammer. If not, you'll have to use a dent puller. Go slowly and work the metal a little at a time. Get the panel as straight as possible before applying filler.

1 This dent is typical of one that can be pulled out or hammered out from behind. Remove the headlight cover, headlight assembly and turn signal housing.

2 Drill a series of holes ½ the size of the end of the dent puller along the stress line. Make some trial pulls and assess the results. If necessary, drill more holes and try again. Do not hurry.

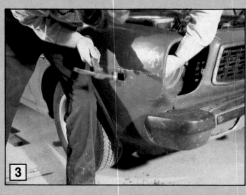

3 If possible, use a body hammer and block to shape the metal back to its original contours. Get the metal back as close to its original shape as possible. Don't depend on body filler to fill dents.

4 Using an 80-grit grinding disc on an electric drill, grind the paint from the surrounding area down to bare metal. Use a new grinding pad to prevent heat buildup that will warp metal.

5 The area should look like this when you're finished grinding. Knock the drill holes in and tape over small openings to keep plastic filler out.

6 Mix the body filler (see Body Repair Tips). Spread the body filler evenly over the entire area (see Body Repair Tips). Be sure to cover the area completely.

7 Let the body filler dry until the surface can just be scratched with your fingernail. Knock the high spots from the body filler with a body file ("Cheese-grater"). Check frequently with the palm of your hand for high and low spots.

8 Check to be sure that trim pieces that will be installed later will fit exactly. Sand the area with 40-grit paper.

9 If you wind up with low spots, you may have to apply another layer of filler.

10 Knock the high spots off with 40-grit paper. When you are satisfied with the contours of the repair, apply a thin coat of filler to cover pin holes and scratches.

11 Block sand the area with 40-grit paper to a smooth finish. Pay particular attention to body lines and ridges that must be well-defined.

12 Sand the area with 400 paper and then finish with a scuff pad. The finished repair is ready for priming and painting (see Painting Tips).

Materials and photos courtesy of Ritt Jones Auto Body, Prospect Park, PA.

REPAIRING RUST HOLES

There are many ways to repair rust holes. The fiberglass cloth kit shown here is one of the most cost efficient for the owner because it provides a strong repair that resists cracking and moisture and is relatively easy to use. It can be used on large and small holes (with or without backing) and can be applied over contoured areas. Remember, however, that short of replacing an entire panel, no repair is a guarantee that the rust will not return.

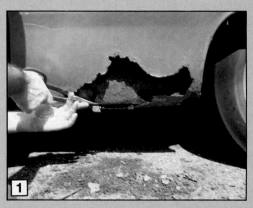

1 Remove any trim that will be in the way. Clean away all loose debris. Cut away all the rusted metal. But be sure to leave enough metal to retain the contour or body shape.

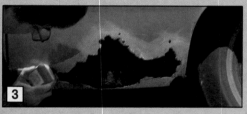

2 Grind away all traces of rust with a 24-grit grinding disc. Be sure to grind back 3-4 inches from the edge of the hole down to bare metal and be sure all traces of paint, primer and rust are removed.

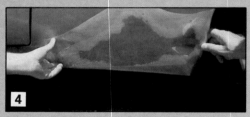

3 Block sand the area with 80 or 100 grit sandpaper to get a clear, shiny surface and feathered paint edge. Tap the edges of the hole inward with a ball peen hammer.

4 If you are going to use release film, cut a piece about 2-3″ larger than the area you have sanded. Place the film over the repair and mark the sanded area on the film. Avoid any unnecessary wrinkling of the film.

Cut 2 pieces of fiberglass matte to match the shape of the repair. One piece should be about 1″ smaller than the sanded area and the second piece should be 1″ smaller than the first. Mix enough filler and hardener to saturate the fiberglass material (see Body Repair Tips).

6 Lay the release sheet on a flat surface and spread an even layer of filler, large enough to cover the repair. Lay the smaller piece of fiberglass cloth in the center of the sheet and spread another layer of filler over the fiberglass cloth. Repeat the operation for the larger piece of cloth.

7 Place the repair material over the repair area, with the release film facing outward. Use a spreader and work from the center outward to smooth the material, following the body contours. Be sure to remove all air bubbles.

8 Wait until the repair has dried tack-free and peel off the release sheet. The ideal working temperature is 60°-90° F. Cooler or warmer temperatures or high humidity may require additional curing time. Wait longer, if in doubt.

9 Sand and feather-edge the entire area. The initial sanding can be done with a sanding disc on an electric drill if care is used. Finish the sanding with a block sander. Low spots can be filled with body filler; this may require several applications.

10 When the filler can just be scratched with a fingernail, knock the high spots down with a body file and smooth the entire area with 80-grit. Feather the filled areas into the surrounding areas.

11 When the area is sanded smooth, mix some topcoat and hardener and apply it directly with a spreader. This will give a smooth finish and prevent the glass matte from showing through the paint.

12 Block sand the topcoat smooth with finishing sandpaper (200 grit), and 400 grit. The repair is ready for masking, priming and painting (see Painting Tips).

Materials and photos courtesy Marson Corporation, Chelsea, Massachusetts

PAINTING TIPS

Preparation

1 SANDING — Use a 400 or 600 grit wet or dry sandpaper. Wet-sand the area with a 1/4 sheet of sandpaper soaked in clean water. Keep the paper wet while sanding. Sand the area until the repaired area tapers into the original finish.

2 CLEANING — Wash the area to be painted thoroughly with water and a clean rag. Rinse it thoroughly and wipe the surface dry until you're sure it's completely free of dirt, dust, fingerprints, wax, detergent or other foreign matter.

3 MASKING — Protect any areas you don't want to overspray by covering them with masking tape and newspaper. Be careful not get fingerprints on the area to be painted.

4 PRIMING — All exposed metal should be primed before painting. Primer protects the metal and provides an excellent surface for paint adhesion. When the primer is dry, wet-sand the area again with 600 grit wet-sandpaper. Clean the area again after sanding.

Painting Techniques

P aint applied from either a spray gun or a spray can (for small areas) will provide good results. Experiment on an old piece of metal to get the right combination before you begin painting.

SPRAYING VISCOSITY (SPRAY GUN ONLY) — Paint should be thinned to spraying viscosity according to the directions on the can. Use only the recommended thinner or reducer and the same amount of reduction regardless of temperature.

AIR PRESSURE (SPRAY GUN ONLY) — This is extremely important. Be sure you are using the proper recommended pressure.

TEMPERATURE — The surface to be painted should be approximately the same temperature as the surrounding air. Applying warm paint to a cold surface, or vice versa, will completely upset the paint characteristics.

THICKNESS — Spray with smooth strokes. In general, the thicker the coat of paint, the longer the drying time. Apply several thin coats about 30 seconds apart. The paint should remain wet long enough to flow out and no longer; heavier coats will only produce sags or wrinkles. Spray a light (fog) coat, followed by heavier color coats.

DISTANCE — The ideal spraying distance is 8"-12" from the gun or can to the surface. Shorter distances will produce ripples, while greater distances will result in orange peel, dry film and poor color match and loss of material due to overspray.

OVERLAPPING — The gun or can should be kept at right angles to the surface at all times. Work to a wet edge at an even speed, using a 50% overlap and direct the center of the spray at the lower or nearest edge of the previous stroke.

RUBBING OUT (BLENDING) FRESH PAINT — Let the paint dry thoroughly. Runs or imperfections can be sanded out, primed and repainted.

Don't be in too big a hurry to remove the masking. This only produces paint ridges. When the finish has dried for at least a week, apply a small amount of fine grade rubbing compound with a clean, wet cloth. Use lots of water and blend the new paint with the surrounding area.

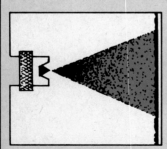

WRONG

Thin coat. Stroke too fast, not enough overlap, gun too far away.

CORRECT

Medium coat. Proper distance, good stroke, proper overlap.

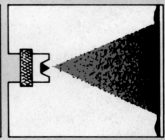

WRONG

Heavy coat. Stroke too slow, too much overlap, gun too close.

Test and Procedure	Results and Indications	Proceed to
5.9—Uncommon fuel system malfunctions: See below:	If the problem is solved: If the problem remains, remove and recondition the carburetor.	6.1

Condition	Indication	Test	Prevailing Weather Conditions	Remedy
Vapor lock	Engine will not restart shortly after running.	Cool the components of the fuel system until the engine starts. Vapor lock can be cured faster by draping a wet cloth over a mechanical fuel pump.	Hot to very hot	Ensure that the exhaust manifold heat control valve is operating. Check with the vehicle manufacturer for the recommended solution to vapor lock on the model in question.
Carburetor icing	Engine will not idle, stalls at low speeds.	Visually inspect the throttle plate area of the throttle bores for frost.	High humidity, 32–40° F.	Ensure that the exhaust manifold heat control valve is operating, and that the intake manifold heat riser is not blocked.
Water in the fuel	Engine sputters and stalls; may not start.	Pump a small amount of fuel into a glass jar. Allow to stand, and inspect for droplets or a layer of water.	High humidity, extreme temperature changes.	For droplets, use one or two cans of commercial gas line anti-freeze. For a layer of water, the tank must be drained, and the fuel lines blown out with compressed air.

Section 6—Engine Compression
See Chapter 3 for service procedures

6.1—Test engine compression: Remove all spark plugs. Block the throttle wide open. Insert a compression gauge into a spark plug port, crank the engine to obtain the maximum reading, and record.	If compression is within limits on all cylinders: If gauge reading is extremely low on all cylinders: If gauge reading is low on one or two cylinders: (If gauge readings are identical and low on two or more adjacent cylinders, the head gasket must be replaced.)	7.1 6.2 6.2

Checking compression

6.2—Test engine compression (wet): Squirt approximately 30 cc. of engine oil into each cylinder, and retest per 6.1.	If the readings improve, worn or cracked rings or broken pistons are indicated: If the readings do not improve, burned or excessively carboned valves or a jumped timing chain are indicated: NOTE: *A jumped timing chain is often indicated by difficult cranking.*	See Chapter 3 7.1

Section 7—Engine Vacuum
See Chapter 3 for service procedures

Test and Procedure	Results and Indications	Proceed to
7.1—Attach a vacuum gauge to the intake manifold beyond the throttle plate. Start the engine, and observe the action of the needle over the range of engine speeds.	See below.	See below

INDICATION: normal engine in good condition

Proceed to: 8.1

Normal engine
Gauge reading: steady, from 17–22 in./Hg.

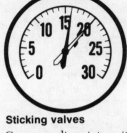

INDICATION: sticking valves or ignition miss

Proceed to: 9.1, 8.3

Sticking valves
Gauge reading: intermittent fluctuation at idle

INDICATION: late ignition or valve timing, low compression, stuck throttle valve, leaking carburetor or manifold gasket

Proceed to: 6.1

Incorrect valve timing
Gauge reading: low (10–15 in./Hg) but steady

INDICATION: improper carburetor adjustment or minor intake leak.

Proceed to: 7.2

Carburetor requires adjustment
Gauge reading: drifting needle

INDICATION: ignition miss, blown cylinder head gasket, leaking valve or weak valve spring

Proceed to: 8.3, 6.1

Blown head gasket
Gauge reading: needle fluctuates as engine speed increases

INDICATION: burnt valve or faulty valve clearance. Needle will fall when defective valve operates

Proceed to: 9.1

Burnt or leaking valves
Gauge reading: steady needle, but drops regularly

INDICATION: choked muffler, excessive back pressure in system

Proceed to: 10.1

Clogged exhaust system
Gauge reading: gradual drop in reading at idle

INDICATION: worn valve guides

Proceed to: 9.1

Worn valve guides
Gauge reading: needle vibrates excessively at idle, but steadies as engine speed increases

---

White pointer = steady gauge hand   Black pointer = fluctuating gauge hand

Test and Procedure	Results and Indications	Proceed to
7.2—Attach a vacuum gauge per 7.1, and test for an intake manifold leak. Squirt a small amount of oil around the intake manifold gaskets, carburetor gaskets, plugs and fittings. Observe the action of the vacuum gauge.	If the reading improves, replace the indicated gasket, or seal the indicated fitting or plug: If the reading remains low:	**8.1** **7.3**
7.3—Test all vacuum hoses and accessories for leaks as described in 7.2. Also check the carburetor body (dashpots, automatic choke mechanism, throttle shafts) for leaks in the same manner.	If the reading improves, service or replace the offending part(s): If the reading remains low:	**8.1** **6.1**

Section 8—Secondary Electrical System
See Chapter 2 for service procedures

Test and Procedure	Results and Indications	Proceed to
8.1—Remove the distributor cap and check to make sure that the rotor turns when the engine is cranked. Visually inspect the distributor components.	Clean, tighten or replace any components which appear defective.	**8.2**
8.2—Connect a timing light (per manufacturer's recommendation) and check the dynamic ignition timing. Disconnect and plug the vacuum hose(s) to the distributor if specified, start the engine, and observe the timing marks at the specified engine speed.	If the timing is not correct, adjust to specifications by rotating the distributor in the engine: (Advance timing by rotating distributor opposite normal direction of rotor rotation, retard timing by rotating distributor in same direction as rotor rotation.)	**8.3**
8.3—Check the operation of the distributor advance mechanism(s): To test the mechanical advance, disconnect the vacuum lines from the distributor advance unit and observe the timing marks with a timing light as the engine speed is increased from idle. If the mark moves smoothly, without hesitation, it may be assumed that the mechanical advance is functioning properly. To test vacuum advance and/or retard systems, alternately crimp and release the vacuum line, and observe the timing mark for movement. If movement is noted, the system is operating.	If the systems are functioning: If the systems are not functioning, remove the distributor, and test on a distributor tester:	**8.4** **8.4**
8.4—Locate an ignition miss: With the engine running, remove each spark plug wire, one at a time, until one is found that doesn't cause the engine to roughen and slow down.	When the missing cylinder is identified:	**4.1**

Section 9—Valve Train
See Chapter 3 for service procedures

Test and Procedure	Results and Indications	Proceed to
9.1—Evaluate the valve train: Remove the valve cover, and ensure that the valves are adjusted to specifications. A mechanic's stethoscope may be used to aid in the diagnosis of the valve train. By pushing the probe on or near push rods or rockers, valve noise often can be isolated. A timing light also may be used to diagnose valve problems. Connect the light according to manufacturer's recommendations, and start the engine. Vary the firing moment of the light by increasing the engine speed (and therefore the ignition advance), and moving the trigger from cylinder to cylinder. Observe the movement of each valve.	Sticking valves or erratic valve train motion can be observed with the timing light. The cylinder head must be disassembled for repairs.	**See Chapter 3**
9.2—Check the valve timing: Locate top dead center of the No. 1 piston, and install a degree wheel or tape on the crankshaft pulley or damper with zero corresponding to an index mark on the engine. Rotate the crankshaft in its direction of rotation, and observe the opening of the No. 1 cylinder intake valve. The opening should correspond with the correct mark on the degree wheel according to specifications.	If the timing is not correct, the timing cover must be removed for further investigation.	**See Chapter 3**

Section 10—Exhaust System

Test and Procedure	Results and Indications	Proceed to
10.1—Determine whether the exhaust manifold heat control valve is operating: Operate the valve by hand to determine whether it is free to move. If the valve is free, run the engine to operating temperature and observe the action of the valve, to ensure that it is opening.	If the valve sticks, spray it with a suitable solvent, open and close the valve to free it, and retest. If the valve functions properly: If the valve does not free, or does not operate, replace the valve:	10.2 10.2
10.2—Ensure that there are no exhaust restrictions: Visually inspect the exhaust system for kinks, dents, or crushing. Also note that gases are flowing freely from the tailpipe at all engine speeds, indicating no restriction in the muffler or resonator.	Replace any damaged portion of the system:	11.1

Section 11—Cooling System
See Chapter 3 for service procedures

Test and Procedure	Results and Indications	Proceed to
11.1—Visually inspect the fan belt for glazing, cracks, and fraying, and replace if necessary. Tighten the belt so that the longest span has approximately ½″ play at its midpoint under thumb pressure (see Chapter 1).	Replace or tighten the fan belt as necessary:	**11.2**

Checking belt tension

11.2—Check the fluid level of the cooling system.	If full or slightly low, fill as necessary:	**11.5**
	If extremely low:	**11.3**
11.3—Visually inspect the external portions of the cooling system (radiator, radiator hoses, thermostat elbow, water pump seals, heater hoses, etc.) for leaks. If none are found, pressurize the cooling system to 14–15 psi.	If cooling system holds the pressure:	**11.5**
	If cooling system loses pressure rapidly, reinspect external parts of the system for leaks under pressure. If none are found, check dipstick for coolant in crankcase. If no coolant is present, but pressure loss continues:	**11.4**
	If coolant is evident in crankcase, remove cylinder head(s), and check gasket(s). If gaskets are intact, block and cylinder head(s) should be checked for cracks or holes.	
	If the gasket(s) is blown, replace, and purge the crankcase of coolant:	**12.6**
	NOTE: *Occasionally, due to atmospheric and driving conditions, condensation of water can occur in the crankcase. This causes the oil to appear milky white. To remedy, run the engine until hot, and change the oil and oil filter.*	
11.4—Check for combustion leaks into the cooling system: Pressurize the cooling system as above. Start the engine, and observe the pressure gauge. If the needle fluctuates, remove each spark plug wire, one at a time, noting which cylinder(s) reduce or eliminate the fluctuation.	Cylinders which reduce or eliminate the fluctuation, when the spark plug wire is removed, are leaking into the cooling system. Replace the head gasket on the affected cylinder bank(s).	

Pressurizing the cooling system

Test and Procedure	Results and Indications	Proceed to
11.5—Check the radiator pressure cap: Attach a radiator pressure tester to the radiator cap (wet the seal prior to installation). Quickly pump up the pressure, noting the point at which the cap releases.	If the cap releases within ± 1 psi of the specified rating, it is operating properly:	**11.6**
	If the cap releases at more than ± 1 psi of the specified rating, it should be replaced:	**11.6**

Checking radiator pressure cap

Test and Procedure	Results and Indications	Proceed to
11.6—Test the thermostat: Start the engine cold, remove the radiator cap, and insert a thermometer into the radiator. Allow the engine to idle. After a short while, there will be a sudden, rapid increase in coolant temperature. The temperature at which this sharp rise stops is the thermostat opening temperature.	If the thermostat opens at or about the specified temperature:	**11.7**
	If the temperature doesn't increase: (If the temperature increases slowly and gradually, replace the thermostat.)	**11.7**
11.7—Check the water pump: Remove the thermostat elbow and the thermostat, disconnect the coil high tension lead (to prevent starting), and crank the engine momentarily.	If coolant flows, replace the thermostat and retest per 11.6:	**11.6**
	If coolant doesn't flow, reverse flush the cooling system to alleviate any blockage that might exist. If system is not blocked, and coolant will not flow, replace the water pump.	

Section 12—Lubrication
See Chapter 3 for service procedures

Test and Procedure	Results and Indications	Proceed to
12.1—Check the oil pressure gauge or warning light: If the gauge shows low pressure, or the light is on for no obvious reason, remove the oil pressure sender. Install an accurate oil pressure gauge and run the engine momentarily.	If oil pressure builds normally, run engine for a few moments to determine that it is functioning normally, and replace the sender.	—
	If the pressure remains low:	**12.2**
	If the pressure surges:	**12.3**
	If the oil pressure is zero:	**12.3**
12.2—Visually inspect the oil: If the oil is watery or very thin, milky, or foamy, replace the oil and oil filter.	If the oil is normal:	**12.3**
	If after replacing oil the pressure remains low:	**12.3**
	If after replacing oil the pressure becomes normal:	—

Test and Procedure	Results and Indications	Proceed to
12.3—Inspect the oil pressure relief valve and spring, to ensure that it is not sticking or stuck. Remove and thoroughly clean the valve, spring, and the valve body.	If the oil pressure improves: If no improvement is noted:	— **12.4**
12.4—Check to ensure that the oil pump is not cavitating (sucking air instead of oil): See that the crankcase is neither over nor underfull, and that the pickup in the sump is in the proper position and free from sludge.	Fill or drain the crankcase to the proper capacity, and clean the pickup screen in solvent if necessary. If no improvement is noted:	**12.5**
12.5—Inspect the oil pump drive and the oil pump:	If the pump drive or the oil pump appear to be defective, service as necessary and retest per 12.1: If the pump drive and pump appear to be operating normally, the engine should be disassembled to determine where blockage exists:	**12.1** **See Chapter 3**
12.6—Purge the engine of ethylene glycol coolant: Completely drain the crankcase and the oil filter. Obtain a commercial butyl cellosolve base solvent, designated for this purpose, and follow the instructions precisely. Following this, install a new oil filter and refill the crankcase with the proper weight oil. The next oil and filter change should follow shortly thereafter (1000 miles).		

TROUBLESHOOTING EMISSION CONTROL SYSTEMS

See Chapter 4 for procedures applicable to individual emission control systems used on specific combinations of engine/transmission/model.

TROUBLESHOOTING THE CARBURETOR
See Chapter 4 for service procedures

Carburetor problems cannot be effectively isolated unless all other engine systems (particularly ignition and emission) are functioning properly and the engine is properly tuned.

Condition	Possible Cause
Engine cranks, but does not start	1. Improper starting procedure 2. No fuel in tank 3. Clogged fuel line or filter 4. Defective fuel pump 5. Choke valve not closing properly 6. Engine flooded 7. Choke valve not unloading 8. Throttle linkage not making full travel 9. Stuck needle or float 10. Leaking float needle or seat 11. Improper float adjustment
Engine stalls	1. Improperly adjusted idle speed or mixture **Engine hot** 2. Improperly adjusted dashpot 3. Defective or improperly adjusted solenoid 4. Incorrect fuel level in fuel bowl 5. Fuel pump pressure too high 6. Leaking float needle seat 7. Secondary throttle valve stuck open 8. Air or fuel leaks 9. Idle air bleeds plugged or missing 10. Idle passages plugged **Engine Cold** 11. Incorrectly adjusted choke 12. Improperly adjusted fast idle speed 13. Air leaks 14. Plugged idle or idle air passages 15. Stuck choke valve or binding linkage 16. Stuck secondary throttle valves 17. Engine flooding—high fuel level 18. Leaking or misaligned float
Engine hesitates on acceleration	1. Clogged fuel filter 2. Leaking fuel pump diaphragm 3. Low fuel pump pressure 4. Secondary throttle valves stuck, bent or misadjusted 5. Sticking or binding air valve 6. Defective accelerator pump 7. Vacuum leaks 8. Clogged air filter 9. Incorrect choke adjustment (engine cold)
Engine feels sluggish or flat on acceleration	1. Improperly adjusted idle speed or mixture 2. Clogged fuel filter 3. Defective accelerator pump 4. Dirty, plugged or incorrect main metering jets 5. Bent or sticking main metering rods 6. Sticking throttle valves 7. Stuck heat riser 8. Binding or stuck air valve 9. Dirty, plugged or incorrect secondary jets 10. Bent or sticking secondary metering rods. 11. Throttle body or manifold heat passages plugged 12. Improperly adjusted choke or choke vacuum break.
Carburetor floods	1. Defective fuel pump. Pressure too high. 2. Stuck choke valve 3. Dirty, worn or damaged float or needle valve/seat 4. Incorrect float/fuel level 5. Leaking float bowl

Condition	Possible Cause
Engine idles roughly and stalls	1. Incorrect idle speed 2. Clogged fuel filter 3. Dirt in fuel system or carburetor 4. Loose carburetor screws or attaching bolts 5. Broken carburetor gaskets 6. Air leaks 7. Dirty carburetor 8. Worn idle mixture needles 9. Throttle valves stuck open 10. Incorrectly adjusted float or fuel level 11. Clogged air filter
Engine runs unevenly or surges	1. Defective fuel pump 2. Dirty or clogged fuel filter 3. Plugged, loose or incorrect main metering jets or rods 4. Air leaks 5. Bent or sticking main metering rods 6. Stuck power piston 7. Incorrect float adjustment 8. Incorrect idle speed or mixture 9. Dirty or plugged idle system passages 10. Hard, brittle or broken gaskets 11. Loose attaching or mounting screws 12. Stuck or misaligned secondary throttle valves
Poor fuel economy	1. Poor driving habits 2. Stuck choke valve 3. Binding choke linkage 4. Stuck heat riser 5. Incorrect idle mixture 6. Defective accelerator pump 7. Air leaks 8. Plugged, loose or incorrect main metering jets 9. Improperly adjusted float or fuel level 10. Bent, misaligned or fuel-clogged float 11. Leaking float needle seat 12. Fuel leak 13. Accelerator pump discharge ball not seating properly 14. Incorrect main jets
Engine lacks high speed performance or power	1. Incorrect throttle linkage adjustment 2. Stuck or binding power piston 3. Defective accelerator pump 4. Air leaks 5. Incorrect float setting or fuel level 6. Dirty, plugged, worn or incorrect main metering jets or rods 7. Binding or sticking air valve 8. Brittle or cracked gaskets 9. Bent, incorrect or improperly adjusted secondary metering rods 10. Clogged fuel filter 11. Clogged air filter 12. Defective fuel pump

TROUBLESHOOTING FUEL INJECTION PROBLEMS

Each fuel injection system has its own unique components and test procedures, for which it is impossible to generalize. Refer to Chapter 4 of this Repair & Tune-Up Guide for specific test and repair procedures, if the vehicle is equipped with fuel injection.

TROUBLESHOOTING ELECTRICAL PROBLEMS

See Chapter 5 for service procedures

For any electrical system to operate, it must make a complete circuit. This simply means that the power flow from the battery must make a complete circle. When an electrical component is operating, power flows from the battery to the component, passes through the component causing it to perform its function (lighting a light bulb), and then returns to the battery through the ground of the circuit. This ground is usually (but not always) the metal part of the car or truck on which the electrical component is mounted.

Perhaps the easiest way to visualize this is to think of connecting a light bulb with two wires attached to it to the battery. If one of the two wires attached to the light bulb were attached to the negative post of the battery and the other were attached to the positive post of the battery, you would have a complete circuit. Current from the battery would flow to the light bulb, causing it to light, and return to the negative post of the battery.

The normal automotive circuit differs from this simple example in two ways. First, instead of having a return wire from the bulb to the battery, the light bulb returns the current to the battery through the chassis of the vehicle. Since the negative battery cable is attached to the chassis and the chassis is made of electrically conductive metal, the chassis of the vehicle can serve as a ground wire to complete the circuit. Secondly, most automotive circuits contain switches to turn components on and off as required.

Every complete circuit from a power source must include a component which is using the power from the power source. If you were to disconnect the light bulb from the wires and touch the two wires together (don't do this) the power supply wire to the component would be grounded before the normal ground connection for the circuit.

Because grounding a wire from a power source makes a complete circuit—less the required component to use the power—this phenomenon is called a short circuit. Common causes are: broken insulation (exposing the metal wire to a metal part of the car or truck), or a shorted switch.

Some electrical components which require a large amount of current to operate also have a relay in their circuit. Since these circuits carry a large amount of current, the thickness of the wire in the circuit (gauge size) is also greater. If this large wire were connected from the component to the control switch on the instrument panel, and then back to the component, a voltage drop would occur in the circuit. To prevent this potential drop in voltage, an electromagnetic switch (relay) is used. The large wires in the circuit are connected from the battery to one side of the relay, and from the opposite side of the relay to the component. The relay is normally open, preventing current from passing through the circuit. An additional, smaller, wire is connected from the relay to the control switch for the circuit. When the control switch is turned on, it grounds the smaller wire from the relay and completes the circuit. This closes the relay and allows current to flow from the battery to the component. The horn, headlight, and starter circuits are three which use relays.

It is possible for larger surges of current to pass through the electrical system of your car or truck. If this surge of current were to reach an electrical component, it could burn it out. To prevent this, fuses, circuit breakers or fusible links are connected into the current supply wires of most of the major electrical systems. When an electrical current of excessive power passes through the component's fuse, the fuse blows out and breaks the circuit, saving the component from destruction.

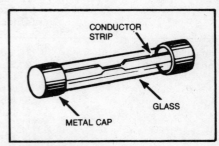

Typical automotive fuse

A circuit breaker is basically a self-repairing fuse. The circuit breaker opens the circuit the same way a fuse does. However, when either the short is removed from the circuit or the surge subsides, the circuit breaker resets itself and does not have to be replaced as a fuse does.

A fuse link is a wire that acts as a fuse. It is normally connected between the starter relay and the main wiring harness. This connection is usually under the hood. The fuse link (if installed) protects all the

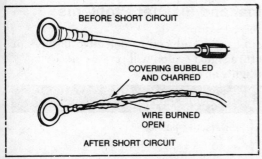

BEFORE SHORT CIRCUIT

COVERING BUBBLED
AND CHARRED

WIRE BURNED
OPEN

AFTER SHORT CIRCUIT

Most fusible links show a charred, melted insulation when they burn out

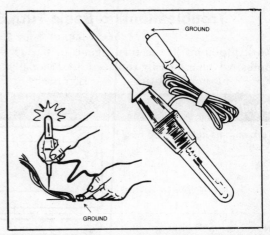

GROUND

GROUND

The test light will show the presence of current when touched to a hot wire and grounded at the other end

chassis electrical components, and is the probable cause of trouble when none of the electrical components function, unless the battery is disconnected or dead.

Electrical problems generally fall into one of three areas:

1. The component that is not functioning is not receiving current.

2. The component itself is not functioning.

3. The component is not properly grounded.

The electrical system can be checked with a test light and a jumper wire. A test light is a device that looks like a pointed screwdriver with a wire attached to it and has a light bulb in its handle. A jumper wire is a piece of insulated wire with an alligator clip attached to each end.

If a component is not working, you must follow a systematic plan to determine which of the three causes is the villain.

1. Turn on the switch that controls the inoperable component.

2. Disconnect the power supply wire from the component.

3. Attach the ground wire on the test light to a good metal ground.

4. Touch the probe end of the test light to the end of the power supply wire that was disconnected from the component. If the component is receiving current, the test light will go on.

NOTE: *Some components work only when the ignition switch is turned on.*

If the test light does not go on, then the problem is in the circuit between the battery and the component. This includes all the switches, fuses, and relays in the system. Follow the wire that runs back to the battery. The problem is an open circuit between the

battery and the component. If the fuse is blown and, when replaced, immediately blows again, there is a short circuit in the system which must be located and repaired. If there is a switch in the system, bypass it with a jumper wire. This is done by connecting one end of the jumper wire to the power supply wire into the switch and the other end of the jumper wire to the wire coming out of the switch. If the test light lights with the jumper wire installed, the switch or whatever was bypassed is defective.

NOTE: *Never substitute the jumper wire for the component, since it is required to use the power from the power source.*

5. If the bulb in the test light goes on, then the current is getting to the component that is not working. This eliminates the first of the three possible causes. Connect the power supply wire and connect a jumper wire from the component to a good metal ground. Do this with the switch which controls the component turned on, and also the ignition switch turned on if it is required for the component to work. If the component works with the jumper wire installed, then it has a bad ground. This is usually caused by the metal area on which the component mounts to the chassis being coated with some type of foreign matter.

6. If neither test located the source of the trouble, then the component itself is defective. Remember that for any electrical system to work, all connections must be clean and tight.

Troubleshooting Basic Turn Signal and Flasher Problems

See Chapter 5 for service procedures

Most problems in the turn signals or flasher system can be reduced to defective flashers or bulbs, which are easily replaced. Occasionally, the turn signal switch will prove defective.

F = Front   R = Rear   ● = Lights off   ○ = Lights on

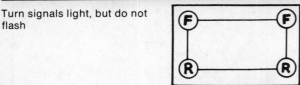

Condition	Possible Cause
Turn signals light, but do not flash	Defective flasher
No turn signals light on either side	Blown fuse. Replace if defective. Defective flasher. Check by substitution. Open circuit, short circuit or poor ground.
Both turn signals on one side don't work	Bad bulbs. Bad ground in both (or either) housings.
One turn signal light on one side doesn't work	Defective bulb. Corrosion in socket. Clean contacts. Poor ground at socket.
Turn signal flashes too fast or too slowly	Check any bulb on the side flashing too fast. A heavy-duty bulb is probably installed in place of a regular bulb. Check the bulb flashing too slowly. A standard bulb was probably installed in place of a heavy-duty bulb. Loose connections or corrosion at the bulb socket.
Indicator lights don't work in either direction	Check if the turn signals are working. Check the dash indicator lights. Check the flasher by substitution.
One indicator light doesn't light	On systems with one dash indicator: See if the lights work on the same side. Often the filaments have been reversed in systems combining stoplights with taillights and turn signals. Check the flasher by substitution. On systems with two indicators: Check the bulbs on the same side. Check the indicator light bulb. Check the flasher by substitution.

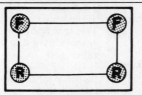
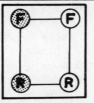
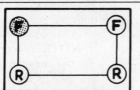
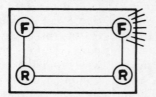

Troubleshooting Lighting Problems

See Chapter 5 for service procedures

Condition	Possible Cause
One or more lights don't work, but others do	1. Defective bulb(s) 2. Blown fuse(s) 3. Dirty fuse clips or light sockets 4. Poor ground circuit
Lights burn out quickly	1. Incorrect voltage regulator setting or defective regulator 2. Poor battery/alternator connections
Lights go dim	1. Low/discharged battery 2. Alternator not charging 3. Corroded sockets or connections 4. Low voltage output
Lights flicker	1. Loose connection 2. Poor ground. (Run ground wire from light housing to frame) 3. Circuit breaker operating (short circuit)
Lights "flare"—Some flare is normal on acceleration—If excessive, see "Lights Burn Out Quickly"	High voltage setting
Lights glare—approaching drivers are blinded	1. Lights adjusted too high 2. Rear springs or shocks sagging 3. Rear tires soft

Troubleshooting Dash Gauge Problems

Most problems can be traced to a defective sending unit or faulty wiring. Occasionally, the gauge itself is at fault. See Chapter 5 for service procedures.

Condition	Possible Cause
COOLANT TEMPERATURE GAUGE	
Gauge reads erratically or not at all	1. Loose or dirty connections 2. Defective sending unit. 3. Defective gauge. To test a bi-metal gauge, remove the wire from the sending unit. Ground the wire for an instant. If the gauge registers, replace the sending unit. To test a magnetic gauge, disconnect the wire at the sending unit. With ignition ON gauge should register COLD. Ground the wire; gauge should register HOT.
AMMETER GAUGE—TURN HEADLIGHTS ON (DO NOT START ENGINE). NOTE REACTION	
Ammeter shows charge Ammeter shows discharge Ammeter does not move	1. Connections reversed on gauge 2. Ammeter is OK 3. Loose connections or faulty wiring 4. Defective gauge

Condition	Possible Cause

OIL PRESSURE GAUGE

Gauge does not register or is inaccurate	1. On mechanical gauge, Bourdon tube may be bent or kinked. 2. Low oil pressure. Remove sending unit. Idle the engine briefly. If no oil flows from sending unit hole, problem is in engine. 3. Defective gauge. Remove the wire from the sending unit and ground it for an instant with the ignition ON. A good gauge will go to the top of the scale. 4. Defective wiring. Check the wiring to the gauge. If it's OK and the gauge doesn't register when grounded, replace the gauge. 5. Defective sending unit.

ALL GAUGES

All gauges do not operate All gauges read low or erratically All gauges pegged	1. Blown fuse 2. Defective instrument regulator 3. Defective or dirty instrument voltage regulator 4. Loss of ground between instrument voltage regulator and frame 5. Defective instrument regulator

WARNING LIGHTS

Light(s) do not come on when ignition is ON, but engine is not started Light comes on with engine running	1. Defective bulb 2. Defective wire 3. Defective sending unit. Disconnect the wire from the sending unit and ground it. Replace the sending unit if the light comes on with the ignition ON. 4. Problem in individual system 5. Defective sending unit

Troubleshooting Clutch Problems

It is false economy to replace individual clutch components. The pressure plate, clutch plate and throwout bearing should be replaced as a set, and the flywheel face inspected, whenever the clutch is overhauled. See Chapter 6 for service procedures.

Condition	Possible Cause
Clutch chatter	1. Grease on driven plate (disc) facing 2. Binding clutch linkage or cable 3. Loose, damaged facings on driven plate (disc) 4. Engine mounts loose 5. Incorrect height adjustment of pressure plate release levers 6. Clutch housing or housing to transmission adapter misalignment 7. Loose driven plate hub
Clutch grabbing	1. Oil, grease on driven plate (disc) facing 2. Broken pressure plate 3. Warped or binding driven plate. Driven plate binding on clutch shaft
Clutch slips	1. Lack of lubrication in clutch linkage or cable (linkage or cable binds, causes incomplete engagement) 2. Incorrect pedal, or linkage adjustment 3. Broken pressure plate springs 4. Weak pressure plate springs 5. Grease on driven plate facings (disc)

Troubleshooting Clutch Problems (cont.)

Condition	Possible Cause
Incomplete clutch release	1. Incorrect pedal or linkage adjustment or linkage or cable binding 2. Incorrect height adjustment on pressure plate release levers 3. Loose, broken facings on driven plate (disc) 4. Bent, dished, warped driven plate caused by overheating
Grinding, whirring grating noise when pedal is depressed	1. Worn or defective throwout bearing 2. Starter drive teeth contacting flywheel ring gear teeth. Look for milled or polished teeth on ring gear.
Squeal, howl, trumpeting noise when pedal is being released (occurs during first inch to inch and one-half of pedal travel)	Pilot bushing worn or lack of lubricant. If bushing appears OK, polish bushing with emery cloth, soak lube wick in oil, lube bushing with oil, apply film of chassis grease to clutch shaft pilot hub, reassemble. NOTE: Bushing wear may be due to misalignment of clutch housing or housing to transmission adapter
Vibration or clutch pedal pulsation with clutch disengaged (pedal fully depressed)	1. Worn or defective engine transmission mounts 2. Flywheel run out. (Flywheel run out at face not to exceed 0.005″) 3. Damaged or defective clutch components

Troubleshooting Manual Transmission Problems
See Chapter 6 for service procedures

Condition	Possible Cause
Transmission jumps out of gear	1. Misalignment of transmission case or clutch housing. 2. Worn pilot bearing in crankshaft. 3. Bent transmission shaft. 4. Worn high speed sliding gear. 5. Worn teeth or end-play in clutch shaft. 6. Insufficient spring tension on shifter rail plunger. 7. Bent or loose shifter fork. 8. Gears not engaging completely. 9. Loose or worn bearings on clutch shaft or mainshaft. 10. Worn gear teeth. 11. Worn or damaged detent balls.
Transmission sticks in gear	1. Clutch not releasing fully. 2. Burred or battered teeth on clutch shaft, or sliding sleeve. 3. Burred or battered transmission mainshaft. 4. Frozen synchronizing clutch. 5. Stuck shifter rail plunger. 6. Gearshift lever twisting and binding shifter rail. 7. Battered teeth on high speed sliding gear or on sleeve. 8. Improper lubrication, or lack of lubrication. 9. Corroded transmission parts. 10. Defective mainshaft pilot bearing. 11. Locked gear bearings will give same effect as stuck in gear.
Transmission gears will not synchronize	1. Binding pilot bearing on mainshaft, will synchronize in high gear only. 2. Clutch not releasing fully. 3. Detent spring weak or broken. 4. Weak or broken springs under balls in sliding gear sleeve. 5. Binding bearing on clutch shaft, or binding countershaft. 6. Binding pilot bearing in crankshaft. 7. Badly worn gear teeth. 8. Improper lubrication. 9. Constant mesh gear not turning freely on transmission mainshaft. Will synchronize in that gear only.

Condition	Possible Cause
Gears spinning when shifting into gear from neutral	1. Clutch not releasing fully. 2. In some cases an extremely light lubricant in transmission will cause gears to continue to spin for a short time after clutch is released. 3. Binding pilot bearing in crankshaft.
Transmission noisy in all gears	1. Insufficient lubricant, or improper lubricant. 2. Worn countergear bearings. 3. Worn or damaged main drive gear or countergear. 4. Damaged main drive gear or mainshaft bearings. 5. Worn or damaged countergear anti-lash plate.
Transmission noisy in neutral only	1. Damaged main drive gear bearing. 2. Damaged or loose mainshaft pilot bearing. 3. Worn or damaged countergear anti-lash plate. 4. Worn countergear bearings.
Transmission noisy in one gear only	1. Damaged or worn constant mesh gears. 2. Worn or damaged countergear bearings. 3. Damaged or worn synchronizer.
Transmission noisy in reverse only	1. Worn or damaged reverse idler gear or idler bushing. 2. Worn or damaged mainshaft reverse gear. 3. Worn or damaged reverse countergear. 4. Damaged shift mechanism.

TROUBLESHOOTING AUTOMATIC TRANSMISSION PROBLEMS

Keeping alert to changes in the operating characteristics of the transmission (changing shift points, noises, etc.) can prevent small problems from becoming large ones. If the problem cannot be traced to loose bolts, fluid level, misadjusted linkage, clogged filters or similar problems, you should probably seek professional service.

Transmission Fluid Indications

The appearance and odor of the transmission fluid can give valuable clues to the overall condition of the transmission. Always note the appearance of the fluid when you check the fluid level or change the fluid. Rub a small amount of fluid between your fingers to feel for grit and smell the fluid on the dipstick.

If the fluid appears:	It indicates:
Clear and red colored	Normal operation
Discolored (extremely dark red or brownish) or smells burned	Band or clutch pack failure, usually caused by an overheated transmission. Hauling very heavy loads with insufficient power or failure to change the fluid often result in overheating. Do not confuse this appearance with newer fluids that have a darker red color and a strong odor (though not a burned odor).
Foamy or aerated (light in color and full of bubbles)	1. The level is too high (gear train is churning oil) 2. An internal air leak (air is mixing with the fluid). Have the transmission checked professionally.
Solid residue in the fluid	Defective bands, clutch pack or bearings. Bits of band material or metal abrasives are clinging to the dipstick. Have the transmission checked professionally.
Varnish coating on the dipstick	The transmission fluid is overheating

TROUBLESHOOTING DRIVE AXLE PROBLEMS

First, determine when the noise is most noticeable.

Drive Noise: Produced under vehicle acceleration.

Coast Noise: Produced while coasting with a closed throttle.

Float Noise: Occurs while maintaining constant speed (just enough to keep speed constant) on a level road.

External Noise Elimination

It is advisable to make a thorough road test to determine whether the noise originates in the rear axle or whether it originates from the tires, engine, transmission, wheel bearings or road surface. Noise originating from other places cannot be corrected by servicing the rear axle.

ROAD NOISE

Brick or rough surfaced concrete roads produce noises that seem to come from the rear axle. Road noise is usually identical in Drive or Coast and driving on a different type of road will tell whether the road is the problem.

TIRE NOISE

Tire noise can be mistaken as rear axle noise, even though the tires on the front are at fault. Snow tread and mud tread tires or tires worn unevenly will frequently cause vibrations which seem to originate elsewhere; *temporarily, and for test purposes only,* inflate the tires to 40–50 lbs. This will significantly alter the noise produced by the tires, but will not alter noise from the rear axle. Noises from the rear axle will normally cease at speeds below 30 mph on coast, while tire noise will continue at lower tone as speed is decreased. The rear axle noise will usually change from drive conditions to coast conditions, while tire noise will not. Do not forget to lower the tire pressure to normal after the test is complete.

ENGINE/TRANSMISSION NOISE

Determine at what speed the noise is most pronounced, then stop in a quiet place. With the transmission in Neutral, run the engine through speeds corresponding to road speeds where the noise was noticed. Noises produced with the vehicle standing still are coming from the engine or transmission.

FRONT WHEEL BEARINGS

Front wheel bearing noises, sometimes confused with rear axle noises, will not change when comparing drive and coast conditions. While holding the speed steady, lightly apply the footbrake. This will often cause wheel bearing noise to lessen, as some of the weight is taken off the bearing. Front wheel bearings are easily checked by jacking up the wheels and spinning the wheels. Shaking the wheels will also determine if the wheel bearings are excessively loose.

REAR AXLE NOISES

Eliminating other possible sources can narrow the cause to the rear axle, which normally produces noise from worn gears or bearings. Gear noises tend to peak in a narrow speed range, while bearing noises will usually vary in pitch with engine speeds.

Noise Diagnosis

The Noise Is:	Most Probably Produced By:
1. Identical under Drive or Coast	Road surface, tires or front wheel bearings
2. Different depending on road surface	Road surface or tires
3. Lower as speed is lowered	Tires
4. Similar when standing or moving	Engine or transmission
5. A vibration	Unbalanced tires, rear wheel bearing, unbalanced driveshaft or worn U-joint
6. A knock or click about every two tire revolutions	Rear wheel bearing
7. Most pronounced on turns	Damaged differential gears
8. A steady low-pitched whirring or scraping, starting at low speeds	Damaged or worn pinion bearing
9. A chattering vibration on turns	Wrong differential lubricant or worn clutch plates (limited slip rear axle)
10. Noticed only in Drive, Coast or Float conditions	Worn ring gear and/or pinion gear

Troubleshooting Steering & Suspension Problems

Condition	Possible Cause
Hard steering (wheel is hard to turn)	1. Improper tire pressure 2. Loose or glazed pump drive belt 3. Low or incorrect fluid 4. Loose, bent or poorly lubricated front end parts 5. Improper front end alignment (excessive caster) 6. Bind in steering column or linkage 7. Kinked hydraulic hose 8. Air in hydraulic system 9. Low pump output or leaks in system 10. Obstruction in lines 11. Pump valves sticking or out of adjustment 12. Incorrect wheel alignment
Loose steering (too much play in steering wheel)	1. Loose wheel bearings 2. Faulty shocks 3. Worn linkage or suspension components 4. Loose steering gear mounting or linkage points 5. Steering mechanism worn or improperly adjusted 6. Valve spool improperly adjusted 7. Worn ball joints, tie-rod ends, etc.
Veers or wanders (pulls to one side with hands off steering wheel)	1. Improper tire pressure 2. Improper front end alignment 3. Dragging or improperly adjusted brakes 4. Bent frame 5. Improper rear end alignment 6. Faulty shocks or springs 7. Loose or bent front end components 8. Play in Pitman arm 9. Steering gear mountings loose 10. Loose wheel bearings 11. Binding Pitman arm 12. Spool valve sticking or improperly adjusted 13. Worn ball joints
Wheel oscillation or vibration transmitted through steering wheel	1. Low or uneven tire pressure 2. Loose wheel bearings 3. Improper front end alignment 4. Bent spindle 5. Worn, bent or broken front end components 6. Tires out of round or out of balance 7. Excessive lateral runout in disc brake rotor 8. Loose or bent shock absorber or strut
Noises (see also "Troubleshooting Drive Axle Problems")	1. Loose belts 2. Low fluid, air in system 3. Foreign matter in system 4. Improper lubrication 5. Interference or chafing in linkage 6. Steering gear mountings loose 7. Incorrect adjustment or wear in gear box 8. Faulty valves or wear in pump 9. Kinked hydraulic lines 10. Worn wheel bearings
Poor return of steering	1. Over-inflated tires 2. Improperly aligned front end (excessive caster) 3. Binding in steering column 4. No lubrication in front end 5. Steering gear adjusted too tight
Uneven tire wear (see "How To Read Tire Wear")	1. Incorrect tire pressure 2. Improperly aligned front end 3. Tires out-of-balance 4. Bent or worn suspension parts

HOW TO READ TIRE WEAR

The way your tires wear is a good indicator of other parts of the suspension. Abnormal wear patterns are often caused by the need for simple tire maintenance, or for front end alignment.

Excessive wear at the center of the tread indicates that the air pressure in the tire is consistently too high. The tire is riding on the center of the tread and wearing it prematurely. Occasionally, this wear pattern can result from outrageously wide tires on narrow rims. The cure for this is to replace either the tires or the wheels.

This type of wear usually results from consistent under-inflation. When a tire is under-inflated, there is too much contact with the road by the outer treads, which wear prematurely. When this type of wear occurs, and the tire pressure is known to be consistently correct, a bent or worn steering component or the need for wheel alignment could be indicated.

Feathering is a condition when the edge of each tread rib develops a slightly rounded edge on one side and a sharp edge on the other. By running your hand over the tire, you can usually feel the sharper edges before you'll be able to see them. The most common causes of feathering are incorrect toe-in setting or deteriorated bushings in the front suspension.

When an inner or outer rib wears faster than the rest of the tire, the need for wheel alignment is indicated. There is excessive camber in the front suspension, causing the wheel to lean too much putting excessive load on one side of the tire. Misalignment could also be due to sagging springs, worn ball joints, or worn control arm bushings. Be sure the vehicle is loaded the way it's normally driven when you have the wheels aligned.

Cups or scalloped dips appearing around the edge of the tread almost always indicate worn (sometimes bent) suspension parts. Adjustment of wheel alignment alone will seldom cure the problem. Any worn component that connects the wheel to the suspension can cause this type of wear. Occasionally, wheels that are out of balance will wear like this, but wheel imbalance usually shows up as bald spots between the outside edges and center of the tread.

Second-rib wear is usually found only in radial tires, and appears where the steel belts end in relation to the tread. It can be kept to a minimum by paying careful attention to tire pressure and frequently rotating the tires. This is often considered normal wear but excessive amounts indicate that the tires are too wide for the wheels.

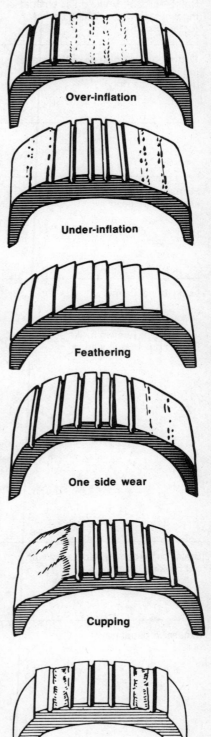

Over-inflation

Under-inflation

Feathering

One side wear

Cupping

Second-rib wear

Troubleshooting Disc Brake Problems

Condition	Possible Cause
Noise—groan—brake noise emanating when slowly releasing brakes (creep-groan)	Not detrimental to function of disc brakes—no corrective action required. (This noise may be eliminated by slightly increasing or decreasing brake pedal efforts.)
Rattle—brake noise or rattle emanating at low speeds on rough roads, (front wheels only).	1. Shoe anti-rattle spring missing or not properly positioned. 2. Excessive clearance between shoe and caliper. 3. Soft or broken caliper seals. 4. Deformed or misaligned disc. 5. Loose caliper.
Scraping	1. Mounting bolts too long. 2. Loose wheel bearings. 3. Bent, loose, or misaligned splash shield.
Front brakes heat up during driving and fail to release	1. Operator riding brake pedal. 2. Stop light switch improperly adjusted. 3. Sticking pedal linkage. 4. Frozen or seized piston. 5. Residual pressure valve in master cylinder. 6. Power brake malfunction. 7. Proportioning valve malfunction.
Leaky brake caliper	1. Damaged or worn caliper piston seal. 2. Scores or corrosion on surface of cylinder bore.
Grabbing or uneven brake action— Brakes pull to one side	1. Causes listed under "Brakes Pull". 2. Power brake malfunction. 3. Low fluid level in master cylinder. 4. Air in hydraulic system. 5. Brake fluid, oil or grease on linings. 6. Unmatched linings. 7. Distorted brake pads. 8. Frozen or seized pistons. 9. Incorrect tire pressure. 10. Front end out of alignment. 11. Broken rear spring. 12. Brake caliper pistons sticking. 13. Restricted hose or line. 14. Caliper not in proper alignment to braking disc. 15. Stuck or malfunctioning metering valve. 16. Soft or broken caliper seals. 17. Loose caliper.
Brake pedal can be depressed without braking effect	1. Air in hydraulic system or improper bleeding procedure. 2. Leak past primary cup in master cylinder. 3. Leak in system. 4. Rear brakes out of adjustment. 5. Bleeder screw open.
Excessive pedal travel	1. Air, leak, or insufficient fluid in system or caliper. 2. Warped or excessively tapered shoe and lining assembly. 3. Excessive disc runout. 4. Rear brake adjustment required. 5. Loose wheel bearing adjustment. 6. Damaged caliper piston seal. 7. Improper brake fluid (boil). 8. Power brake malfunction. 9. Weak or soft hoses.

Troubleshooting Disc Brake Problems (cont.)

Condition	Possible Cause
Brake roughness or chatter (pedal pumping)	1. Excessive thickness variation of braking disc. 2. Excessive lateral runout of braking disc. 3. Rear brake drums out-of-round. 4. Excessive front bearing clearance.
Excessive pedal effort	1. Brake fluid, oil or grease on linings. 2. Incorrect lining. 3. Frozen or seized pistons. 4. Power brake malfunction. 5. Kinked or collapsed hose or line. 6. Stuck metering valve. 7. Scored caliper or master cylinder bore. 8. Seized caliper pistons.
Brake pedal fades (pedal travel increases with foot on brake)	1. Rough master cylinder or caliper bore. 2. Loose or broken hydraulic lines/connections. 3. Air in hydraulic system. 4. Fluid level low. 5. Weak or soft hoses. 6. Inferior quality brake shoes or fluid. 7. Worn master cylinder piston cups or seals.

Troubleshooting Drum Brakes

Condition	Possible Cause
Pedal goes to floor	1. Fluid low in reservoir. 2. Air in hydraulic system. 3. Improperly adjusted brake. 4. Leaking wheel cylinders. 5. Loose or broken brake lines. 6. Leaking or worn master cylinder. 7. Excessively worn brake lining.
Spongy brake pedal	1. Air in hydraulic system. 2. Improper brake fluid (low boiling point). 3. Excessively worn or cracked brake drums. 4. Broken pedal pivot bushing.
Brakes pulling	1. Contaminated lining. 2. Front end out of alignment. 3. Incorrect brake adjustment. 4. Unmatched brake lining. 5. Brake drums out of round. 6. Brake shoes distorted. 7. Restricted brake hose or line. 8. Broken rear spring. 9. Worn brake linings. 10. Uneven lining wear. 11. Glazed brake lining. 12. Excessive brake lining dust. 13. Heat spotted brake drums. 14. Weak brake return springs. 15. Faulty automatic adjusters. 16. Low or incorrect tire pressure.

Condition	Possible Cause
Squealing brakes	1. Glazed brake lining. 2. Saturated brake lining. 3. Weak or broken brake shoe retaining spring. 4. Broken or weak brake shoe return spring. 5. Incorrect brake lining. 6. Distorted brake shoes. 7. Bent support plate. 8. Dust in brakes or scored brake drums. 9. Linings worn below limit. 10. Uneven brake lining wear. 11. Heat spotted brake drums.
Chirping brakes	1. Out of round drum or eccentric axle flange pilot.
Dragging brakes	1. Incorrect wheel or parking brake adjustment. 2. Parking brakes engaged or improperly adjusted. 3. Weak or broken brake shoe return spring. 4. Brake pedal binding. 5. Master cylinder cup sticking. 6. Obstructed master cylinder relief port. 7. Saturated brake lining. 8. Bent or out of round brake drum. 9. Contaminated or improper brake fluid. 10. Sticking wheel cylinder pistons. 11. Driver riding brake pedal. 12. Defective proportioning valve. 13. Insufficient brake shoe lubricant.
Hard pedal	1. Brake booster inoperative. 2. Incorrect brake lining. 3. Restricted brake line or hose. 4. Frozen brake pedal linkage. 5. Stuck wheel cylinder. 6. Binding pedal linkage. 7. Faulty proportioning valve.
Wheel locks	1. Contaminated brake lining. 2. Loose or torn brake lining. 3. Wheel cylinder cups sticking. 4. Incorrect wheel bearing adjustment. 5. Faulty proportioning valve.
Brakes fade (high speed)	1. Incorrect lining. 2. Overheated brake drums. 3. Incorrect brake fluid (low boiling temperature). 4. Saturated brake lining. 5. Leak in hydraulic system. 6. Faulty automatic adjusters.
Pedal pulsates	1. Bent or out of round brake drum.
Brake chatter and shoe knock	1. Out of round brake drum. 2. Loose support plate. 3. Bent support plate. 4. Distorted brake shoes. 5. Machine grooves in contact face of brake drum (Shoe Knock). 6. Contaminated brake lining. 7. Missing or loose components. 8. Incorrect lining material. 9. Out-of-round brake drums. 10. Heat spotted or scored brake drums. 11. Out-of-balance wheels.

Troubleshooting Drum Brakes (cont.)

Condition	Possible Cause
Brakes do not self adjust	1. Adjuster screw frozen in thread. 2. Adjuster screw corroded at thrust washer. 3. Adjuster lever does not engage star wheel. 4. Adjuster installed on wrong wheel.
Brake light glows	1. Leak in the hydraulic system. 2. Air in the system. 3. Improperly adjusted master cylinder pushrod. 4. Uneven lining wear. 5. Failure to center combination valve or proportioning valve.

Mechanic's Data

General Conversion Table

Multiply By	To Convert	To	
		LENGTH	
2.54	Inches	Centimeters	.3937
25.4	Inches	Millimeters	.03937
30.48	Feet	Centimeters	.0328
.304	Feet	Meters	3.28
.914	Yards	Meters	1.094
1.609	Miles	Kilometers	.621
		VOLUME	
.473	Pints	Liters	2.11
.946	Quarts	Liters	1.06
3.785	Gallons	Liters	.264
.016	Cubic inches	Liters	61.02
16.39	Cubic inches	Cubic cms.	.061
28.3	Cubic feet	Liters	.0353
		MASS (Weight)	
28.35	Ounces	Grams	.035
.4536	Pounds	Kilograms	2.20
—	To obtain	From	Multiply by

Multiply By	To Convert	To	
		AREA	
.645	Square inches	Square cms.	.155
.836	Square yds.	Square meters	1.196
		FORCE	
4.448	Pounds	Newtons	.225
.138	Ft./lbs.	Kilogram/meters	7.23
1.36	Ft./lbs.	Newton-meters	.737
.112	In./lbs.	Newton-meters	8.844
		PRESSURE	
.068	Psi	Atmospheres	14.7
6.89	Psi	Kilopascals	.145
		OTHER	
1.104	Horsepower (DIN)	Horsepower (SAE)	.9861
.746	Horsepower (SAE)	Kilowatts (KW)	1.34
1.60	Mph	Km/h	.625
.425	Mpg	Km/1	2.35
—	To obtain	From	Multiply by

Tap Drill Sizes

National Coarse or U.S.S.

Screw & Tap Size	Threads Per Inch	Use Drill Number
No. 5	40	39
No. 6	32	36
No. 8	32	29
No. 10	24	25
No. 12	24	17
$1/4$	20	8
$5/16$	18	F
$3/8$	16	$5/16$
$7/16$	14	U
$1/2$	13	$27/64$
$9/16$	12	$31/64$
$5/8$	11	$17/32$
$3/4$	10	$21/32$
$7/8$	9	$49/64$

National Coarse or U.S.S.

Screw & Tap Size	Threads Per Inch	Use Drill Number
1	8	$7/8$
$1\frac{1}{8}$	7	$63/64$
$1\frac{1}{4}$	7	$17/64$
$1\frac{1}{2}$	6	$1^{11}/32$

National Fine or S.A.E.

Screw & Tap Size	Threads Per Inch	Use Drill Number
No. 5	44	37
No. 6	40	33
No. 8	36	29
No. 10	32	21

National Fine or S.A.E.

Screw & Tap Size	Threads Per Inch	Use Drill Number
No. 12	28	15
$1/4$	28	3
$6/16$	24	1
$3/8$	24	Q
$7/16$	20	W
$1/2$	20	$29/64$
$9/16$	18	$33/64$
$5/8$	18	$37/64$
$3/4$	16	$11/16$
$7/8$	14	$13/16$
$1\frac{1}{8}$	12	$1^{3}/64$
$1\frac{1}{4}$	12	$1^{11}/64$
$1\frac{1}{2}$	12	$1^{27}/64$

Drill Sizes In Decimal Equivalents

Inch	Decimal	Wire	mm
1/64	.0156		.39
	.0157		.4
	.0160	78	
	.0165		.42
	.0173		.44
	.0177		.45
	.0180	77	
	.0181		.46
	.0189		.48
	.0197		.5
	.0200	76	
	.0210	75	
	.0217		.55
	.0225	74	
	.0236		.6
	.0240	73	
	.0250	72	
	.0256		.65
	.0260	71	
	.0276		.7
	.0280	70	
	.0292	69	
	.0295		.75
	.0310	68	
1/32	.0312		.79
	.0315		.8
	.0320	67	
	.0330	66	
	.0335		.85
	.0350	65	
	.0354		.9
	.0360	64	
	.0370	63	
	.0374		.95
	.0380	62	
	.0390	61	
	.0394		1.0
	.0400	60	
	.0410	59	
	.0413		1.05
	.0420	58	
	.0430	57	
	.0433		1.1
	.0453		1.15
	.0465	56	
3/64	.0469		1.19
	.0472		1.2
	.0492		1.25
	.0512		1.3
	.0520	55	
	.0531		1.35
	.0550	54	
	.0551		1.4
	.0571		1.45
	.0591		1.5
	.0595	53	
	.0610		1.55
1/16	.0625		1.59
	.0630		1.6
	.0635	52	
	.0650		1.65
	.0669		1.7
	.0670	51	
	.0689		1.75
	.0700	50	
	.0709		1.8
	.0728		1.85

Inch	Decimal	Wire	mm
	.0730	49	
	.0748		1.9
	.0760	48	
	.0768		1.95
5/64	.0781		1.98
	.0785	47	
	.0787		2.0
	.0807		2.05
	.0810	46	
	.0820	45	
	.0827		2.1
	.0846		2.15
	.0860	44	
	.0866		2.2
	.0886		2.25
	.0890	43	
	.0906		2.3
	.0925		2.35
	.0935	42	
3/32	.0938		2.38
	.0945		2.4
	.0960	41	
	.0965		2.45
	.0980	40	
	.0981		2.5
	.0995	39	
	.1015	38	
	.1024		2.6
	.1040	37	
	.1063		2.7
	.1065	36	
	.1083		2.75
7/64	.1094		2.77
	.1100	35	
	.1102		2.8
	.1110	34	
	.1130	33	
	.1142		2.9
	.1160	32	
	.1181		3.0
	.1200	31	
	.1220		3.1
1/8	.1250		3.17
	.1260		3.2
	.1280		3.25
	.1285	30	
	.1299		3.3
	.1339		3.4
	.1360	29	
	.1378		3.5
	.1405	28	
9/64	.1406		3.57
	.1417		3.6
	.1440	27	
	.1457		3.7
	.1470	26	
	.1476		3.75
	.1495	25	
	.1496		3.8
	.1520	24	
	.1535		3.9
	.1540	23	
5/32	.1562		3.96
	.1570	22	
	.1575		4.0
	.1590	21	
	.1610	20	

Inch	Decimal	Wire & Letter	mm
	.1614		4.1
	.1654		4.2
	.1660	19	
	.1673		4.25
	.1693		4.3
	.1695	18	
11/64	.1719		4.36
	.1730	17	
	.1732		4.4
	.1770	16	
	.1772		4.5
	.1800	15	
	.1811		4.6
	.1820	14	
	.1850	13	
	.1850		4.7
	.1870		4.75
3/16	.1875		4.76
	.1890		4.8
	.1890	12	
	.1910	11	
	.1929		4.9
	.1935	10	
	.1960	9	
	.1969		5.0
	.1990	8	
	.2008		5.1
	.2010	7	
13/64	.2031		5.16
	.2040	6	
	.2047		5.2
	.2055	5	
	.2067		5.25
	.2087		5.3
	.2090	4	
	.2126		5.4
	.2130	3	
	.2165		5.5
7/32	2188		5.55
	.2205		5.6
	.2210	2	
	.2244		5.7
	.2264		5.75
	.2280	1	
	.2283		5.8
	.2323		5.9
	.2340	A	
15/64	.2344		5.95
	.2362		6.0
	.2380	B	
	.2402		6.1
	.2420	C	
	.2441		6.2
	.2460	D	
	.2461		6.25
	.2480		6.3
1/4	.2500	E	6.35
	.2520		6.
	.2559		6.5
	.2570	F	
	.2598		6.6
	.2610	G	
	.2638		6.7
17/64	.2656		6.74
	.2657		6.75
	.2660	H	
	.2677		6.8

Inch	Decimal	Letter	mm
	.2717		6.9
	.2720	I	
	.2756		7.0
	.2770	J	
	.2795		7.1
	.2810	K	
9/32	.2812		7.14
	.2835		7.2
	.2854		7.25
	.2874		7.3
	.2900	L	
	.2913		7.4
	.2950	M	
	.2953		7.5
19/64	.2969		7.54
	.2992		7.6
	.3020	N	
	.3031		7.7
	.3051		7.75
	.3071		7.8
	.3110		7.9
5/16	.3125		7.93
	.3150		8.0
	.3160	O	
	.3189		8.1
	.3228		8.2
	.3230	P	
	.3248		8.25
	.3268		8.3
21/64	.3281		8.33
	.3307		8.4
	.3320	Q	
	.3346		8.5
	.3386		8.6
	.3390	R	
	.3425		8.7
11/32	.3438		8.73
	.3445		8.75
	.3465		8.8
	.3480	S	
	.3504		8.9
	.3543		9.0
	.3580	T	
	.3583		9.1
23/64	.3594		9.12
	.3622		9.2
	.3642		9.25
	.3661		9.3
	.3680	U	
	.3701		9.4
	.3740		9.5
3/8	.3750		9.52
	.3770	V	
	.3780		9.6
	.3819		9.7
	.3839		9.75
	.3858		9.8
	.3860	W	
	.3898		9.9
25/64	.3906		9.92
	.3937		10.0
	.3970	X	
	.4040	Y	
13/32	.4062		10.31
	.4130	Z	
	.4134		10.5
27/64	.4219		10.71

Inch	Decimal	mm
	.4331	11.0
7/16	.4375	11.11
	.4528	11.5
29/64	.4531	11.51
15/32	.4688	11.90
	.4724	12.0
31/64	.4844	12.30
	.4921	12.5
1/2	.5000	12.70
	.5118	13.0
33/64	.5156	13.09
17/32	.5312	13.49
	.5315	13.5
35/64	.5469	13.89
	.5512	14.0
9/16	.5625	14.28
	.5709	14.5
37/64	.5781	14.68
	.5906	15.0
19/32	.5938	15.08
39/64	.6094	15.47
	.6102	15.5
5/8	.6250	15.87
	.6299	16.0
41/64	.6406	16.27
	.6496	16.5
21/32	.6562	16.66
	.6693	17.0
43/64	.6719	17.06
11/16	.6875	17.46
	.6890	17.5
45/64	.7031	17.85
	.7087	18.0
23/32	.7188	18.25
	.7283	18.5
47/64	.7344	18.65
	.7480	19.0
3/4	.7500	19.05
49/64	.7656	19.44
	.7677	19.5
25/32	.7812	19.84
	.7874	20.0
51/64	.7969	20.24
	.8071	20.5
13/16	.8125	20.63
	.8268	21.0
53/64	.8281	21.03
27/32	.8438	21.43
	.8465	21.5
55/64	.8594	21.82
	.8661	22.0
7/8	.8750	22.22
	.8858	22.5
57/64	.8906	22.62
	.9055	23.0
29/32	.9062	23.01
59/64	.9219	23.41
	.9252	23.5
15/16	.9375	23.81
	.9449	24.0
61/64	.9531	24.2
	.9646	24.5
31/32	.9688	24.6
	.9843	25.0
63/64	.9844	25.0
1	1.0000	25.4

Index